P9-EEQ-757

Here is a warning of danger ahead, of a new thunder on the right which threatens liberals and conservatives with sound and fury, with votes and cash. Alan Crawford, a young conservative journalist, wrote this book because he was alarmed at what he saw and heard on his right. Without political party or organizational base in the 1950s and 1960s, the New Right is now, Crawford says, an institutionalized, disciplined, well-financed political network that capitalizes on the passions behind single-issue causes and skillfully commands the use of the increasingly powerful Political Action Committees. Its leadership, mostly white, mostly middle-class, are using their new-found power to tip elections, veto legislation, and initiate referenda. They have their eye on the presidency.

Crawford identifies and describes the New Right's leaders and their umbrella groups, its youth corps and women's auxiliaries, its "think tanks," congressional lobbies, tax-exempt foundations, public-interest law firms, fundamentalist Protestant allies, periodicals, and fund-raising apparatus. Direct-mail solicitation is at the core of the New Right; no longer dependent on wealthy conservatives, it collects millions in small contributions from blue-collar workers and housewives, a modern corruption of American populism.

THUNDER ON THE RIGHT

THE "NEW RIGHT" AND THE POLITICS OF RESENTMENT

Alan Crawford

PANTHEON BOOKS,
NEW YORK

Library of Congress Cataloging in Publication Data

Crawford, Alan, 1953-
  Thunder on the right.

  Bibliography: p.
  Includes index.
    1. Conservatism--United States. 2. United
States--Politics and government--1945-
  I. Title.
JA84.U5C68   320.5'2'0973   79-3305
ISBN 0-394-50663-4

Manufactured in the United States of America

First Edition

Grateful acknowledgment is made to the following for permission to reprint from previously published material:

Connaught Coyne: Lyrics to "Back to Back" on p. 22 and "God Bless Free Enterprise" on p. 211. Reprinted by permission from *Glory Be, There Goes Another! Songs of the Militant Extreme*, prepared for the Young Americans for Freedom Convention, Houston, Texas, 1971, by Vincent Joseph Rigdon and Connaught Coyne. Copyright © 1971.

Firing Line: Excerpts on pp. 18-20 from *Firing Line* television taping of September 2, 1977, "Young Americans for Freedom." Reprinted by permission of *Firing Line*, the Southern Educational Communications Association, Columbia, South Carolina.

Macmillian Publishing Co., Inc.: Excerpts from "Bryan, Bryan, Bryan, Bryan" by Vachel Lindsay. Reprinted by permission of Macmillan Publishing Co., Inc., from *Collected Poems of Vachel Lindsay.* Copyright 1920 by Macmillan Publishing Co., Inc., renewed 1948 by Elizabeth C. Lindsay.

The Reader's Digest Association, Inc.: Excerpts from "Unforgettable John Wayne" by Ronald Reagan, *The Reader's Digest*, October 1979. Copyright © 1979 by The Reader's Digest Association, Inc.

Mark Russell: Lyrics from "Rule Reagannia" by Mark Russell.

South Boston Information Center: Lyrics from "Southie Bay." Reprinted by permission of the South Boston Information Center, Boston, Massachusetts.

Western Islands: Excerpts from "An Interview with Senator Roger Jepsen" by John Rees, which first appeared in the March 28, 1979, issue of *The Review of the News* (Belmont, Massachusetts 02178). By permission of the publisher.

To my mother and my father

The temper and integrity with which the political fight is waged is more important for the health of a society than any particular policy.

—Reinhold Niebuhr

Discontent, anger, and insecurity fuel these efforts. The New Right has no positive program but flourishes on backlash politics, seeking to veto whatever threatens its vision of its way of life—busing, textbooks, women's liberation, abolition of capital punishment, gay rights, gun control, loss of the Panama Canal. Not conservative, it feeds on social protest and encourages class hostility. Its heroes are rugged frontiersmen of the new Old West; its enemies are moderates, liberals, and true conservatives of whatever party.

Alan Crawford is a former editor of *New Guard*, the journal of Young Americans for Freedom, and has been assistant editor of *Conservative Digest*. He was an aide to Senator James Buckley.

Contents

Preface

It surprises me, to a certain extent, that I should have had to write this book at all. I would have thought that some conservative journalist of far greater stature would have come forward to speak frankly on the New Right and its damaging effect on the conservative cause. When no one did, I did, in a sense, to clear my name.

I have written this book because I am a conservative myself, convinced that the activities of the New Right have the potential of being far more damaging to the conservative cause than anything the liberal opposition might do, in much the same way that Joseph McCarthy and Richard Nixon set back the cause of anticommunism.

This book, consequently, represents my own attempt to come to terms with my experiences on the Right. From 1973 through 1979 I worked for *Human Events, Conservative Digest,* Young Americans for Freedom, and New York Senator James L. Buckley (a genuine conservative, Buckley), attending receptions, parties, conventions, and luncheons.

Unfortunately, the more I saw, the less I liked, and the more convinced I became that the political activities of the New Right (which came to dominate the conservative community during those years) were not only unconservative but anticonservative, for reasons that follow.

If it is the responsibility of liberals to expose the radicals, revolutionaries, opportunists, and demagogues who operate in or try to infiltrate their ranks, then it is no less the responsibility of conservatives to disavow and dissociate themselves from the radicals, reactionaries, and hucksters who work their side of the street. In that spirit, I call on liberal journalists to subject to similar scrutiny their own organizations (and their fund-raising activities) before assuming on the evidence presented in this book that such activities are peculiar to the Right.

There are clearly many identifiable right-wing organizations in America reflecting in different degrees the nation's turn to the right, but not all can be treated here. I have, for example, excluded some of those that, my evidence suggests, are outside the mainstream of American politics, too small in following, or so far to the right as to border on fascism, and, as such, irrelevant to the broader currents this book attempts to analyze. I have excluded the Ku Klux Klan, the Liberty Lobby, and the American Nazi Party, whose neofascist ideology is at the farthest point in the right-wing continuum; they are too extreme to reflect the ideology or concerns of the New Right itself. The John Birch Society, however, is included here because of the extent to which its membership (and, in some cases, leadership) overlaps that of the New Right. The splinter American Independent party is given only passing reference, in the context of a brief attempt by New Right leaders to seize its organizational structure.

It seems to me that the New Right represents a serious threat to the nation only to the extent that presumably responsible leaders fail to address the conditions that have given rise to the tensions and anxieties that the New Right so effectively exploits; the New Right, after all, cannot create these tensions. At least it is addressing them, and I see no one else who is. If we must suffer Joe McCarthys, we should bear in mind we must do so only when responsible leaders fail to come to terms with the anxieties such demagogues exploit.

Finally, I would direct the attention of my New Right critics to the words of my dear friend Peter Viereck (a veteran of controversies far more consequential than these) that "any attempt to scrape the barnacles off an excellent but aging boat is never considered an attack upon it. Except by the barnacles."

I would like to express my deepest appreciation for the encouragement and unflagging support of the Reverend Daniel McEver, Arch C. Puddington, Kent Christopher Owen, E. Scott Royce, Edward W. Tallman, and John C. Topping, Jr. And to Jeannette Hopkins, that "tough taskmaster" and extraordinary editor with whom the opportunity to work has been an honor as well as an education.

ALAN CRAWFORD
New York City, 1979

THUNDER ON THE RIGHT

1

The New Right Network

*Organization is our bag. We preach and teach
nothing but organization.*
— PAUL WEYRICH, Committee for
the Survival of a Free Congress

America is lurching to the right. Alarmed by the build-up of
Soviet military strength, some fear for the nation's future.
Many Americans are fearful of crime. They are distressed by
rising taxes and double-digit inflation. Still others worry that
their schools will be destroyed by busing. The list of code
words that refer to the object of their fears seems endless:
forced busing, abortion, gun control, permissiveness, gay
rights, women's lib, the surrender of the Panama Canal, reverse discrimination, and on and on. Many Americans, especially lower-middle-class Americans of the Midwest, South,

and West, arc convinced that existing leaders have failed to confront these issues. As the allegiance of Americans to the two major political parties continues to decline, they turn for the redress of grievances to new structures of political power and new leaders.

Rising to address—and exploit—these anxieties is a new set of self-appointed leaders, men and women of the New Right. One Republican political professional estimated in 1977 that the New Right now constitutes the "fourth most powerful political force in America," behind the two major parties and organized labor. These leaders and the organizations they represent seek radical social and political change, and, unlike previous radicals of the Right, they have built a political and organizational network through which to further those aims.

Until the 1960s, there had been almost no relevant right-wing organization in America; rightists could be found in nonideological groups such as the Republican party or the National Association of Manufacturers, but there were no ideologically conservative groups as such, with the exception of the Americans for Constitutional Action, a Capitol Hill–based organization that issued ratings of senators and congressmen, and stood "against collective morality and a socialized economy through centralization of power." In the 1950s and 1960s, the John Birch Society and other far-out groups emerged, but John P. Roche, dean of the Fletcher School of Law and Diplomacy at Tufts University, and one-time president of Americans for Democratic Action, argued in *The New Leader* that the " 'menace' from the right" was "in effective political terms [a] mythical bogey, a vapor of the perfervid liberal imagination" with no home in American politics—no institutional base, no party, no real understanding or serious interest in the political process beyond the level of theater. In any list of realistic fears, Roche sardonically said, fear of the "radical Right" would rank twenty-third, "between the fear of being eaten by piranhas and the fear of college presidents."

Richard J. Whalen, an aide to President Richard Nixon, made much the same point in his book *Taking Sides* (1974).

> It might almost be said that conservatism gained ground in the 1950s and early 1960s in spite of efforts to organize. The movement of organized "conservative" groups was long on self-appointed leaders who were egotists, dogmatists, hucksters and eccentrics, all engaged in a childish sandbox politics and being very noisy about it. Often referred to by liberals as "the radical Right," such organizations were more accurately described as the irrelevant Right.

By the 1970s, the Right had been transformed into an institutionalized, disciplined, well-organized, and well-financed movement of loosely knit affiliates. Collecting millions of dollars in small contributions from blue-collar workers and housewives, the New Right feeds on discontent, anger, insecurity, and resentment, and flourishes on backlash politics. Through its interlocking network, it seeks to veto whatever it perceives to threaten its way of life—busing, women's liberation, gay rights, pornography, loss of the Panama Canal—and promotes a beefed-up defense budget, lower taxes, and reduced federal regulation of small business. Moreover, the New Right exploits social protest and encourages class hostility by trying to fuel the hostilities of lower-middle-class Americans against those above and below them on the economic ladder. Wholly bipartisan, though predominantly Republican, the New Right network supports whoever shares its desire for radical political change and its resentments of the status quo. As such, the New Right is anything but conservative.

The New Right affiliates include large, multipurpose umbrella groups like the American Conservative Union and the Conservative Caucus; organizations, like Young Americans for Freedom, designed to train young leaders; educational "think tanks" like the Heritage Foundation; periodicals and publishing houses like *Conservative Digest* and Green Hill Publications; tax-exempt legal foundations and public-interest law firms like the Washington Legal Foundation; congressional lobbies like Christian Voice; research arms like the National Conservative Research and Education Foundation; groups to provide research for right-wing state legislators, like the American Legislative Exchange Council; and, on the fringes, a vast array of single-issue groups, ad hoc or long-run, that work on an informal basis with the more established political bodies. The New Right also includes numerous political action committees (PACs) dedicated to financing the political campaigns of like-minded candidates and wrecking those of moderates or liberals.

Direct-mail solicitation of small sums is at the core of the Right's new organizational sophistication, and the leaders of the New Right have mastered the art by taking their message directly into the living rooms of their constituents via their mailboxes. Through the accumulation of lists of supporters, they have built a national following to which they can appeal for money to bankroll their organizations and which they can mobilize for political action.

Although it would be a mistake to assume that this New Right is a monolithic conspiratorial network with a single purpose—it is no more monolithic and single-purposed, nor conspiratorial, I suspect, than the liberal community—the New Right-wingers do not work at cross-purposes. They have been, to a considerable extent, effective in linking into a national network many of the local groups organized from time to time in response to specific concerns. Their leaders are fundraiser Richard A. Viguerie, Paul Weyrich of the Committee for the Survival of a Free Congress, Howard Phillips of the Conservative Caucus, John T. Dolan of the National Conservative Political Action Committee, Reed Larson of the National Right to Work Committee, journalists Patrick J. Buchanan and William Rusher, single-issue activists such as Phyllis Schlafly of Stop-ERA, and representatives of fundamentalist evangelists such as the Reverend Jerry Falwell.

They meet regularly with right-wing congressmen and senators to plot strategy and establish goals for their movement. Often, at these meetings, leadership of local controversies involving textbook selection or gay rights or abortion will participate.

The New Right calls *itself* the New Right, a designation chosen by close associates of Richard A. Viguerie to distinguish its leadership from what they believe to be the slightly effete conservative leadership of the East Coast—for example, William F. Buckley, Jr., and his *National Review.* The New Right and the more traditional conservatives are engaged in a struggle for the soul of their shared constituency, and the New Right has won the first skirmishes. Its emergence has dismayed many conservatives who fear that a reactionary New Right, willing to work with groups like the John Birch Society, will lead American conservatism back into what Richard J. Whalen has called the sandbox. They regard the New Right as anti-intellectual, insensitive to questions of civil liberties, hostile to reforms, more concerned with using political processes for social protest than with improving the quality of life in America by informed public policy and ameliorative social programs. Because they believe New Right dominance could mean the end of a responsible conservatism in America, the conservatives have viewed with encouragement and optimism the rise of the "neoconservative" intellectual movement of ex-liberal scholars like Irving Kristol in New York and others in the Eastern universities; the New Right itself is deeply suspicious of any Eastern elitists and sees little ground for cooperation.

LAST OUTPOST OF THE OLD RIGHT

The most active and responsible of the right-of-center umbrella groups—an organization that has courted neoconservatives like Kristol and yet worked with New Right activists like Phyllis

Schlafly—is the American Conservative Union, founded in 1964 specifically to institutionalize the Draft Goldwater movement. Now equipped with satellite research groups and fundraising apparatus, it was originally the brainchild of such stalwart traditional conservatives as William F. Buckley, Jr., James J. Kilpatrick, and M. Stanton Evans, whose influence in the organization has declined as that of the New Right, with its neopopulist tinge, has grown. Though the American Conservative Union functions as an adjunct of New Right groups, there remains within it a substantial number of conservatives who try to maintain it, along with the *National Review,* as an outpost of traditional conservatism.

The American Conservative Union claims 300,000 members. With a growing budget, the American Conservative Union spearheaded the anti–Panama Canal treaties effort in 1977 and 1978. In its first year of lobbying, the union spent more than $1.4 million, purchasing antiratification commercials on several hundred radio and television stations across the country, publishing ads in major newspapers, and mailing more than 2.4 million letters to mobilize sentiment against what they called the surrender of American property. Ronald Reagan's campaign for the Republican presidential nomination in 1976, and the public outcry against the Panama Canal treaties, proved a boon to the group. In 1978, it increased its fund-raising revenues by 33 percent over those of the previous year, boosting income from contributions to $3.1 million. It stepped up its state activities, adding affiliates—forty-two in mid-1979—in Nebraska, Tennessee, Oregon, and Alabama. Smaller local affiliates were organized in Florida, Texas, New Jersey, Missouri, Georgia, and North and South Carolina, with the aid of two full-time field representatives.

The organization is most effective on Capitol Hill. Alone among right-wing groups, it has learned the advantages of coalition on selected issues with liberal organizations, a tactic that might have been viewed as tantamount to treason by New

Rightists. It was the founder of the coalition Ad Hoc Committee for Airline Regulatory Reform, collaborating with Ralph Nader's Congress Watch and the Americans for Democratic Action. In 1977, the committee lobbied successfully for passage of the Airline Regulatory Reform Act.

The organization favors free-market economics and strong national defense; it sponsors frequent educational seminars and a research arm, the Education Research Institute, which sponsors, in turn, the National Journalism Center, under the direction of former American Conservative Union chairman M. Stanton Evans. This last Capitol Hill–based operation trains young right-of-center writers, in the hope of placing them in professional positions as news reporters. The American Conservative Union is itself a training ground for future political leaders. It took pride in the victory of Jeffrey Bell, once political director of the American Conservative Union, over liberal Republican Senator Clifford Case in the 1977 New Jersey Republican primary.

With genuine conservatives like *Human Events* editor Thomas Winter on its board, the American Conservative Union has remained more responsible and moderate than most New Right groups, despite its obsession with symbolic issues like the Panama Canal treaties, on which it takes predictably rigid positions. It was, however, diverted from serious matters of public policy in 1977 and 1978 when, during Illinois Congressman Philip Crane's tenure as chairman, Crane supporters attempted to transform the organization into a vehicle for his bid for the GOP presidential nomination. Crane's ambitions became too much even for some of his early supporters on the group's governing board. He was replaced as chairman by Maryland Republican Congressman Robert E. Bauman. "With Crane in charge, the whole ACU operation remained predictably obsessed with drumbeating and not the least interested in having a genuine impact on American government and policy," according to one long-time ACU board member. "We had a genuine opportunity back then to get ACU out of the silly anti–New Deal politics that possess these unreconstructed McKinleyites like Phil Crane. But the McKinleyites maintained control—and this tendency toward what I call social protest prevails even today in the organization and, as you'd expect, followed Crane into his quixotic bid for the GOP nomination."

FROM CONSERVATIVE TO NEW RIGHT

The replacement of Philip Crane as chairman of the American Conservative Union was a reflection of an attempt by traditional conservatives within the Washington, D.C., area to minimize the influence of New Right leaders like Colorado brewer Joseph Coors, his Washington political operative Paul Weyrich, and fundraiser Richard A. Viguerie—all of whom were too close to Crane for comfort. The traditional conservatives are convinced that the Viguerie–Coors–Weyrich faction intends to dominate the American Conservative Union. Viguerie, for example, repeatedly tried to buy *Human Events,* the well-established weekly with which the Conservative Union is closely associated. When rebuffed, he founded his own magazine, *Conservative Digest,* in 1975.

The attempt by New Right leaders to control the organization can be traced to Coors's decision in 1971 to bankroll right-wing organizations. That year he sent Jack Wilson, a personal aide, to Washington to look for promising organizations for Coors to support. Coors met Weyrich, then press secretary to former Colorado Senator Gordon Allott, and came to rely for advice on the former broadcast journalist. During the next two years, Coors contributed about $200,-000 to the Analysis Research Corporation, which had been established to conduct research for conservatives in Congress. Internal feuding reduced the effectiveness of the group, and Coors then invested in another research group, the Robert

M. Schuchman Foundation, a tax-exempt center for public interest law in Washington, named for a youthful conservative activist who died at the age of twenty-seven. Coors began to pump money into this group, much to the discomfort of a number of conservatives on the Schuchman Foundation board, who feared that the brewer's influence was altering the charitable organization's activities, and placing too much emphasis on political projects. As one observer told me: "What Weyrich and Coors really wanted was a vehicle for their activities, which included a certain degree of lobbying and political action. It was less expensive, of course, if they could conduct this business under the tax exemption that the foundation enjoyed—but this could risk revocation of that exemption, or worse."

This issue came to a head in January 1974 at a Shuchman Foundation board meeting in Washington. Members of the board concerned about legal ramifications—a group that included *Human Events* editor Thomas Winter and Washington attorneys Daniel Joy and Douglas Caddy—demanded answers of Coors. As one participant said at the meeting: "We could all be subject to a degree of personal liability for some of the things that are being done in the name of this organization, and we want it out in the open now. We want no part of it."

Shortly thereafter, Coors withdrew his financial support, and the Schuchman Foundation became inactive. In its place Coors and Weyrich formed the Heritage Foundation, incorporated in the District of Columbia in 1973. Although Paul Weyrich, who described himself to me as "a political mechanic" lacking a college education, was its first president, the Heritage Foundation surprised many observers by becoming a rather respectable research institution. It issued many solid studies and analyses to the press and to House and Senate offices; it was once under the direction of Edwin J. Feulner, Republican Study Committee chief. It publishes the highly regarded *Policy Review*, a quarterly featuring articles by Dr. Walter Williams, a black economist from Temple University; psychiatrist and author Ernest van den Haag; and defense analyst Eugene V. Rostow; it has been praised as a "worthy addition to the world of political commentary" by neoconservative Democratic Senator Daniel Patrick Moynihan of New York. But it is unusual for a research institution to have a "staff ideology," as the Heritage Foundation has. Its studies invariably confirm the notions to which its conservative colleagues and trustees, who include Coors, Wilson, former Reagan aide Frank Walton, and California industrialist J. Robert Fluor, are already committed. The founder's real interest, in the author's view based on observation of a year or more, appears to be less with balanced public policy research and more with the provision of support for New Right opinions.*

The power struggle within the Schuchman Foundation was not unlike that within another right-of-center organization, the American Legislative Exchange Council, a fledgling alliance of state legislators put together by Juanita Bartnett, an Illinois Republican activist who was its first executive director. ALEC, as the group is called, was also the target of a takeover by a Weyrich-led group that came in with outside funding, which they used to seize control of the organization.

As Bartnett has recalled, she was approached in 1974 by Illinois State Representative Donald Totten, who asked her to help organize the group, which would function as a clearinghouse of legislative research for state legislators. When Mrs. Bartnett began to solicit funds, a representative of the Heritage Foundation independently contacted Richard Larry, an em-

---

*In 1979, I asked the director of another and much smaller educational institute linked to a large conservative organization if his group ever commissioned a study the results of which did not uphold the preconceived right-wing position. He said, yes, a study of gun control legislation failed to support the conservative position. I asked if the study was published. "No," he replied. "We axed it."

ployee of the Sarah Scaife Family Charitable Trusts—an arm of the Mellon fortune of Pennsylvania, which routinely funds conservative causes.

Obtaining the needed funds from the Scaife Foundation, the new group dismissed Mrs. Bartnett from her position (she subsequently sued the organization, which settled out of court), and moved it to Washington, D.C., from Chicago, and added to its board Weyrich, Frank Walton of the Heritage Foundation, and Edwin Feulner. Mrs. Bartnett asked Weyrich,

> "why Scaife wanted to invest $80,000 in ALEC" and he told me: "Juanita, ALEC is the *only* state legislative organization in the country—of our persuasion—which has a 501-C-3 [the Internal Revenue Service designation indicating a tax exempt status]. If they took ALEC to Washington and did a good job, they (Walton, Feulner, Weyrich) could go back to SKAIF [*sic*] and get SKAIF to set up a Political Action Committee to finance state legislative campaign races. He assured me that he was not trying to "buy" the state legislators, but the possibility of some campaign funding for them was there.

Another member of the organization's board also expressed concern that the Scaife Foundation might seek to control the organization. He telephoned the spokesmen, who told him that the organization he represented "operates on the Golden Rule —whoever has the gold rules."

Sure enough, gold did rule. The Weyrich faction prevailed, and the organization, funded by the Scaife Foundation, moved to Washington where it became an adjunct of the growing New Right network. "They really wanted to get rid of me because I knew what they were trying to do with the organization and they knew I would have no part of it," Bartnett told me. She concluded, from examining records of telephone calls and methods of payment within the organization, that they wanted to use the tax exemption status as a shelter under which to conduct political activity. "They were trying, when they fired me, to turn the organization into an arm of the Reagan campaign, by funneling tax deductible contributions through ALEC to be used to finance pro-Reagan activities."

From July 1974 through January 1976, the American Legislative Exchange Council operated from Totten's office, and, according to Bartnett, it paid no rent. "On more than one occasion I was reimbursed for activities that were being performed for ALEC—and not for official state business." Vouchers I have seen, with which Totten arranged for her payment, list Bartnett as a legislative aide when, in fact, according to her, she was employed solely by ALEC. "I made any number of calls—long-distance calls—at the expense of the State Representative's office, because I was instructed to use the state rep's line for the ALEC calls."

In a September 1978 mailing, the American Legislative Exchange Council's Washington headquarters urged its Pennsylvania office to reject the District of Columbia voting rights amendment, then under consideration by the Pennsylvania legislature. Included in the mailing were a Heritage Foundation study, a press release from Senator Richard Schweiker, a clipping of an article by Senator Orrin Hatch of Utah, and editorials from various newspapers—all unanimously adopted by ALEC board members urging "the legislatures of the fifty states to reject the proposed constitutional amendment granting congressional and senatorial representation to the District of Columbia."

Several years earlier, in 1975, a letter from ALEC's attorney at the time, Michael M. Ushijima, to the Internal Revenue Service had described the functions of ALEC as follows:

> The organization would make no attempt whatsoever to oppose or support pending legislation other than providing research material to member legislators as regards model legislation. The organization would take no steps nor devote any funds or personnel to the support or opposition of pending legislation, or the support, opposition, or introduction of any model legislation provided to any member.

CAMPAIGN TREASURIES

Among the immediate consequences of this internecine power struggle on the Right was the creation of the Committee for the Survival of a Free Congress, formed by Weyrich and Coors in 1974. Before the committee was formed, Weyrich had urged the brewer to contribute to the Conservative Victory Fund of the American Conservative Union; he told Coors, however, that he believed the organization was not as effective as it should be because it employed no field representatives. At Weyrich's suggestion, Coors began to contribute to the new political action committee, which Weyrich then headed. He had left the Heritage Foundation to become more actively involved in political campaigns. With Viguerie as fundraiser, "CSFC raised twice as much money as the Conservative Victory Fund did in the same period of time," Weyrich told the *Washington Post.* Coors also contributed money of some of his employees. "How did Coors raise the money?" the *Post* asked. "He just goes around the office and collects it," Weyrich answered.

Now housed in a renovated garage behind the Library of Congress in Washington, the Committee for the Survival of a Free Congress is one of the best financed of the New Right's political action committees (federally sanctioned campaign finance organizations). In large part, it can be credited with the election of New Right Republican Senator Orrin Hatch of Utah in 1977. It does not, however, contribute to the campaigns of incumbents. As Weyrich told *Conservative Digest:* "If a conservative congressman cannot turn the million dollars' worth of prerogatives he receives every two years to his political advantage the way incumbent liberals do, then there is nothing CSFC can do to help him." Such hard-headed politics, as well as skillful placement of well-trained field representatives, accounts for the group's success, which even *Human Events,* the weekly most closely associated with the competitive Conservative Victory Fund, noted: "The Committee for the Survival of a Free Congress deserves credit for establishing outstanding precinct organizations in numerous campaigns."

This New Right group's ideology is suggested by its analysis of the 1977 House of Representatives, which identified 32 percent of all congressmen as "radicals," with those considered "very liberal" coming in second. A similar pattern held in the Senate, whose "radicals" included liberals Edmund Muskie of Maine, Jacob Javits of New York, and Clifford Case of New Jersey. Neoconservative Moynihan of New York, centrist Henry Jackson of Washington, moderate William Proxmire of Wisconsin, and even West Virginia's Robert C. Byrd, a former member of the Ku Klux Klan, were labeled "very liberal."

Another major New Right political arm is the National Conservative Political Action Committee, which raised more money than any other conservative group in 1976—a sum in excess of $3 million. Its modern offices in Rosslyn, Virginia, house four full-time employees and as many as forty part-time workers, led by executive director John T. Dolan, who came up through the ranks of the Young Republicans.

Most responsible for its creation, however, was Charles Black, formerly an aide to the right-wing North Carolina Senator Jesse Helms, and, in 1979, employed by the Reagan campaign. In 1977 and 1978, Black served as political director of the Republican National Committee. The National Conservative Political Action Committee relies heavily on "in-kind" contributions to the candidates it supports. "What's the NCPAC secret?" asked a fund-raising letter by Helms (March 11, 1977). "They provide campaign experts—in press relations, voter surveys, TV advertising, campaign management, and more—instead of merely dumping cash into a campaign and hoping for the best." "One of the reasons for the solid success record of NCPAC is their insistence on providing more than just financial assistance in a campaign," the letter by Helms continued. "NCPAC prefers to give technical political assistance to a campaign, thereby insuring that campaigns are run on a sound basis." Helms praised its "cadre . . . of top professional consultants." *Human Events* credited the 1978 election of Republican Senator Gordon Humphrey of New Hampshire to last-minute efforts by the organization.

The National Conservative Political Action Committee is committed to supporting Democrats as well as Republicans, and about 10 percent of the candidates who received contributions in 1978 were Democrats. When I asked how NCPAC plans to find Democrats conservative enough to support in future races, Dolan, himself a Republican, told me, "We're gonna have to recruit 'em."

The only partisan political action committee of the Right dead set against backing Democrats is Citizens for the Republic, formed with the money left over from the 1976 Reagan campaign. It began with nearly $1 million, a list of 183,-000 contributors to the Reagan effort, and Reagan's exceedingly marketable name. In the fall of 1978, according to a Citizens for the Republic fund-raising letter, the NBC Nightly News described it as "the most advanced presidential campaign ever, this far before an election," prompting the letter's explanation: "The fact is, CFTR is in no way a Reagan campaign organization. Under federal law, it cannot be. But there is no question that it has quickly become the most effective multicandidate political action committee in our nation." True or not, there can be little question that it greatly enhanced the Californian's chances to become the GOP standard-bearer in 1980. According to the *Washington Post,* it footed the bills when Reagan toured the country week after week in 1978 to promote the candidacies of Republican hopefuls, taping as many as fifty-four radio endorsements and twelve television spots in one week. The committee also spent thousands of dollars in 1978 to promote other GOP candidates; it sponsored seminars, placed campaign workers in a number of GOP campaigns, and published a twice-monthly newsletter, which claims it "prints the news one seldom finds—but should—in the mass media."

In addition to the major political action committees of the New Right, dozens more, much smaller but well financed, are concentrating their efforts in regional campaigns. An example is the Western Intermountain Network Political Action Committee (see Chapter 2). WIN-PAC, as it is called, contributes money to right-wing office-seekers in Montana and other Mountain States.

THE CADETS

Young Americans for Freedom, an organization of aggressive young patriots, is the most active and well organized of the right-wing youth corps, and quite possibly its best financed, although its heyday was in the wild sixties. Despite its conservative heritage—it was founded in 1960 by William F. Buckley—it has become increasingly influenced by New Rightist attitudes, a natural development, perhaps, since other early leaders included Howard Phillips and Richard A. Viguerie. The organization was intended to be an institutionalized protest by junior GOPers convinced that Richard Nixon had "sold out" to the hated Rockefeller in 1960 at the Republican National Convention. In the early days it was a New York City–based organization, operating out of conservative fundraiser Marvin Leibman's Madison Avenue offices. But since that time it has expanded its scope to include active chapters in the South and West. Its salad days may be long past; in recent years it has been characterized by what otherwise sympathetic writer Richard J. Whalen has called "cannibalistic" attitudes, which have resulted in "unseemly brawling" among its leaders.

YAF leaders pass lengthy resolutions at their conventions but avoid certain specific controversies, as, for example, a position for or against the decriminalization of marijuana, a subject on which their opinions might carry some genuine weight. Instead, the organization concerns itself with matters of global import—a questionable preoccupation, as suggested by the following exchange on William F. Buckley's "Firing Line" television program between liberal commentator Jeff Greenfield and

a number of YAF spokesmen on the occasion of the group's
1977 convention:

> Greenfield: Do you all agree with the proposition that the war
> in Vietnam was a case of an American commitment that should
> have been kept and was not—that is, that the war essentially
> was a worthy cause?
>
> Frank Donatelli (outgoing YAF executive director): With
> some modifications.
>
> Greenfield: Okay, sir. How many of you enlisted in the armed
> forces of the United States? (None had.)
>
> John Buckley (YAF's newly elected national chairman): [A
> strong commitment to the war] wouldn't necessarily require
> that we individually go out and wage the war physically if you're
> trying to allude to the extent to which we were willing to back
> up, by our own sacrifices, our commitment to that event. I think
> that among ourselves and among the rest of the leadership of
> those folks on the college campus who favor the U.S. position in
> the war certainly revealed the extent of that sacrifice in terms of
> grades and in terms of being active in the battle on campuses.
>
> Greenfield: No, I'm sorry, John. I don't think getting a C-plus
> instead of an A is equivalent to slogging through the mud in
> Vietnam.

Later, Greenfield asked:

> [Is there anything in the YAF program] that an outsider might
> be surprised at? To ask the question less charitably, is there
> anything about any YAF positions one would not be able to call
> "knee-jerk" conservative or utterly predictable?
>
> Donatelli: Well, I would say that there are a large number—the
> voluntary military which we once again have reaffirmed our
> support for—
>
> Greenfield: Excuse me, but I was specifically going to exempt
> that on grounds of self-interest. [Laughter]

Donatelli: The question you asked was, "Is there anything unpredictable?"

Greenfield: Yes, I think it's utterly predictable.

On the marijuana question, Greenfield suggested that he found it odd that a conservative

would . . . want to place in the hands of a state prosecutor—a government official, if you want to load it—the power to send somebody to jail for smoking a marijuana cigarette.

Robert Heckman: But that was not our position we took at this convention. We did not take a position on decriminalization of marijuana.

Donatelli: We felt that with the very large division in our ranks as to the merits of the question that this was something that we should not compel YAF as an organization to take a position on.

William F. Buckley, Jr.: Very libertarian.

Greenfield: It's like anarchists not meeting because they cannot agree on a time.

For a young person's organization, YAF seems complacent —perhaps for the very good reason that it has almost ceased to be a young person's organization. With less and less contact with college campuses, it operates out of a wooded estate in the rolling hills of northern Virginia and not, as one might assume, from a rented room with a battered mimeograph machine in some rundown Capitol Hill townhouse or Cambridge apartment. Before purchasing the land in Virginia, Young Americans for Freedom maintained offices in an elegant apartment building near Washington, D.C.'s Embassy Row. For its conventions, it selects costly and lavish hotels. Its membership seems to be getting older and older, and its rolls smaller. Although it claims to have 55,000 members, a 7 February 1979 mailing from the office of its director of state and chapter services to members of its national board reported membership at 6,582, up 3 percent since 1 November 1978. Only three of the California chapters—to take one state as typical of all—are located on college campuses, none in the high schools, and sixteen in communities. When this writer was employed by YAF in 1976 as editor of its monthly magazine *New Guard,* one member of the governing board had teenage children; and those members who were under thirty were, for the most part, professionals in the process of building comfortable careers as attorneys or professional political operatives, their days as campus counterrevolutionaries long past. YAF has demonstrated decreasing interest in educational programs, with most of its activity in the late seventies being devoted to advancing the political careers of its tight clique of leaders. All of this has prompted Leibman to suggest to me that the organization, which he calls "boring and bureaucratized," ought to close its doors. Its national conventions are so tightly controlled that not once in the past sixteen years has a candidate not endorsed by the national office been elected.

The 1976 Reagan campaign looked like Old Home Week to the YAFers. A number of Reagan's closest aides—including Charles Black, Loren Smith, David Keene, and fundraiser Bruce Eberle—are YAF alumni, as is Maryland Congressman Robert Bauman, who was elected chairman of the American Conservative Union in 1979. Another alumnus is Tom Charles Huston, who left politics to practice law in Indianapolis in the mid-1970s and is the author of the infamous plan to create an extralegal secret police independent of the FBI, intended to operate at the sole discretion of the president. "Use of this technique is clearly illegal," wrote Huston, then a White House security expert, in a memo urging President Nixon to authorize the plan (Nixon signed it on 23 July 1970). Huston was executive director of Young Americans for Freedom in 1965–1966.

At the organization's 1979 convention at Washington, D.C.'s Shoreham Americana, a mock presidential election was held, with the Wisconsin chairman reporting six votes for former Senator Joseph McCarthy, "a man who truly believes it's better to be dead than Red." Despite the tough talk suggested by the fight song

> *Back to back, belly to belly,*
> *Burn their bodies with Napalm jelly,*
> *Back to back, belly to belly,*
> *It's a Hanoi jamboree!*
> *Joan Baez was singin' a song,*
> *Favorin' the Viet Cong.*
> *Put the goo to every leftwinger,*
> *Joan Baez was a real torch singer!*

YAF members tend to be docile and obedient, not much given to carrying out threats. As conservative writer Noel Parmentel, Jr., has written in *Esquire*, while "enthusiastic (even unto ecstasy)," the Young Americans for Freedom

> are hopelessly schizoid as a disciplined political group. On the one hand, they display orthodox *Führer-prinzip*, fawning upon the New Right's big guns to the point of bystander discomfort. But this embarrassing servility toward their betters is more than counterbalanced by their "stilettos-out" intramural policy. . . .
>
> While patriotism appeals to these boys, the rest of us will have to manage to keep it a Republic without much assistance from YAF. They drink beer but are poor *Putsch* material. Mainly, the YAFs couldn't punch their way through a soaking-wet copy of *Human Events*.

Increasing in stature as a right-wing organization is the Young Republican National Federation, which—with the Teenage Republicans and the College Republicans—represents the official youth arm of the GOP. The Young Republicans have been controlled by party right-wingers since 1955; in 1977, the organization elected as its national chairman Roger J. Stone, a former Reagan campaign worker who served as treasurer of the National Conservative Political Action Committee. The right-wingers first took control during the Eisenhower years when William Rusher, now *National Review* publisher, and GOP strategist F. Clifton White arranged the election of John Ashbrook, now a conservative Ohio congressman, to the Young Republicans' top spot. The coalition that backed Ashbrook, Rusher wrote, was "more or less frankly an anti-Rockefeller, anti-Eastern and anti-liberal" alliance. "Despite its junior status," columnist M. Stanton Evans has written,

> the YRNF has been an accurate indicator of past trends in general—presaging trends that have later taken hold in the senior GOP.
> In 1963, for instance, the YR convention in San Francisco saw the first organizational victory for forces aligned with Senator Barry Goldwater. In that contest, Goldwater-backed [Donald E. "Buz"] Lukens, later an Ohio Congressman, was elected chairman over a candidate with formal conservative credentials (then as now required in YR politics) but who had the backing of the Rockefeller wing. Lukens' win foreshadowed the rising Goldwater strength inside the party.

The 1977 Young Republicans' election was especially revealing. Contending for the chairmanship were Richard Evans, a right-winger from Louisville, Kentucky, and Roger Stone, the former National Conservative Political Action Committee treasurer from Alexandria, Virginia. Stone, with endorsements from Senators Jake Garn of Utah and Paul Laxalt of Nevada, put together a well-organized campaign that had support from Reagan aides Black, Keene, and John Sears, the GOP national campaign manager. Disinterested observers were stunned to learn of Stone's past activities from Walter Cronkite on his CBS Evening News on the evening of Stone's election. According to the Senate Watergate report, Stone, while employed as a "scheduler" in the office of Herbert L. "Bart" Porter at the Committee to Re-Elect the President (CREEP), had been deeply involved in the Nixon committee's "dirty tricks" campaign. He used an alias ("Jason Rainer") to recruit a young agent to infiltrate several 1972 Democratic election campaigns. The agent, Michael McMinoway of Louisville, was not told for whom he was working, but he reported back to Stone; and the information was relayed, in turn, to Porter, then eventually to H. R. Haldeman in the White House and John Mitchell at CREEP. When White House aide Charles Colson suggested to colleagues that someone be sent to New Hampshire to make a contribution to the 1972 presidential primary challenge of California Congressman Pete McClosky, "on behalf of some radical group," as the Senate Watergate report put it, Stone received the assignment. Instructed by Porter to give $135 cash to the McClosky effort there in the name of the Gay Liberation Front, he persuaded Porter that he should give the cash contribution instead in the name of the Young Socialist Alliance. Stone and Porter then drafted an anonymous letter to William Loeb's *Manchester Union Leader*, enclosing a photocopy of the receipt Stone had received from the McClosky campaign worker. Loeb, assuming its authenticity, printed the letter along with a front-page editorial critical of McClosky.

A number of the Young Republicans were distressed by these shenanigans, anxious to cleanse themselves of the taint of the Nixon scandal. The Stone supporters, with the help of their Washington connections, successfully portrayed the Young Republicans campaign as an ideological battle, painting Evans —a Reagan delegate to the 1976 Republican presidential convention in Kansas City—as a captive of the Rockefeller "liberals." Confronted by such a technically skillful campaign, Evans was badly beaten at the polls; once again, the "candidate of the Conservative Movement," as apologists for Stone's Watergate past called him, maintained control of the Young Republicans. Stone promptly put into practice an intensive direct-mail fundraising program; revenues increased from about $34,000 for the two-year period ending in 1975 to $491,000 from 1977 to the fall of 1978. The organization became active on other fronts as well, putting heavy emphasis on the training of young political leaders. As a consequence, the 1979 Young Republican Leadership Conference was dominated by the New Right. The convention presented an "Americanism" award to former Nixon aide Patrick Buchanan, who once advocated, according to the Senate Watergate report, that the White House secretly sponsor the candidacy of a black for president in 1972 to drain votes from Nixon's Democratic challenger.

A third key element of the right-wing youth movement is the Committee for Responsible Youth Politics, an organization for which Viguerie raises money; it is under the direction of Morton Blackwell, for years a Viguerie employee and editor of *The New Right Report.* This organization, which conducts seminars to train young activists in campaign management techniques, contributes to political campaigns and places its graduates on key Senate and congressional campaign staffs. One self-described Republican "progressive," who has attended campaign management schools conducted by many Republican groups, gives credit where it is due. The committee's seminars, he told me, are "very good. Blackwell knows his business." The one disturbing element, he said, is that the teachers at the sessions "make it clear enough that they believe some of the dirtier aspects of campaigning are just politics, and to be encouraged on the basis that the other side does it, too." According to the Senate Watergate report, the individual responsible for recommending agent Michael McMinoway to Roger Stone for the Nixon committee's "dirty tricks" campaign was Morton Blackwell.

PRO-BUSINESS GROUPS

Learning from the successes of their liberal counterparts, the New Rightists by the late 1970s had discovered the advantages of fighting on all fronts. Taking a page from Ralph Nader and the environmentalists, the New Rightists formed their own "public interest law firms" in the 1970s, expanding their organizational activities into the broader area of tax-exempt foundations. The most important of these is the Pacific Legal Foundation, founded in 1973 by Ronald Zumbrun, an adviser to California Governor Reagan on welfare reform. The Pacific

Legal Foundation maintains a staff of more than twenty lawyers; in 1979, it operated on a budget of $2 million a year,
according to its own annual report. Right-wing legal fronts,
their leaders readily admit, were started to counteract the growing influence of such organizations as the Sierra Club and the
Environmental Defense Fund. "We are trying to show that
there are different ideas about what is the 'public interest,' "
explained the director of the Pacific Legal Foundation's Washington office in *Conservative Digest.* California industrialist
J. Robert Fluor said: "We felt somebody had to be there in
court to give the other side; a lot of times, in the case of jobs,
for instance, we felt the public interest wasn't really represented by the public interest law firms." Originally concerned
with abuses of welfare programs, a matter of great concern to
businessmen who display little hostility to government subsidies to business, the organization has recently moved into the
larger area of governmental regulation. By 1978, the Pacific
Legal Foundation had participated in 150 court cases, many
involving environmental standards. The group challenged the
search procedures of the Occupational Safety and Health Administration, and succeeded in reversing an Environmental
Protection Agency decision to ban the use of pesticides in
Northwestern forests. The Pacific Legal Foundation, according to an article by Julian Weiss in *Conservative Digest,* believes

> that, whenever government issues a regulation or sets policies,
> some analysis of costs and benefits should be made. Decisions
> by EPA and OSHA bureaucrats have cost thousands of jobs.
> . . . In each case, PLF asks the court to take into account the
> loss of employment, burdens of high prices passed on to con-
> sumers, or consequences of government meddling in the pri-
> vate sector.

Another public interest law firm, the Washington Legal
Foundation, is headed by former Nixon Administration lawyer
Don Popeo, who has called Ralph Nader "the most dangerous

man in America since Lee Harvey Oswald." In 1976, Popeo's group, more blatantly political than the Pacific Legal Foundation, sued to prevent President Carter from implementing the Panama Canal treaties until the U.S. House of Representatives also approved them. Acting with the support of sixty congressmen, it lost in the U.S. Court of Appeals. It also sued to overturn a recent ruling by the Federal Election Commission, which, the Washington Legal Foundation held, allowed the Democratic National Committee to use large contributions to pay off old campaign debts. Like the Pacific Legal Foundation, the group is also involved in the fight to protect business and industry from costly governmental regulations; and, in 1977, it successfully persuaded a federal court to order a jury trial for a mine operator fined by the Federal Mining Enforcement and Safety Administration for violations of safety regulations.

There are, in all, about ten rightist legal organizations, and most side primarily with business interests in court. The board of trustees of the Pacific Legal Foundation is chiefly composed of representatives of large corporations.

A rightist consumer group that openly courts financial backing from business and industry is the Consumer Alert Council, directed by Barbara Keating, an American Conservative Union board member. Formed in 1977, Consumer Alert has worked with the Pacific Legal Foundation to redefine consumerism; according to Mrs. Keating, this will benefit both business and the average American. Mrs. Keating is trying, with some success, to sell the American people on the notion that governmental regulations imposed at the behest of Naderite and other groups are harmful to the consumer. "The cost of regulating business is always passed along to the consumer in higher prices," she told me. The common hamburger, she tells American lawmakers in frequent legislative testimony, is now affected by 41,000 regulations, 200 legal statutes, and 111,000 precedent-setting court decisions. Consumer Alert appeals to citizens' groups as well as business and industry for much of its funding, choosing to avoid massive direct-mail fund raising.

One rightist organization that does not like to be regarded as a front for business interests, although the courts see it as such, is the National Right to Work Committee and its legal arm, the National Right to Work Legal Defense Foundation. Founded in 1955 by then–Congressman Fred Hartley, co-sponsor of the Taft-Hartley Act, the National Right to Work Committee is led by Reed Larson, who was first involved in right-to-work disputes as state chairman of the Kansas Chamber of Commerce. His group claims 1.25 million members; and so great is the volume of mail that pours forth from its offices that it has been awarded its own zip code. To maintain this heavy direct-mail fund-raising operation, it spends an estimated $2 million each year on postage alone. Although Larson has insisted that his organization is interested only in the issue of compulsory unionism, it has nevertheless been involved since the mid-sixties in legislative battles touching all aspects of the American trade union movement. In 1976, for example, President Gerald Ford was ready to sign into law the common situs picketing bill, a measure having little bearing on right-to-work, until Larson's membership deluged the White House with letters. Ford vetoed the bill. In 1977, the AFL-CIO put up its own common situs bill and, with a sympathetic President Carter in the Oval Office, the measure was expected to move smoothly through Congress and into law. Again Larson mobilized his troops, and the bill failed even to make it through the House of Representatives. In 1978, the Carter Administration produced a labor law reform package and Larson went into action again. The *Washington Post* reported: LABOR LAW BILL STARTS PAPER BLIZZARD.

In January and February 1978 alone, the committee mailed roughly eight million letters and, in one day, placed full-page advertisements in thirty major newspapers from coast to coast. Committee supporters blanketed the offices of their senators with six million letters, cards, and telegrams urging them to reject the "labor bosses'" bill. The bill was beaten. *Human Events* reported:

Major credit for blocking the "labor law reform act" should go to the National Right to Work Committee. In six months, the committee spent $1.5 million galvanizing opposition to the scheme. The committee placed more than 500 newspaper ads and mailed more than 12 million letters generating heavy mail to wavering Senators.

One prominent conservative activist familiar with the committee's activities told me that it is a "pro-business lobby" whose ostensible purpose of fighting compulsory unionism is, in fact, subordinate to its larger interest in furthering right-wing political causes that go beyond the strict issue of right-to-work. Another activist—employed by the organization—expressed great disappointment with the direction Larson has taken it in recent years, calling it "just another part of the right-wing fund-raising machine."

Similar in function to the National Right to Work Committee is the Public Service Research Council, dedicated to preventing public sector unions. Although Larson has denied it, it is widely believed that this group got off the ground with a loan from the National Right to Work Committee. Larson has acknowledged his role in helping organize the group, even to having recommended to its leadership some members of its board of directors. The Public Service Research Council conceives of itself as a research institution, conducting studies and polls affecting the issue of public sector unions and illegal strikes; the group also goes by the name of Americans Against Union Control of Government. A spokesman has told a *Richmond Times Dispatch* reporter that the two names are interchangeable: "Whereas one sounds more academic, the other can be used to arouse people." And arouse people it does. A 1979 fund-raising letter signed by Senator Jesse Helms informs readers of the "very real possibility of a relative handful of union bosses seizing control of America's government." In order to prevent this catastrophe, the group has formed the Public Service Political Action Committee to contribute money to candidates, with funds raised by Richard Viguerie.

So great has been its success that three times in three years the organization has outgrown its offices; the size of its staff has increased from two to roughly thirty full- and part-time employees.

Two New Right populist lobbies that seek basic changes in America's political structure, though not actively involved in political campaigns, are Populist Forum and Initiative America, both based in Washington. Populist Forum, a shoestring operation that attempts to monitor, co-opt, and encourage right-wing populism, was involved in the textbook controversies in West Virginia and the antibusing protests in South Boston. Initiative America, another low-budget operation, is more specialized in pursuing its populist goals; this group lobbies for the national initiative amendment, a constitutional amendment to allow voters to put issues directly on the ballot.

THE NEW RIGHT'S FOURTH ESTATE

The American Right now has an active, vigorous battery of publications and publicists, ranging from the eminently conservative William F. Buckley and *National Review*—not strictly New Right at all—to the neopopulist monthly *Conservative Digest.* *Human Events,* a Washington-based news weekly, part conservative, part New Right, provides in-depth coverage of Capitol Hill and political campaigns. *Washington Weekly,* a tabloid distributed in the Capitol area, reprints syndicated right-wing columnists and staff-written editorials focusing on the lapses of the established *Washington Post* and *Washington Star,* all served up in a sensationalist and hard-hitting style. Richard A. Viguerie, the New Right fundraiser, publishes *Conservative Digest,* a slick magazine geared to Wallaceites, and *The New Right Report,* a twice-monthly newsletter for right-wing political activists. Outside of Washington, right-of-center newspapers like the *Manchester* (New Hampshire) *Union Leader,* the *Richmond* (Virginia) *News-Leader,* the *Arizona Republic,* and the *Santa Ana* (California) *Register* provide a "movement" perspective for local readers. Their editors sometimes contribute to the national rightist publications. These magazines and newspapers, taken together with such non–New Right establishment publications as *The Wall Street Journal, The Saturday Evening Post,* and *U.S. News and World Report,* ensure that conservative views are well represented in the national news media.

Political commentators also proliferate on the Right. Four of the nation's most widely syndicated columnists—William F. Buckley, James J. Kilpatrick, and Pulitzer Prize winners George F. Will and William Safire—are unapologetic conservatives, but are not New Rightists. They are flanked to their right by a small army of New Right publicists, including former Nixon speech writer Patrick J. Buchanan; John D. Lofton, Jr.; and long-time *Indianapolis News* editor M. Stanton Evans. Of growing stature as a columnist, pollster, and author is Kevin Phillips, another former Nixon aide, whose books *The Emerging Republican Majority* and *Mediacracy: Politics and Power in the Communications Age* have helped to shape right-wing political strategy throughout the 1970s. Less well known right-wing commentators include Lee Edwards, Allan Brownfeld, and libertarian David Brudnoy, who distribute their own newspaper columns.

The right-wingers also have their own publishing houses, where many books that could not have been published elsewhere are well received and publicized through advertisements in periodicals like *Human Events* and *Conservative Digest.* Arlington House in New Rochelle, New York, once an enterprise of the Buckley family, is now independent of the Buckleys, and distributes many of its books through the Conservative Book Club. Although Arlington House has published such successful works as Kevin Phillips's *The Emerging Republican Majority,* it also publishes books of less mainstream appeal, like *Hippies, Drugs and Promiscuity, How To Survive in Your Liberal School,* and *None Dare Call It Witchcraft.* Green Hill Publications of Ottawa, Illinois, run by American Conservative Union activist Jameson Campaigne, publishes paperbacks like

The Gun Owners Political Action Manual, How to Start Your Own School, and North Carolina Senator Jesse Helms's *Where Free Men Shall Stand.*

LAW AND ORDER INTEREST GROUPS

Working closely with the highly sophisticated, Washington, D.C.–based New Right organizations, and constituting a major element of the New Right network, are the many single-issue groups that have, in recent years, come to play such an important role in electoral politics. While often unprofessionally organized, ad hoc, and confined to local controversies, they nevertheless make up an important part of the New Right constituency.

One that is organizationally sophisticated is the single-minded gun lobby, a growing power within New Right politics. The National Rifle Association, a well-financed and lavish operation in downtown Washington, was long assumed to be the leading pro-gun group, but that assumption is no longer valid. The association—which has systematically de-emphasized the gun control issue and put more stress on gun safety, environmentalism, and the like—came under attack in 1977 by hardcore gun enthusiasts and some of the crankier zealots on the Far Right as being too liberal. One result was a power struggle within the 1.2-million-member organization, during which a faction that columnist John Chamberlain called the "ecological revolutionists" almost took control. The association, seeking to raise large sums of money for Western land development, had sought aid from a public relations firm, Oram Associates, which urged the group to change its image by playing down the anti-gun-control activities of its Washington-based Institute for Legislative Action. When the smoke had cleared, the pro-gun forces within the organization had successfully resisted the "ecological revolutionists"; but two new and more militant pro-gun groups benefited from the infighting.

The Citizens Committee for the Right to Keep and Bear

Arms, for example, claims to have doubled its budget—to $1.5 million—in 1978 over the preceding years; its 1979 membership was reported to be 176,000—small, considering its considerable clout on Capitol Hill. Although directed from its headquarters in Bellevue, Washington, where it is part of a growing empire of quasi-political groups associated with New Right entrepreneur Allan M. Gottlieb, its public relations office in the capital is in the capable hands of a tough-talking lobbyist, John Snyder. Snyder edits its blistering newsletter, *Point Blank*.

The second group to profit from the troubles within the National Rifle Association is Gun Owners of America, formed by California Republican State Senator H. L. "Bill" Richardson of Sacramento, a one-time field representative of the John Birch Society. Gun Owners, with Viguerie as its fundraiser, is now under the direction of Larry Pratt, a former executive director of the American Conservative Union. It claims more than 200,000 members. Through its affiliate, Gun Owners Political Action Committee, it supports anti-gun-control candidates.

Also concerned with law and order, the Americans for Effective Law Enforcement, formed in 1966 in Evanston, Illinois, works to counteract the influence of the liberal American Civil Liberties Union. Its founders, including former Chicago Police Chief O. W. Wilson, believed that as long as the ACLU represents the rights of the accused, someone should represent those of the victim and the law enforcement officer. Under the leadership of attorney Frank Carrington (author of two books, *The Defenseless Society* and *The Victims*), the organization dispenses legal aid through its Victims' Rights and Legal Defense Centers, but is most effective, Carrington believes, through its use of *amicus curiae* legal briefs. Said Carrington: "The court has in effect conceded that we are an informed source. We can bring in more empirical or intellectual data. We also bring in other cases to show prejudice." In one case in which the organization submitted an *amicus curiae* brief, it attempted to persuade the court that police officers may enter the residence of a narcotics suspect if the police are in hot pursuit.

It was out of a similar concern for domestic order that the American Security Council—now the most influential group on the right dedicated to a strong national defense—was formed in 1955. Now ensconced in an 850-acre estate in the Blue Ridge Mountains of Virginia, it grossed $1.8 million for the fiscal year ending March 31, 1977, and experienced, it reported, a threefold increase in membership over the preceding four years. Although it was founded to fight internal subversion—hence its name—the group has made the transition from a Cold War outfit concerned with domestic communism to a modern lobby that promotes beefed-up defense budgets quite successfully, as its fund-raising records suggest. It works to mobilize support for development of new missile systems and, in 1978, opposition to cancellation of the B-1 bomber.

Of special significance, perhaps, is the American Security Council's contribution of $386,000 in 1977 for creation of a Center for International Security Studies, one form of which functions in connection with Georgetown University in Washington, D.C., offering a graduate program in National Security Studies.

SINGLE-ISSUE "FAMILY" LOBBIES

The rise of the single-issue groups such as the gun committees and the antiabortion activists—while superficially a blessing to the New Right organizers—has been something of a frustration to them as well. The leaders are enormously grateful that these groups exist and they work with them whenever possible, but efforts to co-opt them into a larger New Right movement have not always been successful. This lack of success certainly characterizes the New Right's links to Right-to-Life (a movement unto itself) and Phyllis Schlafly's 50,000-member Eagle Forum. These women's groups, while temperamentally related, and overlapping other New Right groups, have maintained organizational independence (see Chapter 5).

Schlafly is undoubtedly a right-winger through and through —she serves on the American Conservative Union board and speaks regularly to right-wing groups—but her Stop-ERA Eagles are loyal only to her. She emphatically denies that they are in any significant way adjuncts of "the Conservative Movement." Jealous of the lists of her dedicated supporters, she does not allow their names to be bought or rented, to the dismay of professional list brokers and fundraisers who would dearly love to fuse them into a larger bank of right-wing names. Eagle Forum is supported by five-dollar-and-up membership dues, but Schlafly can almost at will raise thousands of dollars more when the need arises. *Newsweek* reported in 1979 that before the Equal Rights Amendment votes were taken in the Nevada, North Carolina, Florida, and Illinois legislatures, Schlafly issued an emergency call to her followers. One Missouri housewife responded with a check for $2,000, representing the proceeds from the sale of 450 coconut layer cakes she whipped up in two months of nonstop baking.

The Right-to-Life movement is a successful, broad-based, and well-organized national coalition. New Right leaders have been working to seize control of it and turn its political clout to their own uses, but without complete success. The right-to-lifers have their own press, their own political action committee (the National Pro-Life PAC), even their own political party, which in 1978 fielded candidates for the Democratic presidential nomination and the governorship of New York State. In the statewide race, the Right-to-Life party drew more votes than New York's Liberal party and threatened to render the Conservative party obsolete. The chairman of the National Right-to-Life Committee is Dr. Mildred Jefferson, an articulate black surgeon from Boston; its 1976 presidential candidate was Ellen McCormack, a Roman Catholic housewife and Democrat from Long Island.

The right-to-lifers' great strength lies in the fact that they have not diluted their single-minded constituency by trying to make common cause with, say, the gun and free enterprise lobbies; as a result, they may well be one of the most powerful political forces in the country, ranking with the American Medical Association, the AFL-CIO, and the major political parties themselves. Candidates backed by the National Right-to-Life Committee who won in 1978 included Republican Senators Roger Jepsen of Iowa, Jesse Helms of North Carolina, and Rudy Boschwitz of Minnesota, and Republican Congressman Larry Pressler of South Dakota, who announced in 1979 intention to seek the GOP nomination.

With justification, the right-to-lifers are proud of the way their organization cuts across ideological lines, drawing huge support (for example) from New Deal Democrats of the industrial Northeast. They seem wary, therefore, of attempts to influence them by professional right-wingers or efforts to associate them with what appears to be a much narrower constituency. There is little evidence that the right-to-lifers share the same overriding concerns about their country as the more comprehensive New Right activists. Mrs. McCormack, for example, favors gun registration, day care centers for the poor, détente with the Soviets, and abolition of capital punishment —all of which strike the New Right as dangerously liberal.

This is not to suggest the absence of cooperation between the primary New Right organizations and the autonomous single-issue groups. There is cooperation and a significant overlap in the memberships of these organizations. Efforts are made to further this cooperation as, for example, the decision in 1977 to place groups devoted to preservation of the traditional social roles of the family, the churches, and the schools —which are the generalized concerns of the antiabortion, antibusing, anti–Equal Rights Amendment, and anti-gay-rights constituencies—under the more inclusive rubric of the "pro-family" movement. This larger area of concern includes two very active and notable elements of the New Right coalition, the groups that have risen to address the problems of the public schools and the opponents of gay rights. This latter group, in addition, is an offshoot of what seems to be an intensifying interest in politics on the part of a number of fundamentalist Protestant evangelists.

When in 1977 Anita Bryant conducted a successful campaign to repeal by referendum a Dade County, Florida, ordinance that would have prohibited the firing of homosexual teachers in private schools, her efforts were made possible, to a great extent, by the organizational skills of Mike Thompson, a Miami public relations expert who serves as chairman of the Florida Conservative Union and produced the two documentaries for the American Conservative Union that opposed the Panama Canal treaties and SALT II. Out of the Dade County struggles grew Save Our Children, Inc. Protect America's Children, the political arm of the Bryant organization, moved on to similarly successful efforts in Oregon, Minnesota, and Kansas. Seventeen full-time staff members were working for the Bryant organization when I spoke with Ed Rowe, a fundamentalist minister who is executive director of the Bryant organizations, in 1979, and it planned to branch out into production of television and radio specials to publicize "God, family and country" rallies.

The "pro-family" forces also came together in the West Virginia textbook protests of September 1974. The Heritage Foundation sent attorney James McKenna to act as counsel to the protesting parents, and a representative of Populist Forum handled press relations for the protesters. From Texas, the husband and wife team of Mel and Norma Gabler, activists in Texas textbook struggles, lent their support (Mrs. Gabler traveled to West Virginia to help). In 1975, the Heritage Foundation formed the National Congress for Educational Excellence, intended to unite the widely scattered parents' groups, but the effort had only limited success. Jil Wilson, a Wisconsin housewife active in Kenoshans Concerned for Their Schools and People of America Responding to Educational Needs in Today's Society (PARENTS), wrote in a letter to me:

> To make a LONG sad story short Onalee [*sic*] and I and most
> of the board members left this marvelous dream group after
> two years because unfortunately our choice of leadership was
> as far as I can see our only mistake but the individual who was
> President became very possessive and power hungry and for
> someone reason (I am not sure why) she wanted all the board
> members of this national group to be from her surrounding
> community in Texas. The activities that took place were in-
> credible and although I feel we had a court case I and others
> decided that rather than waste our time and money fighting in
> a court case we would just withdraw from the group and go
> home and keep up the good work as we had done in the past.
> Here I was again in the same position except now I had met
> personally with people like Onallee, George Archibald, the
> Marchner girls and others who were active nationally and also
> people from Wis. who also cared enough to do something
> beside tell me to keep up the good work.

The antibusing groups, another element of the pro-family
forces, are more sophisticated than PARENTS. Protesters
from South Boston, for example, have been aided by the Phillips–Viguerie Conservative Caucus and, at Howard Phillips's
suggestion, formed a monthly luncheon group, attended not
only by antibusing activists but also by Dr. Mildred Jefferson,
national chairman of the National Right-to-Life Committee.
In Los Angeles, BUS-STOP launched a full-fledged direct-mail
fund-raising campaign, organized by Arnold Steinberg; once
press secretary to U.S. Senator James L. Buckley of New York,
he runs a political affairs consulting firm in Sherman Oaks,
California.

By far the slickest of these "pro-family" operations, however, are the television evangelists of the South and Southwest, who are focusing increasing attention on conservative
politics. Chief among these is the Rev. Jerry Falwell, the fundamentalist preacher from Lynchburg, Virginia. Through his
new political organization, Moral Majority, Inc., Falwell—
with the help of New Right leader Howard Phillips—is or-

ganizing other right-wing television evangelists and religious leaders into what they hope will be a united front for "God and Country."

INTERLOCKING DIRECTORATES

Coordinating the activities of the far-flung ad hoc "home and family" groups was the task of Conservative Caucus, under the leadership of Howard Phillips and Richard A. Viguerie since 1975. "The answer is not another Washington-centered institution that claims to speak for people all over the country," Phillips explained. "The answer is to build a local structure through which people can speak for themselves." This is not, however, how the organization actually functioned. An early caucus organizer told me that "Howie was very heavy-handed in his approach to the people he attracted to the idea, and the people who had the skills and experience to really put together a political organization resented it. He had a set of rules they had to follow and they couldn't deviate from them in the least." As Phillips learned, it was impossible to bring all the single-issue groups together under one roof. The organizer explained to me: "What he didn't realize is that you just cannot expect the gun owners, for example, to have the same commitment in terms of energy and time and money to the Conservative Caucus that they have to something really tangible, like a gun club or a labor union. It is just not realistic."

The project was also enormously costly, and the heavy mailings that Viguerie made to keep the organization afloat prompted one Washington wag to begin calling the project "Conservatives for Cash." When it was said to be near death because of financial difficulties in 1978, it became known as "Conservative Carcass." It was "always in debt," a close aide of Phillips told me. All the district organizations were ordered to send their funds, which they were expected to raise on their own, to the national headquarters. There any expenditures had to be approved by Howie. If the money was spent, they had to send receipts. Sometimes they were reimbursed and sometimes they weren't. Things got so bad that more and more of the activities of the national office were being paid for—whether the members liked it or not—out of resources raised by the local organizations. If Howie wanted to hold a statewide conference, he would just announce that he was going to do it. Then the local organizations would say they didn't want one, yet—that they were not organizationally prepared. He'd say he didn't care, that they were going to have a conference anyway and he would fly out—at their expense—and pay the speaker out of their funds, too.

The leaders of the New Right meet continually, at luncheons, dinners, over drinks at Capitol Hill receptions, in formal meetings, and at a weekly "Kingston" high command session, named for a banquet room in a Washington hotel where the first such meetings were held. There they discuss tactics and the strategy of the "movement" as a whole with the individual participants, who in never-ending permutations form the governing and advisory boards, officers, and staff of rightist lobbies, political action committees, legal defense funds, and research and education institutes. The same names appear, over and over, on dozens of letterheads on the stationery of groups like the National Right to Work Committee, the American Conservative Union, the Conservative Caucus, the Committee for Responsible Youth Politics, Young Americans for Freedom and the American Security Council, the Heritage Foundation, and others. The most frequent names are Senator Jesse Helms of North Carolina, Congressman Robert Dornan of California, Howard Phillips, Paul Weyrich, Morton Blackwell, Phyllis Schlafly, Barbara Keating, John T. Dolan, Roger Stone, and M. Stanton Evans.

These leaders and others are building a political movement that has already reshaped, in significant ways, the face of Congress, stalled legislation in its tracks, and pushed through initiatives and referenda. It has its eye on the presidency in coming years, vowing, as one New Right leader told me, "to take control of the culture." Unlike right-wing zealots of the recent past, the New Right has built the organizational structure to make good that promise.

2

Plunder on the Right

Reagannia,
Reagannia!
We struggle to exist,
Our country is not on a map,
It's on a mailing list!
— WASHINGTON HUMORIST MARK RUSSELL

Some people say they can't understand what
becomes of all the money that's collected for cam-
paigns.
— GEORGE WASHINGTON PLUNKETT,
Plunkett of Tammany Hall

"The fat cats are dead," according to an obituary pronounce-
ment of Herbert Alexander, a political scientist at Princeton
who is the nation's acknowledged expert on campaign finance.
The new kingmaker, Alexander says, is the specialist who can
arrange for small contributions or can connect a candidacy to
a fund-raising network that can get him qualified for matching
funds quickly. Behind almost all of these networks on the
Right, as one veteran of conservative political struggles told
me, is one man: "The real effect of the Watergate campaign
reforms has been to vastly increase the power of one man—

Richard Viguerie. Once you have limited the amount of money that big contributors can kick in, it becomes necessary to reach thousands of small contributors. And Viguerie, more than anyone else, is the proven master of this."

Who is this powerful Richard Viguerie, operating in his windowless, temperature-controlled, professionally guarded high-rise offices in Falls Church, Virginia? An intense and somewhat diffident, but nevertheless cheerful man with rapidly thinning hair and a wiry physique, Viguerie, a political rightist, handles only mailing list clients who share his political views. The son of a middle-management petrochemical executive from Texas, Viguerie attended law school in Houston but left to work full-time in the late 1950s for Young Americans for Freedom in New York. A businessman, he is also an ideologue; he has said that his political views were formed in admiration of the "two Macs"—Douglas MacArthur and Joseph McCarthy. Beyond great generosity shown some of his employees (he has been known to treat them to European trips for annual "Richard A. Viguerie" golf tournaments in Scotland), he is an unprepossessing individual, not given to lavish tastes or high living. A dedicated family man, he sends his children to a private Christian school run by fundamentalist Protestants, though he is a Roman Catholic. In 1980, he moved from his large home in suburban Virginia to a townhouse in Washington, D.C.'s Georgetown. His lists form a composite of the American Right. He sometimes exercises great control over the political organizations with which he is associated. The consolidation of that control goes far to account for the growth and influence of the New Right. Viguerie is an unanticipated consequence of the Watergate campaign reforms, which, ironically, were supported largely by liberals who hoped to curb the campaign finance abuses of Richard Nixon's Committee to Re-Elect the President.

In October 1974, a post–Watergate Congress enacted sweeping campaign finance reforms, limiting the amount of money individuals were allowed to contribute to political campaigns and extending federal control over the election process.

These reforms set up a system for federal matching funds; they limited the amount of money that can be spent by individual presidential candidates. The Federal Election Commission was created to monitor compliance. Although the new rules were designed to reduce the role that money plays in elections, they did not succeed. They simply shifted the source. The role of the traditional kingmakers in American politics—the "fat cats" —was indeed reduced, but the power of a tiny number of technicians who have learned to raise small amounts of money from large numbers of contributors was vastly increased. Now that individuals are limited to contributions of $1,000 to any candidate in a primary or general election, candidates must seek money from a large number of supporters. Viguerie is the acknowledged expert at reaching those supporters. Direct-mail solicitation is the core of his strategy. "He is a genius at it," another right-wing fundraiser told me.

But Viguerie is not the only direct-mail specialist on the American Right. A number of his former employees have gone forth, like disciples, to spread the new gospel on their own; they did big business in the late 1970s raising money for Republican candidates and right-wing organizations. A handful of newcomers have entered the field as well.

PACS VOBISCUM

The rise of the direct-mail fundraiser has resulted in a proliferation of political action committees (PACs), the federally sanctioned campaign finance organizations through which individuals can band together to promote or oppose candidates or causes. Under the new campaign laws, PACs must make periodic reports of their activities to the Federal Election Commission. In 1974, the number of PACs registered with the commission was 516. In 1976, following passage of the new rules, 650 new PACs entered the field, and by 1977 the total was 1,360. By 1978, when the Supreme Court okayed the formation of PACs by corporations, PACs were growing at the rate of one a day. During this period, they raised more than $77 million, with direct contributions to candidates for federal office totaling more than $30 million. "These are not just numbers," Senator Adlai Stevenson, Jr., of Illinois told his colleagues. "They illustrate a revolutionary element in American politics. The rise of single-issue politics is paralleled by the rise of focused, single-interest funding of campaigns." Thus, no party and no comprehensive program is supported; rather, a single issue, such as opposition to gun control or abortion, is the heart of this fund raising and political action. Candidates are to be elected or defeated on one issue only, reward or revenge.

PACs are not, of course, new to the political scene, no sinister innovation invented by the strategists of the New Right. Labor PACs, like AFL-CIO's Committee on Political Education, have played a prominent role in partisan politics for years. Nor is the clout of these "special interests," as their critics call them, unique to the Right. Harley Staggers, the labor-oriented West Virginia Democrat who heads the House Interstate and Foreign Commerce committee, and no New Rightist, received 82 percent of his total 1978 contributions from PACs of many persuasions. Until the rise of the New Right, Democratic officeholders and incumbents received the majority of PAC contributions. Thus, in the recent past, the PACs served to strengthen the congressional status quo; but, after the campaign reform laws were enacted, small special interests became more bipartisan; much of the money now raised went to New Right candidates—Democrats and Republicans—and causes. The clout of the New Right is a result of their expertise in the field of direct-mail solicitation, an art they have been refining for years and have only recently employed for specifically political purposes. "Direct mail has allowed conservatives to by-pass the liberal media, and go directly into the homes of the conservatives in this country," Viguerie said to the 1977 Conservative Political Action Conference. "There really is a silent majority in this country, and the New Right now has learned how to identify them and communicate with them and mobilize them." "It's our best way to offset the unions' lavishly financed political organizations," Huck Walther of the National Right to Work Committee told *Conservative Digest*, explaining his group's reliance on direct mail. Since 1978, the conservative PACs have actually been raising vastly more money than organized labor.

Direct-mail solicitation is a sophisticated business that has increased in sophistication since Marvin Leibman, a conservative fundraiser in New York City, kept the names and addresses of contributors to Young Americans for Freedom on 3-by-5-inch index cards in the early 1960s. The mailing list is the most important element in the operation; computers maintain the lists of names, addresses, and other relevant information, thus eliminating costly duplication. These computers also make it possible for solicitors to direct their appeals to specific audiences. William Rusher links the resurgence of the American Right to the mailing lists accumulated in the 1950s and 1960s by Leibman and others.

> Prior to the Draft Goldwater movement of the early 1960s, modern conservatism had developed a respectable body of doctrine and academic spokesmen, but lacked organizational clout. The successful drive to take over the Republican party via the Goldwater candidacy provided that clout. Goldwater's landslide defeat by Lyndon Johnson was of course a bone-crushing disappointment, but it did not alter the fact that, in the process of drafting Barry Goldwater, conservatives all over America had gotten to know each other. The mailing lists accumulated during the Goldwater campaign were the foundation of all subsequent organized political activity on the part of American conservatives.

Goldwater was the first major political candidate for whom supporters conducted a large-scale campaign to solicit political contributions through the mails. In the 1964 presidential campaign, his campaign staff mailed more than 15 million fundraising appeals and raised $5.8 million at an estimated cost of slightly more than $1 million. Goldwater received 380,000 responses, with contributions under $100 each, which went far to disprove a long-standing conviction that direct-mail appeals could not be counted on to raise large sums for political campaigns.

The Arizona senator's success, however, was soon surpassed by another presidential hopeful, Alabama Governor George Wallace, in 1968. Wallace's fundraiser was Viguerie, who had been tutored in the art by Leibman when Viguerie was running Young Americans for Freedom's fundraising operation out of Leibman's New York office. For Wallace, Viguerie raised an estimated $6 million, then an unheard-of sum to be accumulated through mailing appeals. Direct mail accounted for 76 percent of the income for the Wallace campaigns.

By the 1972 presidential campaigns, George McGovern— rejected by the Richard A. Viguerie Co. as too liberal when he asked Viguerie to raise money for him—used another direct-mail company to raise more than $15 million, at a cost of about $4.5 million.

By 1976, direct-mail fund raising had become standard procedure in American political campaigns. A constellation of conservative PACs operating with Viguerie's services was raising more money than the Republican National Committee and its House and Senate campaign committees combined; and a staggering $6 million—as much as was raised for Wallace, a presidential candidate, in 1968—was raised for one senatorial candidate. The impact on American politics has been phenomenal. In 1972, existing conservative organizations raised about $250,000 for the congressional races; but by 1976, New Right PACs, excluding the traditional conservative groups, raised $5.6 million.

Unlike most of the older PACs such as the American Medical Association or the AFL-CIO's Committee on Political Education, which supported primarily incumbents, the New Right gave its money to challengers. Victorious insurgents made great inroads in Congress (see Chapter 11). According to a Gannett News Service analysis in 1978, certain New Right

PACs had much more success than liberal or labor groups: The right-wingers, represented in the study by the Committee for the Survival of a Free Congress, backed thirteen winning challengers, while the liberal National Committee for an Effective Congress backed only one winning challenger and eleven losing incumbents. The AFL-CIO's COPE spent five times as much as the Committee for the Survival of a Free Congress, yet nineteen of the incumbents it supported were beaten. The analysis, according to Gannett reporter Pat Ordovensky, showed "that the activist New Right, which has been making steady gains in both houses of Congress, got by far the most for its money in November's voting." Business and corporate PACs did relatively better than the labor and liberal groups, though not nearly as well as the New Right.

Having already amassed a small fortune from his advertising business, Viguerie now maintains a staff of 300 nonunion employees in the offices of the Richard A. Viguerie Co. (RAVCO) in Falls Church, Virginia, a Washington suburb. His apparatus sends out 100 million pieces of mail a year from some 300 mailing lists that contain the names of 25 million Americans. His inner sanctum is guarded by two different security systems, and even Viguerie himself must produce proper identification before guards will let him in. In his office are 3,000 reels of magnetic computer tape containing the names and addresses of more than 10 percent of the population of the United States. Two giant computers, leased for $2,700 per month, operate twenty-four hours a day; high-speed printers and tape units churn out the letters, which are packaged and mailed from various Viguerie businesses in northern Virginia.

Though he began in 1965 with a $400 investment, Viguerie now claims to turn away 90 percent of the potential political clients who approach him; and the business is said to gross about $15 million a year. His start in business is interesting: He handled Young Americans for Freedom's fund raising, but was fired. John Fialka reported in the *Washington Star* that Viguerie took the mailing list with him when he departed. From that inauspicious beginning, he built his flourishing business.

Viguerie's clients, for the most part, have been political right-wingers more interested in issues like busing, gun control, and sexual permissiveness than, for example, free market economics. Among his clients have been Conservative Books for Christian Leaders, No Amnesty for Deserters, Citizens for Decent Literature (now known as Citizens for Decency Through Law), the National Rifle Association, Gun Owners of America, Conservative Caucus, and the National Conservative Political Action Committee—names that reflect Viguerie's personal range of political concerns.

But, as discussed later in this chapter, RAVCO has also been heavily involved in raising money for not-for-profit charities. As a result of his high fund-raising costs, officials in Ohio and New York have pressured him to sign consent orders agreeing to hold his fees to a certain limit, which varies from state to state. Rejecting the notion that his constituency will finally give all they can afford to give and then cut off the flow of money, he maintains that lists of regular contributors can be expected to continue growing by 20 to 25 percent for the next three to five years, reaching eight million Americans by the year 1982. Television figures prominently in his plans. He envisions using thirty-minute television messages, devoting twenty-five minutes to discussion of a political issue and then a fund-raising appeal in the last five minutes. Viewers would be asked to call a toll-free number to pledge donations. He publishes a newsletter, *The New Right Report,* and a monthly magazine, *Conservative Digest;* and he has considered starting a weekly newspaper and venturing into the production of radio programs.

Other New Right fundraisers plying the direct-mail trade (and successfully competing with Viguerie) include Bruce W. Eberle, a long-time activist in Young Americans for Freedom who learned the business as a Viguerie employee and began a direct-mail business of his own in the basement of his home in suburban Virginia in 1974. Within two months, his business had expanded into offices in a commercial building in Virginia. Business continued to boom at such a rate that the growing staff moved again in November 1975, by this time occupying nine offices and a conference room plus graphics department. Eberle formed the Omega Mailing Company that year, and signed a direct-mail contract with the Ronald Reagan presidential campaign. For Reagan, Bruce W. Eberle & Associates raised more money in a shorter period of time than any other presidential candidate. The Reagan campaign ended up in 1976 with a surplus in excess of $1 million. The Eberle staff of almost twenty employees that year took over one-half of the seventh floor of a large office building in fashionable Tyson's Corner, Virginia.

A number of other New Right activists are also getting into the direct-mail business, and an increasing number of clients clamor for their services. Allan M. Gottlieb, an ambitious young New Rightist associated with the Citizens Committee for the Right to Keep and Bear Arms, has handled fundraising for the American Conservative Union and is now building an empire of related businesses in Washington State. H. L. Richardson, a California state senator once employed by the John Birch Society, has his own direct-mail business in Sacramento. Another conservative fundraiser has called Richardson's operation "a carbon copy" of Viguerie's RAVCO.

The mailing lists accumulated by the fundraisers and their clients are often exchanged—usually bought or sold but sometimes loaned. In 1977, for example, State Senator John Briggs of Orange County, California, crusader against homosexuals, used the mailing list built by Anita Bryant's fundraiser to support Proposition 6, his anti-gay rights ballot measure. As Marvin Leibman told me: "Ever since [the direct-mail business] took off, there's been an entire army of hustlers emerge —list brokers, public affairs consultants, copywriters, mailing house operators . . . an entire army!" George Will has referred to the right-wing pen pals as "quasi-political entrepreneurs who have discovered commercial opportunities in merchandising discontent. . . ."

The key to all of these appeals is anger and fear. As Terry

Dolan of the National Conservative Political Action Committee told me, his organization's fund-raising letters try to "make them angry" and "stir up hostilities." The "shriller you are," he said, the easier it is to raise funds. "That's the nature of our beast," he explained. The fund-raising letters of the New Right groups depict a world gone haywire, with liberal villains poised to destroy the American Way of Life. After reciting a list of horrors about to be perpetrated, the signatory—often a prominent right-wing activist or politician —asks for "help" from the recipient, frequently requesting his participation in a survey or poll; then he is asked to contribute and told how his $5 or $10 contribution will be used to further the counterattack on the liberals. In the case of a political campaign, almost invariably launched to defeat some "radical" incumbent, the donor is told that his $10 will be used, for example, to maintain a phonebank for a given period of time. The more specific they can be, the fundraisers have learned, the more likely they will be to receive a contribution. They try to get the donor involved—or at least get him to feel that he is involved.

The letters vary according to the organization and the fundraiser, but, stylistically, there are great similarities. They address "Dear Friend." They employ direct personal warnings of what will happen to "*you.*" They use rhetorical questions. They cast blame on a vaguely identified enemy. They offer a way out. Most could have been written by a single hand. The following letter is from the Americans Against Union Control of Government, signed by executive vice-president Donald Y. Denholm:

> Dear Friend,
> What would you do if your home caught fire right now? Call the Fire Department, right?
> But what if they don't answer?
> What if the phone keeps ringing while flames rage through your home, destroying valued possessions, perhaps even taking the life of a loved one.

That might sound like an impossible nightmare to you. Something that couldn't possibly happen.

But it has already happened.

City after city in America has been shocked recently by illegal strikes, by Police and Firemen unions.

And I wanted to write to you today—before another illegal strike called by the big union bosses endangers you and your family—to tell you how you can help prevent such a disaster.

From the Free Congress Research and Education Foundation, Inc:

Dear Friend:

Do you believe that children should have the right to sue their parents for being "forced" to attend church?

Should children be eligible for minimum wage if they are asked to do household chores?

Do you believe that children should have the right to choose their own family?

As incredible as they might sound, these are just a few of the new "children's rights laws" that could become a reality under a new United Nations program if fully implemented by the Carter Administration.

If radical anti-family forces have their way, this U.N. sponsored program is likely to become an all-out assault on our traditional family structure.

From Save Our Children, Inc., underlined in red and signed by Anita Bryant:

When the homosexuals burn the Holy Bible in public . . . how can I stand by silently.

Dear Friend:

I don't hate the homosexuals!

But as a mother I must protect my children from their evil influence.

. . . Do you realize what they want?

They want to recruit our school children under the protection of the laws of our land!

From Citizens for the Republic, signed by executive director Lyn Nofziger:

Dear Friend:
YOU CAN BET THAT SOMEWHERE IN THE VAST LABYRINTH OF THE FEDERAL BUREAUCRACY THERE'S A FILE ON YOU!
It may be a Social Security record, an FHA record, or an OSHA record.
It may be at HUD or the Department of Agriculture. Or it may be at the Federal Elections Commission.
BIG BROTHER GOVERNMENT WILL GO TO ANY LENGTH TO KEEP A TAB ON YOU . . .

From Americans for LIFE signed by Ohio state representative Donald E. "Buz" Lukens:

Dear Friend:
Please take a second right now to look at the outrageous pro-abortion political propaganda I've enclosed.
And then help me STOP THE BABY KILLERS by signing and mailing the enclosed anti-abortion postcards to your U.S. Senators. (You'll find a list of all U.S. Senators on the back of that sickening baby killer propaganda.)
These anti-life Baby Killers are already organizing, working and raising money to re-elect pro-abortionists like George McGovern, South Dakota . . . Congressman Robert Drinan, Massachusetts . . . Senators John Culver, Iowa . . . Frank Church, Idaho . . . Birch Bayh, Indiana . . . men who apparently think it's perfectly OK to slaughter unborn infants by abortion. . . .
Abortion means killing a living baby, a tiny human being with a beating heart and little fingers . . . killing a baby boy or girl with burning deadly chemicals or a powerful machine that sucks and tears the little infant from its mother's womb.
And to my way of thinking, that's just plain murder. . . .
Yes, I'm harsh when I call [these Senators] Baby Killers, but it's time we exposed them for what they are. If they want to

talk about abortions, then let's unite and perform an abortion
on their political lives.

Abort them at the ballot box and save innocent babies who've
done nothing wrong.

From the Conservative Caucus, signed by Howard Phillips:

Dear Friend:
I think you will appreciate, more than most Americans, what
I am sending you.
I have enclosed two flags: the red, white, and blue of Old
Glory—and the white flag of surrender.
I want to show you, by these two flags, what is at stake for
America under the SALT II Treaty with Russia.
If the U.S. Senate ratifies SALT II (the Strategic Arms
Limitation Treaty negotiated by Kremlin Boss Leonid Brezh-
nev with Jimmy Carter) it will mean the permanent surrender
of the United States of America to the military superiority of
the Soviet Union.
You and I must choose—and the Senate must decide—
whether we will personally accept the White Flag of Surrender
as America's banner.
Or, whether we are prepared to work and sacrifice to keep
Old Glory perpetually raised on high.

In a textbook case of New Right mailbox campaign tactics,
Washington State Congressman John E. (Jack) Cunningham
in a special election in 1977 faced a liberal Democrat, Marvin
Durning, for the congressional seat vacated by Brock Adams,
who had resigned to become President Carter's secretary of
transportation. Going after Durning's blue-collar Democratic
constituents, Republican Cunningham scored the upset of the
year, garnering 54 percent of the vote. He portrayed himself
as a self-made man with Middle-American roots, and depicted
the Harvard-educated Durning as an Ivy League lawyer whose
real allegiance was to the liberal establishment in Washington.
Making jobs "the number one issue," Cunningham accused

Durning of favoring defense cuts and environmental regulations that would cost Washington workers their jobs. He outspent his opponent two-to-one, raising a war chest of $250,000. RAVCO produced "up front" contributions of $5,000 from the National Conservative Political Action Committee and other New Right PACs—with a few strings attached. According to reporter Nick Kotz, writing in *The Atlantic,* the seed money had to be invested with Viguerie later in a direct-mail fund-raising campaign. "Viguerie had the whole piece of cake, and Cunningham is happy because he won. 'You can't tell Viguerie what to do. He is the master of his ship and, if you're going to tie your dinghy to it, you go where he goes.' "

Less than a month after he was elected, Cunningham allowed his name to be used in a national conservative PAC fund-raising appeal, explaining in the mailing brochure that passage of the voter registration bill before Congress would allow George Meany and his "henchmen" to take over the election process. "The union bosses will have their troops out there on the streets on election day, digging up derelicts, vagrants and anyone else who will take a dollar to cast a vote. . . ."

With the money raised by what one right-wing activist disdainfully calls these "panic letters," the fundraisers have built a complex and enormously profitable and interdependent business. Some of the organizations for which Viguerie raises funds are continually in debt to him, for example, yet the employees and officers of these organizations do not appear to be concerned by this burden. In interviews with me in March and May 1979, respectively, Paul Weyrich of the Committee for the Survival of a Free Congress and John T. Dolan of the National Conservative Political Action Committee admitted that each of their organizations owed RAVCO at least $200,-000. They do not worry about such things, Dolan said, because new mailings will keep them afloat. In fact, one professional fundraiser who has worked closely with Viguerie and considers him "a friend," told me he believes RAVCO tolerates the debt for good reasons.

They think Richard is doing them a big favor because they owe him a lot of money and he doesn't make them pay up.

It's like when the guy is winning in poker and says he'll let the loser stay in the game if he'll agree to play for double-or-nothing. Since they owe him money anyway they think he is doing them a favor. What they don't understand is that in the direct-mail business, he has already made a colossal profit off of them and will continue to make more each time he mails for them, whether they pay off the debt or not. He volunteers to keep them going by continuing to mail for them, so they go ahead. There is one way out of the relationship. They can get out at any time they want, but Richard will say: Okay, but can you pay me now? There's not much they can do but keep in the relationship, letting him continue to raise money for them, while he continues to take his cut.

The fundraiser informed me: "The organizations themselves may lose money, but their employees do not. The PAC employees make good money, even if their organizations are always in debt." And another conservative activist who has also been involved in direct-mail fund-raising on a consulting basis explained it this way: "We're creating an entire conservative welfare class in Washington alone—people who cannot do much else who are doing very well off the $10 checks of little old ladies on Social Security."

In 1977, RAVCO raised money for the successful congressional campaign of New Rightist Robert Livingston, the first Republican to represent his Louisiana district since 1874. It was an impressive victory since only 10 percent of the district's voters are Republicans, but Livingston—with RAVCO's help —spent substantially more than his Democratic opponent. A routine investigation by the Federal Election Commission discovered that Livingston's campaign committee owed RAVCO about $40,000. The Federal Election Commission found no evidence of any illegality. It did remark on the unusual way the debt settlement had been reached. The committee's creditor, RAVCO, was also the fundraiser. As an FEC report stated, it "would not in this commercial arrangement seem reasonable for the creditor to go to court to enforce its debt, since the debtor would ultimately have to turn to its fundraiser in order to obtain the money to satisfy the debt." In other words (borrowing from Peter to pay Paul), the debt was paid—with interest—by April 1978.

Some critics suspect that political fundraisers may create organizations solely to function as fronts for direct-mail campaigns and primarily to make money for themselves. But blanket charges are probably not really fair; many individuals involved in these "fronts" are sincere ideologues, using the direct-mail business, however profitable, to build their political movement and to advance the causes for which the funds are raised. (The term "plunder" is used here not to mean necessarily *personal* profit but, rather, the gathering up of peoples' money to use for purposes other than those its owners intend.)

Right-wing PACs frequently loan money to one another, according to reports filed with the Federal Election Commission; and at least one such organization came into existence through extension of a loan from a similar group. The Committee for Responsible Youth Politics, ostensibly a school for the training of young campaign workers, also functions as a political action committee, raising more than $177,000 from 1976 to 1978. Its chairman is Morton C. Blackwell, for years an employee of the Viguerie Company, who left Viguerie in 1979 to work for Senator Gordon Humphrey of New Hampshire. At the same time, when Blackwell was an executive of RAVCO and chairman of the Committee for Responsible Youth Politics, Federal Election Commission reports show, the PAC was frequently in debt to Viguerie. Interlocking relationships of this kind led the National Committee for an Effective Congress to file a complaint with the Federal Election Commission in 1977, charging that the National Conservative Political Action Committee, the Committee for the Survival of a Free Congress, and the Committee for Responsible Youth Politics might be one committee, under RAVCO control and with Viguerie "the central figure." The FEC concluded that each committee is independent.

A few knowledgeable conservatives who have worked closely with many of the PAC leaders told me of one vast operation the individual components of which exist because clients are in debt to their fundraiser. One participant has described to me periodic meetings at which representatives of the various committees meet to decide which candidates are to be supported, and how. "They sit around with their pocket calculators," the participant explained, "and go around the table, discussing different candidates; and one will say: We can give $5,000, and another will say: We can give $1,500, until it is decided. . . ."

Another associate of the PAC leaders told me of less frequent meetings that last an entire weekend and are attended by "the money people on the Right." Called "Red Fox" meetings after a lodge at which the first meeting took place, these sessions map out long-range political strategies. It was at one of these meetings, one participant told me, that Viguerie quipped: "My political principles? That's easy. M-O-N-E-Y."

The limits imposed by the 1974 election laws caused some trouble even for New Right fundraisers. But the way around them was readily at hand. Almost every right-wing organization (like many liberal groups) has formed its own tax-exempt foundation; and John T. (Terry) Dolan of the National Conservative Political Action Committee admitted to me that his group formed the National Conservative Research and Educational Foundation (NCREF) for "our contributors who want to help but can't go over the $5,000 limit." Campaign finance laws permit this maneuver. Thus, contributors may give $5,000 to the National Conservative Political Action Committee and another $5,000 to the National Conservative Research and Educational Foundation.

This has clearly aided the rise of independent expenditure by political action committees (PACs). The U.S. Supreme Court struck down portions of the campaign finance law in 1976, ruling that Congress could not impose spending limits on those who wish to advocate or oppose a candidate's election without prior approval of the candidate. That year, the American Conservative Union's Conservative Victory Fund ran a

$250,000 campaign for Ronald Reagan; Hank Grover, a former state legislator in Texas, spent $63,000 of his own money on pro-Reagan activities. And the National Conservative Political Action Committee informed thousands of its donors in 1979 of its plan to "actually seize control of the U.S. Senate" in 1980 by earmarking more than $700,000 in independent expenditures for campaigns to oppose five "radical" senators, all Democrats. Spokesmen announced that $403,000 was to be used for a campaign to oppose Alan Cranston, with $338,000 of that to be spent on letters to voters—letters, it is assumed, that will ask for still *more* money. Dolan said he hoped the effort would chip away 20 percent of the vote from their intended victims in the primary polls (see Chapter 11). There were also plans afloat to ease some liberal to moderate Republicans out of office.

A New York organization called the Committee to Replace Jacob Javits—some of its members were associated with the Conservative Party of New York—flooded the Senator's Capitol Hill office in 1979 with postcards:

> *DEAR SENATOR JAVITS:*
>
> *HAPPY 75TH BIRTHDAY.*
>
> *WHY NOT QUIT WHILE YOU'RE AHEAD?*
>
> *RETIRE IN 1980!*
>
> *Sincerely,_____*

The group described Javits as "an allegedly Republican United States Senator whose voting record . . . is more liberal than many Democratic senators," and said "it is Jacob Javits' turn to retire or be defeated."

The New Right activists have also maneuvered around the limitations of the new campaign finance law through the formation of PACs associated with presidential candidacies; yet these are actually created to allow the presidential hopeful to campaign for lesser office seekers in his party. These committees allow the expenses of campaigning to be paid through an organization technically not for that purpose. They avoid contribution limits—individuals are prohibited from contributing more than $1,000 to a candidate but they are allowed to give up to $5,000 to a "multi-candidate political action committee," even if it exists primarily to support the campaign activities of a presidential aspirant. They enable a candidate or his allies to raise and spend money to further a campaign without counting it against the maximum spending limits imposed on any candidate who wants to accept federal matching funds. Multi-candidate PACs associated with presidential candidates were expected to raise about $14 million in 1980.

The largest of these committees is Citizens for the Republic, formed in 1977, according to a committee spokesman, with roughly $250,000 left over from Citizens for Reagan, the campaign committee that backed the former California governor for the 1976 GOP nomination. With the services of Bruce Eberle, this group built a list of 300,000 contributors; and its 1978 budget of $2.5 million exceeded that of the political arms of such traditional special interest groups as the AFL-CIO, the American Medical Association, the National Education Association, and the United Auto Workers. It paid Reagan's traveling expenses, allowing him to campaign almost constantly for GOP candidates and thus to collect political IOUs. None of this counted as part of Reagan's own fund-raising activities for the 1980 election, which was to be conducted under different auspices. During the last congressional elections, the Reagan committee gave almost $575,000 to candidates—all of whom would be asked to remember Reagan in 1980.

However effective the New Right has been in building its movement and mobilizing its constituency through direct-mail advertising, this success has come at an enormous cost to those constituents, often unbeknown to most of them. Huge sums of money have been raised to elect or defeat candidates, but much of the money contributed by interested individuals for candidates and causes never goes to the purpose for which it was raised. It ends up at the disposal of the fundraiser, not the candidates or organizations, with the fundraiser deciding what cause to spend it on. Some conservative critics see the booming direct-mail business as small-scale hucksterism that was perfected when right-wing publicists and fundraisers dabbled in charities; linked to political finance, the situation has reached, in many instances, the proportions of a large-scale scandal.

FROM CHARITIES TO CAMPAIGN FINANCE

At least as early as 1970, right-wing fundraisers and public relations experts were involved in charitable fund-raising, often with a political flavor. The transition from not-for-profit fundraising to campaign finance was an easy one. One of the earliest of these quasi-charitable operations was the United Police Fund, a project of right-wing fundraiser Patrick Gorman. The United Police Fund, using the Public Trust Foundation of Chicago as a tax-exempt front, in 1970 distributed appeals showing pictures of the families of dead policemen around the graves of the officers. The purpose of the organization, it was said, was to help the widows and children of the slain law enforcement officers. Its fund-raising letters were signed by Congressman Sam Devine, an Ohio Republican, who later said he had been "deceived" by the promoters, who were running the show with what a congressional investigator called an "unconscionable contract," so high were the fund-raising costs. In two years, the project netted a reported $110,000, almost 90 percent of which went to fundraiser Gorman. The Police Departments of Los Angeles and New York City barred their employees from any involvement with the organization; and the operation, exposed in the press, dissolved.

Viguerie has applied charity fund-raising techniques to single-issue campaigns, with comparable results. In 1971, Viguerie raised money for an anti-smut group called Citizens for Decent Literature. It still exists, without Viguerie and with a new name—Citizens for Decency Through Law, with far-right California Republican Congressman Robert K. Dornan on its governing board. Its founder and director is Charles Keating, a Cincinnati lawyer who, as a member of President Nixon's Commission on Obscenity and Pornography, wrote a dissent to the commission's final report, later accepted by the President and the Senate, which rejected the more liberal conclusions of Keating's colleagues, 60 to 5. Keating refused to discuss his relations with RAVCO with me, but an audit by the Charity Frauds division of the New York State Attorney General's office showed that in 1971 Viguerie raised $1.2 million for Citizens for Decent Literature, 84 percent of which went back to his own company. The next year, RAVCO raised almost as much, taking 81.4 percent home to the fundraiser. An estimated $2.3 million was raised over the two-year period.

In 1977, RAVCO raised funds for a project called the Children's Relief Fund. A program of the Korean Cultural and Freedom Foundation, the Children's Relief Fund is part of the world-wide operation of the controversial Reverend Sun Myung Moon of South Korea. Its president is Colonel Bo Hi Pak, widely regarded as Moon's right-hand man and believed to have close ties to the Korean CIA. On its board of directors is Neil Salonen, president of the Unification Church of America. Fund-raising literature for this organization states: "As I write you this letter thousands of little boys and girls are suffering from the terminal forms of malnutrition. . . . What better gift could you give than a gift to fight suffering and death?" That way, of course, was to send money, and lots of big-hearted Americans did. The New York state auditors discovered that, in all, $1,508,256 came in from the appeals, although less than 6.3 percent ever got back to the needy, starving Asian children. "The disproportionate and wholly inadequate expenditures for program services ($95,674)," the attorney general concluded, "was the direct result of the unconscionably high fees of $920,302 (60 percent of expenses) disbursed to the professional fundraiser Viguerie. . . ."

The state of Ohio brought action against the operation, charging the Korean Cultural and Freedom Foundation with filing a financial statement that was "inaccurate, false and misleading," and Viguerie with failing to register as required by law as a fundraiser in the state. Officials concluded that the project had caused "substantial annoyance, inconvenience and pecuniary injury to residents," and Viguerie agreed to sign a consent order to limit its costs for solicitations within Ohio. As a result of the investigation he was temporarily barred from mailing in Ohio and Connecticut. State officials in Massachusetts, Minnesota, Vermont, Illinois, and Arizona, along with the Internal Revenue Service, the Federal Bureau of Investigation, and the Immigration and Naturalization Service, made special inquiries into the New York investigation.

During roughly the same period, RAVCO was handling the fund-raising for another ostensibly charitable group, Bibles for the World, which exists to distribute Bibles in Asia. This group began direct-mail solicitation in 1976; and reports for the year ending in 1977 show that the solicitation, handled by RAVCO, raised $802,028 at an incredible cost of $889,255. Viguerie's fund-raising costs thus came to about 112 percent of the contributions, leaving the organization worse off than it was before it entered the contract. Needless to say, nothing was left with which to distribute Bibles.

A similar operation came to light in 1975 when Congressman Lionel Van Deerlin, a California Democrat, investigated a number of charitable institutions, and discovered a "charlatan-like operation" called the Underground Bible Fund. This group, he said in congressional hearings,

> undertook to persuade prospective donors that for every $2 that came in there would be five Bibles (distributed) in the native tongue of the Iron Curtain country. Working backward from the maildrop, we couldn't ascertain whether one single Bible had ever been delivered to one single person behind the Iron Curtain, despite more than $200,000 that had been collected.

An aide to Van Deerlin recalls New Right publicist Lee Edwards's involvement in the operation, calling it "a classic case" of a charity that uses a professional fundraiser "who skimmed off as much as 80 percent." The same group that conducted the Underground Bible Fund operation, the Congressman said, was also involved in a scheme called Save Our Symbol, the purpose of which was to convince Americans not to shoot eagles. "All of these were doing quite well," he said, "and we found they were mingling the mailing lists. They culled an excellent list from people who do send in money in response to these appeals. They had quite an ongoing business there, just this one outfit . . . quite a bit of money is being stashed away, which money was obviously well-intended and could have found its way into legitimate charities." Some observers have criticized the extent to which Viguerie controls the mailing lists he builds for clients, to buy or sell as he sees fit—even in the case of not-for-profit charities.

To minimize charity abuses, Democratic Congressman Charles Wilson of California has introduced a bill that would require nonprofit organizations to make public the percentages of their contributions that actually go to the causes they represent. New Right spokesmen began to fight back; *Conservative Digest,* for example, published an article under the by-line of former Arizona Congressman John B. Conlan (Rep.) defending the fundraisers:

> The portions of the bill that deal with expenses and income, the costs of fundraising, and the expenditure of charitable funds raise serious problems. Charitable mailing can be divided into two categories, both with totally divergent purposes and cost of fundraising.
>
> One category of mailing is called "prospecting"—the seeking of new friends and contributors who have never given before. The return from such a mass mailing to prospects would be considered good if it makes a small amount of money or breaks even. A return of 1 or 2 percent is common. Wouldn't this cost, if published in the mailing piece, inhibit the effort to build a list of long-term friends and donors?

The Heritage Foundation also took up the matter. An "issue bulletin" released by the organization argued that the Wilson bill "would discriminate against new charitable organizations and those with necessarily high fund-raising costs," subjecting religious leaders to "vicious" accusations of fraud by the knaves at the U.S. Postal Service.

> Opponents of H.R. 41 fear that this measure is the first step to a legislative strategy to eliminate tax-exempt status for all non-profit organizations.
>
> [By requiring charities to notify their donors of such costs, the Wilson bill] will increase the paperwork on every Christian organization by providing each potential donor with financial statements with each appeal, creating additional costs and inevitably lessening the funds each charity can use for its stated purpose.

Affixed to a picture of Conlan was a caption telling the reader that he "defends charities against Big Government," and at the bottom of the article ran the message: "Reprint permission for this article granted by its publisher." Its publisher: Richard A. Viguerie.

FUNDING THE SINGLE-ISSUE GROUPS

In 1971, Patrick Gorman and Lee Edwards, later to emerge as editor of Richard Viguerie's *Conservative Digest,* started Friends of the FBI, which, in the words of one participant, "produced a Niagara of dollars." Friends of the FBI was put together ostensibly to express support for J. Edgar Hoover, a hero to New Rightists, who was coming under increasing criticism from the liberals and the Left. With the help of Louis Kutner, a Chicago attorney attached to the tax-exempt Commission for International Due Process of Law, the partners prevailed upon Efrem Zimbalist, Jr. (star of television's long-running serial "The FBI") to sign a fund-raising letter. Within four months, they had raised close to $400,000, about two-thirds of which ($256,000) was eaten up in operating expenses. The rest was divided among Kutner, Gorman, and Edwards. Soon Zimbalist became suspicious, claiming he had been "used" by the partners; and his lawyers told the group to stop using their client's name, accusing them in a letter of "fraud and misrepresentation." Pressed to account for the group's activities, the partners announced publication of a study of the FBI, which was subsequently published by the group itself as *Whose FBI?* The organization still exists and has since issued newsletters and a booklet, AMERICA'S INTERNAL SECURITY: ITS DANGEROUS DECLINE AND WHAT TO DO ABOUT IT.

In 1974, Viguerie raised money for the Americans for Effective Law Enforcement, a law-and-order group then operating out of Evanston, Illinois. He raised $198,568 and took 90 percent of the contributions. The next year, when Americans for Effective Law Enforcement stopped using RAVCO, its fund-raising costs dropped to 43 percent of the contributions. Nevertheless, Frank Carrington, its executive director, told me that he was not at all dissatisfied with the earlier relationship, saying he and Viguerie are "still good friends."

His group went into the arrangement "with our eyes open," Carrington said. Americans for Effective Law Enforcement officials were well aware, he said, that the costs of fund-raising would be high, so they tucked away between $400,000 and $500,000 well in advance to cover programs they had planned for the year. Carrington said Viguerie told him that his group would "barely break even," but he admitted that "we didn't know how barely." RAVCO raised $202,000 at a cost of $198,-000, and "we found we were just trading dollars." RAVCO brought thousands of names of new donors that Americans for Effective Law Enforcement could use for its own fund-raising, and the group now has its own "house list" to which it can appeal, without Viguerie. But when Americans for Effective Law Enforcement showed no further interest in continued "prospecting," as the process of seeking new contributors is called, RAVCO canceled the contract. Now RAVCO and

Americans for Effective Law Enforcement share the list of donors; and Viguerie is allowed to use the names for other fund-raising appeals, but only for groups not involved in law enforcement–related issues.

Carrington maintains that the 90 percent figure as a cost of fund-raising for 1974 is misleading. Since his organization already had almost half a million dollars set aside for its program before it used RAVCO's services, he adds that sum to the $4,000 net raised by the direct-mail appeal, which would leave 64 percent of the year's budget for program activities.

A similar report comes from the National Rifle Association, for whom RAVCO raised money in 1975. That year Viguerie agreed to handle the fund-raising for the NRA's Institute for Legislative Action and brought in $5.8 million at a cost of $3.2 million. Even so, a spokesman for the gun lobby said there was no dissatisfaction over the costs. H. K. McGaffin, fiscal director for the Institute for Legislative Action, told me that RAVCO's "prospecting" brought his group an additional 600,000 names. And while the expenses were "tremendous," the mailing "paid for itself" by building the organization's list of contributors. All in all, he said, it was a "pretty good relationship," which ended only because the NRA decided it could handle its own fund-raising from now on, working from the list RAVCO built for it. In the three years that Viguerie worked for the NRA, $12 million rolled in, at what cost McGaffin could not say. NRA was happy with the arrangement and RAVCO was happy with the arrangement. Only the unsuspecting thousands who sent their money thinking it would be used to fight gun control legislation, and not to purchase others' names and addresses, might be offended. And they did not know.

The New Right fundraisers have become more and more deeply involved in political finance. In 1970, Viguerie raised money for rejected Supreme Court nominee G. Harrold Carswell, then seeking the Republican nomination for a Florida Senate seat. Edward J. Gurney, then a GOP senator from Florida, agreed to sign the fund-raising appeals. When they arrived in the mailboxes of prospective contributors, the appeals contained a return envelope addressed to Gurney's suite in the old Senate Office Building in Washington. Federal law at the time provided for a maximum penalty of up to $5,000 in fines and three years in jail for public officials who receive "money or anything of value for any political purpose" in "any room or building occupied in the discharge of official duties." A spokesman for Gurney said all funds would be sent to an address in Florida. It was just a "slip-up" by the mailing house, Gurney's spokesman said. The mailing house was Viguerie's.

Such slip-ups continue. A solicitation from the Citizens Committee for the Right to Keep and Bear Arms, then using the Viguerie mailing house, came under fire in 1977 when several disgruntled members of Congress found their names had been used in a mailing of some 500,000 letters, reading "From Congressman ———." As might be expected, this was not appreciated by the congressmen, who had not given their permission to the anti-gun-control group. "I cannot believe there is anyone in the Congress more opposed to gun control legislation than I am," Republican Congressman Robert S. Walker of Pennsylvania said. "However, I cannot and will not condone this kind of irresponsible special interest appeal for money." Calling the organization's action "highly unethical and grossly ill-conceived," Walker said the appeal "bears my name in a fashion designed to mislead the recipient into believing that I am sanctioning and sponsoring this effort to solicit money." Walker asked Citizens Committee chairman Allan M. Gottlieb to issue a follow-up mailing to set the facts straight; but his response, Walker said, "was to hang up the telephone in the middle of our conversation."

Another congressman to complain was Bob Carr, a Michigan Democrat who opposed the aims of the Citizens Committee. "People all over the United States were misled by this," he said. "It is gross and wanton fraud to use my name in a way that implied that I favor something that I actually oppose." The Citizens Committee finally agreed to return any funds generated by the misleading solicitation, including a statement to the recipient that the previous mailing "may have led you erroneously to believe that your congressional representative had sent the solicitation or had authorized or otherwise concurred in the use of his name on the solicitation." The group's chief lobbyist said: "The company that handled the mailings admitted that it was just a mistake, an accident."

Abuse of congressional letterheads by fundraisers has become so prevalent that at least one congressman—Democrat Berkley Bedell of Iowa—proposed a change in House rules to prohibit any member from mailing on congressional stationery more than 500 copies of any unsolicited message not dealing with official business. Bedell said the use of the letterhead, even when it carries a notice in small print that the message is "not prepared or mailed at public expense," has a tendency "to make people believe that the cause, whatever it is, has been sanctioned by the United States Congress."

A recent case involves the ubiquitous Robert K. Dornan of California who allowed his stationery to be used in a fund-raising appeal for Larry Pratt of the Gun Owners of America, then seeking to raise a staggering $27,850 for his campaign to win a seat in the Virginia House of Delegates. Pratt's organization, which uses RAVCO's fund-raising services, has the dubious distinction of having been hit by the Federal Election Commission with the heaviest fines in FEC history. Fines of $11,000 were imposed in 1978 on Gun Owners and two affiliated PACs for making illegal contributions to the parent committee and for failing to register and report as PACs.

Huge amounts of money have been raised by the New Right PACs, but relatively meager amounts have actually been received by the candidates for whom the money is raised. By and large, the worst offenders have been PACs using RAVCO as their fundraiser. However, some PACs independent of Viguerie must bear responsibility for their own activities. For example, WIN-PAC, the Western Intermountain Network Political Action Committee, was the creation of Stan Burger, an unsuccessful Republican candidate for the U.S. Senate in 1976, who lost to Democratic Congressman John Melcher by a two-to-one margin, despite Burger's having outspent Melcher

$609,000 to $311,000.* Ostensibly established to support Mountain West New Rightists, the committee's 1978 filings with the Federal Election Commission show that it raised $187,101.46, none of which, according to federal political election filings, was contributed to political candidates. Several thousand dollars, however, were paid in salaries and consulting fees to various Burgers, including chairman Stan Burger, in Bozeman and Belgrade, Montana.

Weyrich's Committee for the Survival of a Free Congress in 1976 raised almost $1.7 million to give away around $265,000 with about sixteen cents on the dollar going to the candidates donors thought they were sending their money to support. Two years later, with just under $1.2 million raised, the amount contributed to candidates slipped to $127,000, or a dime on the dollar. The bulk, of course, was split between CSFC and Viguerie-owned companies. The National Conservative Political Action Committee, whose success, its executive director John T. Dolan told me, is measured in terms of its fund-raising, raised even more than the Committee for the Survival of a Free Congress in 1976: $2.5 million, of which about 16 percent, or $386,800, went to candidates. In the 1978 congressional elections, NCPAC raised $1.5 million and contributed $212,000 to candidates.

In 1976, Gun Owners of America raised $2.1 million to contribute $153,000 to candidates—about seven cents on the dollar. Another anti-gun-control group, Gottlieb's Right to Keep and Bear Arms Political Victory Fund, the campaign arm of the Citizens Committee for the Right to Keep and Bear Arms, has a record only slightly better than the other groups. In 1976, it raised $77,000, giving $18,600 or 23 percent to candidates, a percentage that dropped to 12 percent ($26,250) in 1978 when much more—$217,000—was raised through the mails.

---

*A Burger for Senate fund-raising event during the 1976 campaign was arranged for the candidate by the staff of North Carolina Senator Jesse Helms and held on federal property on Capitol Hill. Federal law prohibits the exchange of political contributions on federal property.

Young Americans for Freedom is also in the fund-raising business, with the Fund for a Conservative Majority. In 1976, this organization, known in recent years as Young America's Campaign Committee, raised $458,000 (that's a lot of money for a youth group) to contribute $48,000, or 10 percent of the funds, to candidates. This dropped to 5.8 percent ($17,400)— little more than a nickel on the dollar—in 1978, when the appeal brought in $301,000. During this period, the Eberle company handled the group's fund-raising. The Committee for Responsible Youth Politics, a youth group founded by New Rightist Morton Blackwell, uses RAVCO's services, contributing $22,000 of the almost $88,000 raised in 1976 to candidates, or 25 percent. Two years later, it contributed $7,866 or nearly 32 percent of the $24,700 raised.

Support for limiting the power of the political action committees is already growing on Capitol Hill, and in late 1979 a bill passed the House to lower the amount of money PACs can contribute to individual candidates.

DEFENDERS AND DETRACTORS

"I am a conservative and I used to be associated with Paul Weyrich in the Capitol Hill 'chapter' of the New Right," wrote Washington attorney Louis Ingram, formerly minority counsel to the House Administration Committee, in a letter to all members of the Republican National Committee in 1977. "I am convinced that these people put economic and egotistic self-aggrandizement ahead of national interests." In the letter Ingram enclosed copies of a *National Observer* article analyzing the costs of fund-raising for New Right PACs that used Viguerie's fund-raising services.

One of the most vocal critics of these practices has been M. Stanton Evans, the conservative columnist and author. "As far as I am concerned the real difference between the two elements ('Old' and 'New Right') is fund-raising," Evans told me. "Richard Viguerie and the group with which he is associated believe in massive direct-mail campaigns, involving millions of dollars in overhead and mailing costs to give away thousands." Another critic is conservative Thomas Winter, editor of *Human Events*. "He has an obligation to hold [the costs] down," Winter said. "There's a serious question here."

One conservative PAC operates differently, without questionable activities—the one with which Winter has had the closest association. In 1976, the Conservative Victory Fund, until February 1977 the political arm of the American Conservative Union, raised $231,000 to contribute $101,014 to candidates, a respectable percentage of 44.8, almost fifty cents on the dollar. Two years later, the now-independent committee's record was even better, raising $44,474 with $251,891, or 57 percent, of that going to candidates. Thus, in 1978, Conservative Victory Fund raised roughly one-third of the amount raised by the Committee for the Survival of a Free Congress, yet it gave away almost twice as much as that organization did. The group also provides valuable "in-kind" services, with trained fieldmen assisting in the campaigns to which the Conservative Victory Fund contributes. No plunder here.

The fundraisers of the New Right, however, "rape the public," conservative fundraiser Marvin Leibman told me, in a "hideous" business that constitutes a disgrace to respectable conservatives and conservative causes, posing a threat to their reputation and influence. "There are two kinds of people involved in these scams," another appalled conservative told me. "There are those who climbed on board"—the army of list brokers, copywriters, consultants, and fundraisers—"and the others who pretend it doesn't go on."

It is clear that the fund-raising business itself is becoming a potential political issue. The practitioners are coming under increasing scrutiny from governmental agencies, and there is mounting support for increased regulation of their activities. Even many voters are becoming aware of the nature of the New Right fund-raising operation, and sometimes criticize it.

Covering the race for the 22nd Congressional District seat in Illinois in November 1978, I was amazed at the sophistication of the questions raised by citizens at the public forums at which Dan Crane, the Republican candidate, appeared. Crane, brother of the Illinois Congressman Philip Crane who was running for president, used RAVCO as his fundraiser and received the third-largest contribution in the country from right-wing PACs for that election—$28,900 from the New Right PACs alone—and more from such traditionally conservative groups as the American Medical Association. When Crane appeared in public, he would invariably be deluged with such questions about campaign finance as:

> *How many people, Dan, were invited to be on your "advisory committee"?*—This was a reference to a standard piece of RAVCO fund-raising that attempts to make the prospective donor feel that he is going to play a significant role in the candidate's decisions.

> *How come your opponent and his wife were asked to be on the "advisory committee"?*—Guffaws from the crowds.

> *Hey, Dan, how come we got a letter from your wife postmarked from Washington, D.C.?*—This was a reference to an effective solicitation purporting to be a personal letter from the candidate's wife, Judy, 100,000 of which were mailed into the district. Considered to be the single most effective fund-raising gimmick for congressional campaigns, the "wife letter" is routinely used by RAVCO; and company spokesmen admit that they are designed to appear to have been individually handwritten, but, like most fund-raising material, they are mass-produced. The letters used in the Crane campaign included a photograph of the candidate, his family, and dog, with a reminder from the wife that Crane wrote to the recipient earlier in the month to extend an offer of membership in the candidate's "congressional advisory committee." Some 80,000 of the "advisory committee" letters were mailed.

One disenchanted subscriber to *The New Right Report* wrote:

> The New Right Report is interesting & good, but the price is getting beyond my reach, and what I have read about Mr.

Viguerie becoming a millionaire thru writing letters for candidates does not set well with me. I fear much of the contributions I have made to Sen. Helms' campaigns and 15 some others has gone into his pockets. While many of us are sacrificing to get good men elected, has Mr. V. found a gold mine & is he swimming in wealth at the expense of patriots?

Some contributors to right-wing causes are annoyed at the frequency with which they are approached by the fundraisers. One reader wrote to *U.S. News and World Report* following its interview with Viguerie:

In the February 26 interview with Richard Viguerie on raising dollars for conservatives, there was one question Viguerie did not answer: "Is there a danger that you can ask the same people for money too often?" It is possible, and has been done—to me! I am what you might call a "rock-ribbed conservative Republican," and I've given as much as I can afford, both in money and services, since I was old enough to vote. Recently, in one two-week period, I received 12 requests for money from national and state conservative Republican parties and candidates. That is really killing the golden goose! I get so very irritated that pretty soon I'll end up giving them nothing!

One prominent conservative, who wishes to remain anonymous, said of the fund-raising practices: "How anyone of any sensitivity can bear to read those letters scrawled by little old women on Social Security who are giving up a dollar they cannot afford to part with . . . without feeling bad is unbelievable."

Leibman, the granddaddy of the conservative fundraisers, told me this story:

Apparently, some of the fundraisers down in Washington started hitting up their donors on the telephone. So this one tells me that he got a little old lady on the telephone who apologized because she couldn't afford to give. It seems that she makes ends meet by knitting these little items of some sort, which she sells for $2 apiece, and that plus her Social Security check is what she lives on. So, when the fundraiser hears this, he says: Okay, can you just knit one extra mitten or scarf or whatever, and send the money to us? And she agreed. Can you imagine that? The guy was really proud of himself.

Did the contributors, often sacrificing to send their contributions, understand that most of the money they give would not be passed on to the candidates for whom they believe it is raised? "No," Weyrich said. "I don't think they did."

But Viguerie himself defends the practices of his clients. As he told *U.S. News and World Report:*

The press has been very unsophisticated and loose in understanding direct mail when they think in terms of half the money going to us and half to the client. It would be much more accurate to say that the candidate spent half of his money on direct-mail advertising and half on other needs of the campaign. By the way, about 35 to 40 percent of the cost of direct mail goes for postage alone.

The press is missing the point on direct mail. It is only partly fundraising; it's mostly advertising. Raising money is only one of five or six purposes of our direct-mail advertising letters. The same letter, besides asking people for money, may ask them to vote for a candidate, to volunteer for campaign work, to circulate a petition among their neighbors, to write letters to their senators and congressmen urging them to pass or defeat legislation. Direct-mail advertising is a critically important political tool for conservatives. . . .

You've got to remember that most of the press in this country has a left-of-center bias. And if Walter Cronkite and Katharine Graham of the *Washington Post* fail to tell the people about issues such as common-situs picketing or labor law reform, we're stymied. It's like the tree that fell in the forest and no one heard it. But direct mail can bypass the monopoly the left has in the media, and let us go directly to the people and tell them what the problem is and what to do about it.

The New Right Report, published by Viguerie, has hailed "UNSUNG MERITS OF CONSERVATIVE PACS." "While the money contributed to conservative candidates by burgeoning conservative political action committees is important, their major functions are sometimes less obvious," the publication states. (These include those mentioned by its publisher in *U.S. News and World Report.*)

Some New Right publicists defend their record by comparing it favorably to the Republican party's campaign organizations, some of whose spokesmen have been critical of the New Right's attempts to purge GOP incumbents. In 1977, RAVCO raised a total of $25 million, compared to $20 million raised by the GOP's House and Senate campaign committees. The difference, says Republican fundraiser Wyatt Stewart III, a former RAVCO employee, is what is left over after fund-raising costs are deducted. The Republican committees say they get 70 to 80 percent of what the mail brings in, compared to the 20 percent or so that gets back to the New Right PACs. William Rusher counters that the Republicans can be taken to task for using conservative issues such as the Panama Canal treaties to raise money for candidates who do not support the positions for which the money has been raised.

Specifically addressing the question of discrepancies between the amounts raised and given to candidates, Viguerie reminds reporters that the initial costs of fund-raising are high, but that as the "house list" of an organization or candidate is built up, the costs go down. He once said that when he is first building a list, it costs $1.20 to raise a dollar. He has expressed pride, too, that an early prospect mailing for Wallace in 1974 broke even. That mailing, he said, provided the former Alabama governor with a list of supporters to whom he could turn in the future to appeal for money and was a tremendous success.

Confronted with such figures and the criticisms implied in them, spokesmen for these groups point to the benefits that accrue to groups they raise funds for. "Look, if I had given money and I heard the figures, I'd be disturbed," said Paul

Weyrich of the Committee for the Survival of a Free Congress. "People must understand what we are trying to accomplish." Besides supporting individual right-wing candidates, he said, his organization is working with the others to build an organizational network for future elections. "We spend money to recruit candidates, to train campaign managers, to analyze every vote cast in the House and the Senate, to publish newspapers and weekly reports, and none of this is reflected in the financial reports. People who look at what we spent and how much candidates actually got should look at our total program."

Dolan of the National Conservative Political Action Committee denies any deception. "I don't think it's so bad we spent so much to raise money," he told me. "All the mail we send out does some good. It keeps the issues in front of the voters."

3

The New Old West

And all these in their helpless days,
By the dour East oppressed. . . .
Crucifying half the West,
Till the whole Atlantic coast
Seemed a giant spiders' nest. . . .
And all the way to frightened Maine the old East
heard them call. . . .
Prairie avenger, mountain lion,
Bryan, Bryan, Bryan, Bryan, . . .
Smashing Plymouth Rock with his boulders from
the West. . . .
—Vachel Lindsay,
"Bryan, Bryan, Bryan, Bryan"

The great cult figure of the New Right is John Wayne, the swaggering, tough-talking loner motivated by duty, principle, and a deep sense of justice. Wayne feared no man, respected all women: He displayed the *macho* qualities that are admired and emulated in the political and cultural heroes of the New Right. To them he symbolizes America itself and its role in the world. Wayne's unabashed patriotism, his love-it-or-leave-it belligerence, is the *only* patriotism the New Right recognizes, anything short of it considered nearly treasonable. Some years back, *Human Events* distributed a record album by Wayne

entitled *America, Why I Love Her,* subsequently turned into
a book of quasi-devotional readings. Perhaps Ronald
Reagan, writing in *Reader's Digest* shortly after Wayne's
death in 1979, said it best:

> We called him Duke, and he was every bit the giant off-screen
> he was on. Everything about him—his stature, his style, his
> convictions—conveyed enduring strength. . . .
> As Elizabeth Taylor Warner stated last May when testifying in
> favor of the special gold medal Congress struck for him: "He
> gave the whole world the image of what an American should
> be."
> . . . When war broke out, Duke tried to enlist but was rejected
> because of an old football injury to his shoulder, his age [34],
> and his status as a married father of four. He flew to Washing-
> ton to plead that he be allowed to join the Navy but was turned
> down. So he poured himself into the war effort by making
> inspiration war films—among them *The Fighting Seabees,*
> *Back to Bataan* and *They Were Expendable.* To those back
> home and others around the world he became a symbol of the
> determined American fighting man. . . .
>
> In the 1940s, Duke was one of the few stars with the courage
> to expose the determined bid by a band of communists to take
> control of the film industry. Through a series of violent strikes
> and systematic blacklisting, these people were at times danger-
> ously close to reaching their goals. With theatrical employes'
> union leader Roy Brewer, playwright Morrie Ryskind and oth-
> ers, he formed the Motion Picture Alliance for the Preservation
> of American Ideals to challenge this insidious campaign. Subse-
> quent Congressional investigations in 1947 clearly proved both
> the communist plot and the importance of what Duke and his
> friends did. . . .
>
> Duke went to Vietnam in the early days of the war. He scorned
> VIP treatment, insisting that he visit the troops in the field.
> Once he even had his helicopter land in the midst of a battle.
> When he returned, he vowed to make a film about the heroism
> of the Special Forces soldiers.
> The public jammed theaters to see the resulting film, *The*

Green Berets. The critics, however, delivered some of the harshest reviews ever given a motion picture. *The New Yorker* bitterly condemned the man who made the film. The *New York Times* called it "unspeakable . . . rotten . . . stupid." Yet Duke was undaunted. "That little clique back there in the East has taken great personal satisfaction reviewing my politics instead of my pictures," he often said. "But one day those doctrinaire liberals will wake up to find the pendulum has swung the other way."

. . . Fifteen years ago, when Duke lost a lung in his first bout with cancer, studio press agents tried to conceal the nature of his illness. When Duke discovered this, he went before the public and showed us that a man can fight this dread disease. He went on to raise millions of dollars for private cancer research. Typically, he snorted. "We've got too much at stake to give government a monopoly in the fight against cancer."

Steve Dunleavy, a *National Star* reporter who is nicknamed "Mr. Blood and Guts" for his bellicose prose style, wrote in *Conservative Digest* of Wayne's appeal: "John Wayne *was* a hero. The big man had fought off cancer, commies, intellectuals and general bad guys." Wayne's last film, *The Shootist,* suggested that Wayne himself—unlike the New Rightists who idolize him—knew that the world he symbolized was a world of the past; in it, he played an aging gunslinger dying of cancer in a changed society where primitives like himself were clearly anachronistic.

Of growing stature among the New Right and a potential successor to Wayne is Clint Eastwood, admired chiefly for his role in the film *Dirty Harry,* a neo-vigilante movie about a tough cop who, foiled in his attempt to catch a murderer by constitutionally approved means, takes the law into his own hands. Eastwood, in an interview in *Conservative Digest,* denied that his films glorify violence:

> Hopefully, I always shoot in a good cause. . . . I think audiences were pleased to see me play a detective who was concerned for the victim, a man he has never seen. People are sick and tired

of seeing the criminal glorified and made into an object of
sympathy . . . .
Basic men and women who work hard, bring up families, these
people want order. They don't want mayhem in their lives.
They're concerned about the law, and if a guy is let out on a
technicality, the law was wrong.

In another film, *High Plains Drifter,* Eastwood embodied the
image of the mythic New Right hero as effectively, perhaps,
as Wayne ever did. He played a loner who rides into a corrupt
town and, acting quite on his own, wipes out its rampant
criminal element because the sniveling townsfolk lack the courage to do it themselves. He rides out contemptuous of the town
that is too corrupt and morally flabby to protect itself.

The New Right admires such rugged individualists, all of
them "tough," "gutsy," "mean," "no-nonsense," *"macho"*
loners who stand against Establishment authority, adhering to
an internal code of honor in a world gone soft. It is no coinci-
dence that their political discourse bristles with images of the
mythic U.S. marshal. Fundraiser Viguerie has called John Connally "a man on a white horse," and Kevin P. Phillips praised
Connally as "America's potential Matt Dillon, Washington's
putative Wyatt Earp."

It is a political style that represents the revolt of the New
Old West against the East, a region that feels deeply alienated
from the federal government, which seems at best a meddlesome absentee landlord holding the ranchers, miners, and developers of the West from the political gold they believe they
can pan from the political streams of their mineral-rich land,
if only left alone. The city slickers in Washington, they believe,
do not really know what is best for the West and have no
reason to know; after all, there was no strong central government working its will through a federal bureaucracy when the
hardy settlers built the West—a notion dear to the hearts of
angry Westerners. The federal government, in return for helping to open up the Western states, assumed control over nearly
one billion acres of land that Western developers are anxious

to get back, a source of growing resentment; so is the stepped-up regulation of farming, ranching, and mining by the Bureau of Land Management.

Behind the New Right's glorification of the values and images of the Old West, with its tough sheriffs, lonely mavericks, and rugged individualists, and behind its retreat from history, lies a deep-rooted distaste for our European past that, through the years, has been transformed into a generalized revulsion at the American East as an extension of Europe, and particularly at New York City, that golden door through which Europe's refugees entered their own promised land. "The United States was built by men and women who turned their backs on Europe," said Patrick J. Buchanan, syndicated columnist, former speechwriter for President Nixon, and New Right polemicist. This attitude, common to the New Right, is both unconservative and even anticonservative in its disregard for historical continuity. The practical political applications of this view are apparent in the New Right's contempt for Eastern institutions, universities, banks, the press, and in its chauvinist and interventionist foreign policy, heir to the isolationism of the Midwest of earlier decades.

THE REVOLT AGAINST THE EAST

The anti-Eastern impulse, dating back to the days of the Jacksonian democratic revolt and taking dramatic form in the post–Civil War regional struggles, finds increased expression in New Right politics, which is—at least in part—an organized attempt to revenge the resentments of the South and West against the settled and cosmopolitan East. Hostilities to the East, with its associations of wealth and cultivation, and—in recent years—upper-middle-class and upper-class liberalism, have fixated on such symbols, not only on the East Coast and New York City, but specifically on Wall Street, the Rockefellers, and "international bankers"—once a euphemism for Jewish money merchants with anti-Semitic implications but now, apparently, to the New Old West simply symbolizing Eastern money with European gloss. These special targets of the resentful New Right are viewed as tools of internationalists seeking to link America's fate increasingly with that of other nations —Europe, in particular—in direct denial of the fact that America's fate is already linked to theirs. Thus, New Right hostility to the East represents a refusal to confront unpleasant political realities of the world as it is. British conservative writer Henry Fairlie has noted that this "fear many people have of the East" is not so much an alarm "for their own interests . . . as for their perceptions of the modern world and of their place in it." New Right politics seems intent on reasserting control over the federal government and the American culture, a control that they believe has been wrongly usurped from the common people of the frontier by the aristocratic East. Heirs of an American impulse that views Europe as decadent and despotic, these neopopulists seek to avoid rot and tyranny by a continuous shift of power from the East further and further west, where small-town values, so the myth goes, still dominate.

The notion that the West grew up in isolation without the help of the East is one that conservative columnist George Will of the *Washington Post,* a Midwesterner educated at Princeton and Oxford, finds mildly amusing. Westerners who feel "surrounded and set upon" by Big Brother government, he has written, are obsessed by the idea that "men were brave, women were fair and life was sweet before the tea-sipping, paper-pushing dudes from Washington started butting in." "There is something quaint," Will said, "about the Westerner's insistence that he built the place all by his lonesome, with no help from God or the socialistic East." (The West, in fact, was opened up by the American military and developed by a succession of government agricultural programs, the railroads, and, more recently, by research and development projects of the Defense Department.) Midwest and Western voters, nevertheless, are sending a growing number of angry New Right senators who cherish this myth to represent them in Washington, including James McClure of Idaho, Roger Jepsen

of Iowa, Harrison Schmitt of New Mexico, Orrin Hatch and
Jake Garn of Utah, and Malcolm Wallop of Wyoming, all
Republicans. They join such Republican stalwarts, who also
share this view of history, as Barry Goldwater of Arizona and
Reagan Republican Paul Laxalt of Nevada. Only Goldwater is
an old-timer; McClure was elected in 1972, Garn and Laxalt
in 1974, Schmitt, Hatch, and Wallop in 1976, and Jepsen in
1978.

A romantic search for "that perfect place," "the primeval
landscape," accounts in large part for the New Right's fixation
with the American West and Southwest—that unexplored,
presumably untainted frontier of mountains and plains where
the buffalo roam and the deer and the antelope play, and from
which, more and more, its political leaders (Goldwater, Reagan,
and Connally) have emerged. This, too, is part of an American
tradition that lives on as a kind of fighting faith not only among
the New Rightists but among some traditional Midwestern
conservatives as well. Away from Europe and the decadent
Eastern seaboard with its settled wealth and increasingly cosmopolitan outlook, they represent that part of America about
which conservative historian Stephen Tonsor has written that

> [the archetypal American] has always moved on to the fresh
> start; to the primeval landscape, regaining in our adventurous
> movement our lost innocence and betrayed virtue.
>
> Geographic mobility, no doubt, has been a major factor in
> our history, making the fresh start possible. Over and over again
> we have moved on in quest of that perfect place. . . .

The experience of the New World, Tonsor said, "was above
all else a desire to escape history, an attempt to throw off the
burden of the past and make a fresh start." The American view
of the European past is summed up by the burden carried by
Thoreau's immigrant on the road, "a great deal of baggage;
trumpery which has accumulated from long housekeeping,"
which he has not the courage to discard. "To both the individual and the society [Tonsor writes] Thoreau offers a simple and

easy solution: lay down or burn your burden; escape the past."
Although Tonsor's subject in this essay is the New Left, what
he says applies equally well to the impatient and troubled
American Right. The student radicals of the 1960s, he writes,
in their desire to escape from this burdensome and complex
past, "were far closer to native American populism and know-
nothingism than they were and are to the orthodox certainties
of Marxism. In this flight from history the student radicals are
joined by the main tradition of American culture." Historian
David W. Noble views all of American history as dominated
by this theme:

> The American people believe that their historical experience
> has been uniquely timeless and harmonious because they are
> the descendents of Puritans who, in rejecting the traditions and
> institutions of the Old World, promised never to establish
> traditions and institutions in the New World.

The experience of Americans in the New World, Tonsor concludes, "was such as to encourage the immigrant *to strip off his
European institutional and cultural past* and to become a new
American man. . . . They created a myth of American novelty
and simplicity, virtue and harmony which is constantly threatened with corruption and confusion from the forces of high
culture and history."

It is only natural that right-wingers like Barry Goldwater
have spoken of the Eastern coast with contempt, because, as
Fairlie has written, "it is an Atlantic seaboard; and if it floated
out to sea, it would drift naturally back across the ocean and
attach itself to Europe again." And such a drift would be
deadly: It would connect America, again, to the "fear and
failure" that rightists believe characterize the Old World, with
its trappings of old monarchy and new (socialist) ideas, and
deny the conviction that America began anew, and that it may
still begin anew, as Fairlie puts it, "if that is necessary to
recover its original inspiration." When in his speech to the
Republican National Convention in 1968 Goldwater "drew his

imagery from his own state, and seemed to plead for a desert wind to sweep across the nation and cleanse it, he was raising a hope for the renewal and reinvigoration of American exceptionalism to which many Americans still respond."

In practical political terms, this obsession often has meant an indifference to the plight of foreign nations; at one time this suspicion expressed itself in right-wing isolationism, a primarily Midwestern phenomenon from the 1930s to the 1950s, and bipartisan in its identification. Midwestern Republicans and Democrats shared a reluctance to become involved in "entangling alliances" with other nations. In domestic affairs, the anti-Eastern, anti-European impulse meant a desire to wrest control from the Republican party, especially from its liberal elements, which were associated with the Rockefellers and the East. So inextricably involved were these impulses that it is often impossible to discern where, for the Right, foreign policy ends and domestic policy begins.

This anger and resentment, culminating in the simmering politics of the New Right, can be traced throughout the recent history of American conservatism. It began, in effect, with the defeat of Wilson's crusade for the League of Nations after the First World War, led by Massachusetts Senator Henry Cabot Lodge, and continued in the Republican party of Harding and Coolidge. The America Firsters of the Second World War carried on the tradition. Robert Taft, who became the putative leader of the GOP isolationists of the 1940s and 1950s, after having worked for Hoover's war relief agency in Europe after the First World War, had little patience with affairs on the Continent, and, later, little patience with the liberal East. "European quarrels are everlasting," he wrote of his experience under Hoover. "There is a welter of races there so confused that boundaries cannot be drawn without leaving minorities which are a perpetual source of friction." Callous to the plight of England as Hitler began to menace Europe, he criticized Franklin Roosevelt for dealing with Winston Churchill; he opposed involvement in these "European quarrels" until after Pearl Harbor was bombed. "I feel very strongly that Hitler's defeat is not vital to us," he said. "Even the collapse of England is to be preferred to participation for the rest of our lives in European wars." Accused of being an isolationist, Taft snapped: "If isolation means isolation from European wars, I am an isolationist." In 1947, a writer in *Fortune* magazine wrote that, as Taft saw them, "other countries were merely odd places, full of uncertain plumbing, funny colored money, and people talking languages one can't understand."

Taft's hostility to England and indifference to its plight—his isolationism, like that of so many others, extended to Atlantic countries but not to the Pacific—was a mirror image of his antipathy for the American East. He eventually blamed his inability to win the Republican presidential nomination on abusive treatment by the Eastern newspapers. Commenting on the campaign staff assembled in 1948 by his rival, Thomas Dewey, Taft snorted: "The whole headquarters is run by New Yorkers." The successful 1940 campaign for the nomination of Wendell Willkie, Taft said, was "engineered from Wall Street." He was not far wrong, though; Time Inc. and Henry Luce, who discovered Willkie, were some blocks north of Wall Street.

Anti-Europeanism had now become anti-Easternism. With the war the Republican party had yielded to Eastern-based leadership—Willkie, Dewey, Eisenhower—with a European-directed philosophy. An anti-Europeanism emerged again in the 1950s, this time with an interventionist cast. Suspicious of the United Nations and its agents—Texas led an attack in the 1950s on liberal textbooks that praised UNESCO—wary of foreign aid and even doubtful, until recently, of the wisdom of U.S. support for NATO, the New Right remains as chauvinist in its interventionism as its predecessors were in their isolationism. "When President Nixon announced the bombing resumption in Vietnam and the mining of Haiphong harbor in May 1972," Ronald Radosh, a radical historian, wrote in *Prophets on the Right: Conservative Critics of American Globalism*, "James Buckley endorsed the policy and added that the President 'would be justified in taking far stronger measures.'

One does not have to think long to imagine what John T. Flynn, Robert A. Taft or Oswald Garrison Villard would have had to say about such a blanket endorsement for extending the power of the imperial Presidency . . . Goldwater argues that 'the Founding Fathers vested in the President a discretion to *react* against foreign danger whenever and wherever he sees a threat to the security of the United States.' " Much of the fear Goldwater engendered in the East and among Republican moderates was related to the conviction that the Arizona Republican Senator could not be trusted with the nuclear button.

In the ideological Goldwater candidacy of 1964, in the highly charged anti-Communist campaigns by Richard Nixon in 1960 and, with Agnew, in 1972, plus the attempt by Republican hard-liners to nominate Ronald Reagan for president in 1975, American militance has been a constant of our politics; it will no doubt continue to manifest itself for years to come —perhaps, then, in Wilsonian crusades from the Democratic side as well, in wars to "make the world safe for democracy," in "wars to end all wars." It cannot, certainly, be divorced from the attitudes of, say, Lyndon Johnson—that son of the Texas frontier—nor from the "go anywhere, pay any price" bravado of the Kennedys. Inadequately modulated, it can do great damage, especially in the hands of the xenophobic militants of the New Right.

While traditional GOP conservatives have become increasingly sophisticated in recent years—more aware of the complexity and interdependence of America's interests and those of Western Europe, the Middle East, and Asia—the New Right retains the frontier psychology of the Old West. The "surrender" of the Panama Canal seemed almost an unbearable affront to their pride and sense of America's position in the world, and every major New Right organization in 1977 and 1978 conducted campaigns against ratification of the new Panama Canal treaties.

Galvanized to the threat of World Communism, the Right has responded with a "protracted conflict" strategy of their own, supporting global struggle against the Soviets, suspicious of détente, quick on the trigger, ready to take offense like the Old West sheriffs they so admire. When the Carter Administration in 1979 acknowledged the presence of Soviet troops in Cuba, Illinois Republican Congressman Philip Crane, seeking the GOP nomination in 1980 as a New Rightist, said that President Carter should announce to the Soviets that he is giving them "48 hours" to get the troops out of the Western hemisphere.

Just as liberals have been accused by conservatives of throwing dollars at problems, the Rightists would, in effect, throw bombs. A New Right president, John T. Dolan has promised, would "double the defense spending" and "take on international communism" by committing American troops to Iran, Afghanistan, Angola, Uganda, and Cambodia (when there were problems there).

Fairlie, noting such transformation from isolationism to interventionism, calls it a "mutation." But the motives, he writes, are the same:

> a suspicion of the rest of the world, an impatience with its complexities, and a desire for solutions that are simple. In this situation, the internationalism of the Eastern Establishment is the same and as objectionable as it was before. The "international bankers" and the "Establishment," and even something as vague as "big business," will do almost anything, according to the suspicions of the conservatives, to sustain their financial and trading interests: will traduce and betray, not only exceptional American interests, but an exceptional American faith, if the account books justify it.

Indeed, when the Carter Administration in 1977 unveiled the culmination of years of negotiations—participated in and furthered by three Republican presidents—to alter the terms of the Panama Canal treaties, many on the Right believed that the hidden agenda was an attempt by political leaders to mollify the Panamanian government because the Chase Manhattan and Marine Midland Banks had loaned money to its leaders. Phyllis Schlafly, New Right colleague from the women's auxiliary, appeared on William F. Buckley, Jr.'s "Firing Line" television program to make that charge. When confronted with the fact that Buckley himself supported the new treaties, some rightists concluded that the Buckley family, fearing for their presumed oil investments in the Caribbean, were putting financial interests above those of the nation.

In January 1978, *Human Events* published a tirade entitled "A Banker's Betrayal to Hanoi Butchers" which lashed out at "bankers" and "banks" in general, portraying one Citibank executive as "some modern-day Uriah Heep," "fawning before the Hanoi butchers, rubbing his hands in anticipation of multimillion-dollar orders and totally oblivious to the past and present record of Communist Vietnamese atrocities." This fury extended to the Chase Manhattan Bank as well; its executives felt no more than a "twinge of conscience about opening a Moscow office to do business with the Kremlin murderers. . . . The Chase chirped away about the long hours of negotiations to arrange loans, capped by evenings at the Bolshoi relaxing. And all the while Baptists and Jews were getting their heads broken by the KGB, and writers and artists were being reduced to vegetables via forced drug injections and psychiatric institutes."

As Richard Whalen notes: "In the Middle American region where isolationism had flourished before World War II, to the consternation of Eastern internationalists who then sought a more venturesome foreign policy, the conservative resurgence of the early 1960s brought a reversal of roles. Now accusations of retreat and default flew from west to east. And the target often chosen was the *New York Times*." As early as 1928, Herbert Hoover (brought up on the West Coast but born in Iowa) had quipped, upon defeating Al Smith for the presidency: "I am looking forward to reading *Life, Time*, the *Nation*, and *The New Republic*, and seeing how they take the result. The discomfiture of the Eastern intelligentsia gives me as much pleasure as that of the radical farm leaders."

As might be expected, the financial crisis of New York City

in 1978 brought out the worst in New Rightists. Commenting on the city's financial plight in his syndicated newspaper column, Patrick Buchanan wrote:

> A few years back, when some miserable wretch who was contemplating suicide was poised on the ledge of a Manhattan skyscraper, a crowd of New Yorkers gathered below chanting: "Jump! Jump!" As New York City crawls back toward the abyss of bankruptcy, some Americans feel a similar thrill of anticipation.

The fact is, Buchanan wrote, "like some wines, New Yorkers, especially the Manhattan illuminati, do not travel especially well." Indeed, Buchanan remembers that as a Georgetown University student in the 1950s, he thought of New Yorkers as "a loud, arrogant and cocky lot. With very little to be cocky about." Many of the politicians "have made a negative impression of New York indelible in the national mind."

THE LAST FRONTIER

To the Right, the frontier is not only a symbol and a myth, but —like hated New York City—also a place. The New Old West is a combination of Texas, Arizona, Colorado, and California. It excludes Oregon and most of the Northwest, that civilized, settled region of political liberalism, settled by New Englanders whose descendants now on billboards exhort: "Don't Californicate Oregon!"—a warning to grasping developers who covet the real estate Oregonians want left pristine. The New Right includes, as its ancestral home, the Confederate States, symbol of the South of memory and myth, of military prowess and manly sentiment and primitive backwoodsmen. George Wallace's rough and earthy demeanor well suited rightists in the recent past; John Connally's Texan bravado suits them in the recent present. But the frontier—and the last frontier—of the New Old West is Orange County, Southern California.

The fastest-growing congressional district in the United States is the 40th District, one of three in Orange County, California, with a population burgeoning from 216,000 in 1950 to 703,000 in 1960 and then to 1.42 million in 1970. It is the birthplace of Richard Nixon, the home of anti-gay-rights activist State Senator John V. Briggs, and, overall, a hotbed of political reaction.

Growing government-supported industries (especially the defense industry) and growing public sector employment in connection with the state university system, vastly expanded by Governor Ronald Reagan, has brought with it vast social change and a large number of Democrats. This once-Republican stronghold is up for grabs. A rising La Raza population, too, in the district and the county, along with a growing black population in Los Angeles to the north, has caused serious insecurities among middle- and lower-middle-class white residents. The economic boom of the twenty-year period in which population increased is over. According to *The Almanac of American Politics* 1978, a standard reference for political observers:

> The fantastic growth that has made Orange County possible has also produced surroundings that convey little of permanence; the 40th district is full of shopping centers and subdivisions which did not exist ten years ago and which in another ten may be decaying.
>
> Even more frightening to people who seek order and calm, Orange County has not been able to restore the old values of a left behind Midwest or South, or to produce anything satisfactory to take their place. Orange Countians who sought a bucolic life are baffled by the habits of their own children, who prefer rock music to whatever their parents might like, who do not sneak off to drink beer, but openly smoke marijuana. The beleaguered residents of Orange County are the bedrock of southern California conservatism. They are men and women who have achieved modest success by their own standards. When that success and those values were sneered at by outsiders and by their own children, they sought comfort in politics.

And they found it, for a while at least, in the politics of Ronald Reagan and Richard Nixon.

Goldwater, Reagan, and Nixon, in their individual ways, told Orange County what it wanted to hear—that its values and its way of life were the finest in the world.* They encouraged the population's comfort and complacency. Yet declining support for the traditional Republican party in Southern California and the simultaneous rise of competing far-right groups attest to the anxieties of these Americans. Orange County and Southern California are, as such, the microcosm community and state of the New Right. There, a rootless, boomtown atmosphere has given rise to a political tradition that is anything but classicly conservative. The setting for the San Clemente White House, Orange County is also the home of Gary Allen, the author of *None Dare Call It Conspiracy*, a best-selling book much admired by members of the John Birch Society. Television evangelists have huge followings here; so does former Democratic Mayor Sam Yorty of Los Angeles, who hosts a popular weekly television talk show that celebrates God and Country. John Wayne lived just down the coast near Seal Beach, not far from Gary Allen's home. The 40th is also the congressional district once represented by Jon Schmitz, a Bircher who, in 1972, sought the presidency on the Wallaceite American Independent party ticket. This is the home of the *Santa Ana Register*, the maverick daily (estimated circulation 400,000) that, in accordance with its libertarian stance, has advocated the legalization of heroin yet has denounced Nixon as too liberal in his economic policies. Its antigovernment position dates back to the 1940s when it criticized FDR's policy of sequestering American citizens of Japanese descent in "relocation camps." Its chief editorial writer, Kenneth Grubbs, once active in Young Americans for Freedom and earlier employed at the nearby Knotts' Berry Farm resort (where he

---

*Even Democrat Jerry Brown, seeking the governorship in 1972, ran a cut-taxes, antigovernment campaign.

distributed right-wing propaganda), carries on the tradition by
espousing free-market economics and civil libertarian positions
on "victimless crimes," like drug abuse and prostitution, that
are voluntarily engaged in by their "victims" and are hence
beyond the appropriate reach of the law. In this, its position
is identical to that of the American Civil Liberties Union.

Grubbs's libertarianism, however, is offset in the county by
the stern morality of the local Birchers, who supported Briggs's
Proposition 6, a ballot measure to root out presumed homosexual teachers from the public schools. The Birchites and libertarians, though often at war, represent the tradition of "entrepreneurial radicalism" (as Richard Hofstadter has described
the rugged individualist tradition), but the Birchites represent
as well a backlash against the "hot-tub" morality of Hollywood
and its "laid-back" lifestyles.

Because of these anxieties, Orange County is fertile New
Right territory: The right-wing attitudes of its inhabitants are
not those of moneyed oil men but of status-conscious Middle
Americans who see their world slowly changing and their pre-
cious positions in that world challenged. They are suspicious,
slightly intimidated individuals who, wishing they had greater
control over their lives, harken back to the days when men like
John Wayne could take control; they are people looking for
leaders like him.

Orange County is a stronghold of two political movements
—at first quite different, it would seem—which, in fact, have
striking similarities. They represent the New Right at its two
extremes. Orange County has long been known as a frontier
of the John Birch Society but, in recent years, the libertarian
movement has found a home there as well. The John Birch
Society's headquarters is in Massachusetts, home of its founder, but its heart is in Orange County. The society is reportedly
undergoing a resurgence as the nation moves to the right.
Founded in 1958 by candy manufacturer Robert Welch and
named for the "first victim of the Cold War," a Christian
missionary and American intelligence officer killed in Korea,
the society's past heyday (with roughly 600,000 members)

came in the early 1960s. Losing membership after Barry Goldwater was crushed at the polls, it continued to put forth the Bircher conspiratorial spectre, which holds that the American government, in Welch's words, is "sixty to eighty percent" dominated by Communists. This feverish notion has undergone revision. Today Birchers hold that the secret rulers of America are "the insiders," a mysterious cabal of rich bankers, including David Rockefeller, who are only using Communism as a means of achieving world domination.

The society now operates on a budget estimated to be about $8 million a year; it publishes two magazines—the weekly *Review of the News* and the monthly *American Opinion;* it runs bookstores, a speaker's bureau, and even summer camps for teen-agers. Its organizational model is strikingly similar to the old American Communist Party. The group's primary project of the late 1970s was tax reduction, spearheaded by TRIM (Tax Reform Immediately) committees in 300 congressional districts.

Society members insist that theirs is an "educational enterprise" and not a political lobby, primarily intent on alerting Americans to the perils they face. These perils include weakening national defenses but, more important, the rule by leaders who owe their allegiance not to the United States but to a shared vision of one world government. Committed to such a view, Birchers are highly suspicious individuals who view reform of almost any kind as advancing the interests of the "insiders." As such, they tend to be obstructionists; their goals are almost wholly negative, seeking to oppose measures on a local level that are ordinarily viewed as "progressive." They are against busing and gun control, "regionalism," and the income tax—and *for* "patriotism."

In the early 1960s—when Welch gained great notoriety by announcing that Dwight Eisenhower was a "Communist"—conservatives were compelled to dissociate themselves from the organization. Many Birchers considered themselves "conservatives," but many Republican politicians, who found the John Birch Society among their supporters, were uncomfortable with the new ally. William F. Buckley, Jr., led an assault in the pages of *National Review* on the conspiracy-minded zealots, writing them out of the conservative camp. Frank Meyer, conservative philosopher and once a Communist party functionary, took the society on in 1962:

> The false analysis and conspiratorial mania of the John Birch Society has moved beyond diversion and waste of the devotion of its members to the mobilization of that devotion in ways directly anti-conservative and dangerous to the interests of the United States. It is no longer possible to consider the Society merely as moving towards legitimate objectives in a misguided way. However worthy the original motivations of those who have joined it and who apologize for it, it is time for them to recognize that the John Birch Society is rapidly losing whatever it had in common with patriotism or conservatism—and to do so before their own minds become warped by adherence to its unrolling psychosis of conspiracy.

Seymour Martin Lipset, professor of political science and sociology at Stanford University, has said that he believes the society's influence has always been exaggerated. "It looks like they had mass appeal at one time," he told *The Wall Street Journal,* "but it was more journalistic attention than anything they were doing." However, in the fifteen years that have passed since *National Review* conservatives wrote the Birchers out of "the movement," the Birchers seem to have wormed their way back in along the frontier of the New Right. The New Right leaders seem to welcome them. The New Rightists may indeed feel more comfortable with the primitive Birchers than they do with *National Review* types, whom they regard as effete Easterners; indeed, when this author worked at *Conservative Digest* in 1975, the editors kept back copies of both Birch periodicals, the *American Opinion* and the *Review of the News,* in the office, but not back copies of the more moderate conservative weekly *Human Events.*

At least two New Right heroes—Georgia Congressman

Larry McDonald and former New Hampshire Governor (but Georgia-born) Meldrim Thomson—are members of the Birch Society, and Robert Welch has claimed that Phyllis Schlafly was once a member, though she has denied it. H. L. Richardson, the founder of the New Right lobby Gun Owners of America, was once employed by the Birchers.

Orange County is also a frontier outpost stockade of the libertarian movement which, in the mid-1960s, split with the traditional conservatives over, among other issues, the draft and the Vietnam War—both of which most libertarians opposed. At the 1969 convention of Young Americans for Freedom in St. Louis, the libertarians walked out, jeered as "laissez-fairies" by the traditionalists, who did not take kindly to the libertarians' more permissive attitudes toward homosexuality and other "victimless crimes." "They wore these little buttons with 'Laissez-faire' written on them," a former Young Americans for Freedom leader told me, "and the traditionalists used the slogan to ridicule them more for their obsession with free-market economics than for anything else." These disciples of "Objectivist" author Ayn Rand formed their Libertarian party in 1972 and, within six years, had their own think tank, the Cato Foundation, and their own publications—*Inquiry, Reason,* and *Libertarian Review*—all based in California.

In 1972, the Libertarians ran for president University of Southern California philosophy professor John Hospers, who appeared on two states' ballots and received about 5,000 votes —and one electoral vote, when Nixon elector Roger MacBride bolted and voted for Hospers. In 1976, MacBride was the party's presidential nominee and, managing to get on thirty-two ballots, he won 175,000 votes. In the off-year elections of 1978, the party picked up 1.3 million votes in a variety of state and local contests, even winning a seat in the Alaska legislature. Most impressive, however, was the following of Ed Clark in the 1978 California gubernatorial election, where he received nearly 400,000 votes—the best showing for a third-party candidate in California in more than three decades. While libertarian positions on public policy issues may at first sound like a hodgepodge of the Old Right and the New Left, they are, in fact, utterly consistent. Stressing freedom of the individual above all other values—a freedom, they believe, that is diminished when an individual must give up a portion of his earnings for public use—they favor an unregulated economy; the legalization of drugs; an end to all laws governing private behavior between consenting adults; return to the gold standard; "freedom of choice" in abortion; the right to commit suicide; and abolition of the Central Intelligence Agency, the Federal Bureau of Investigation, the Occupational Safety and Health Administration, and Social Security. Ironically, the libertarians have attracted a large number of New Leftists for reasons not unlike those cited by Tonsor on the New Left and the primeval landscape; the leftists in the Libertarian party are attracted by its consistency, its antimilitarism, and its permissive attitudes toward drugs. When the possibility of the military draft was revived in 1978, the membership lists of Students for a Libertarian Society (a deliberate counterpart to Students for a Democratic Society) swelled.

The libertarians see themselves as rugged individualists who do not need the federal government to look out for their interests. If the New Rightists and the Birchers have John Wayne as their ideal, the libertarians have Gary Cooper—the brilliant, impulsive architect Howard Roark of the film version of Ayn Rand's *The Fountainhead,* a man who overcomes great social opposition to achieve his individual artistic vision. Borderline anarchists, they share a dogmatic opposition to state action and state spending that has led them to reconsider the defense expenditures of the Cold War and the Vietnam era. In the late 1970s they adopted many of the conclusions of New Left revisionist historians—anti–Cold War, neo-isolationist. Disinclined to support a costly defense establishment, they have now decided that the Soviet Union is not an aggressive power to be greatly feared—a position for which they have been severely chastised by *National Review,* a former ally. In their noninterventionism, a retreat from behind the American border, they resemble the 1950s right-wing critics of American globalism like Robert Taft.

It is in their domestic policy, however, that the individualism of the libertarians is most apparent; here, they favor unrestrained economic development and the elimination of public services like welfare and the postal service. Private suppliers can provide whatever services individuals feel are necessary; for government to provide them, they regard as an unconscionable intrusion. Only on the question of nuclear power does there seem to be a great debate among libertarians, which has found a tenuous resolution. Libertarians of the left oppose and fear nuclear power, pointing to potential dangers and the involvement of the federal government in its development, while those of the right favor it as a technological advance that should not be hampered by government.

Unlike the Birchers, the libertarians are an upbeat and optimistic group of high achievers, often affluent and, in their social and cultural attitudes, quite liberal. There is a large homosexual contingency within the group and an Association of Libertarian Feminists. Their 1979 convention* was a boisterous affair at the swanky Bonaventure Hotel in Los Angeles; marijuana circulated freely at the banquet honoring the presidential nominee, while delegates discussed esoteric matters of economic policy and the wickedness of the CIA. Speakers were a mixed lot, former Senator Eugene McCarthy, syndicated columnist Nicholas von Hoffman, anti-war activist Ron Kovic, and right-wing polemicist John Lofton.

Unlike domestic libertarians of the Frank Meyer persuasion, the new libertarians (many of them members of the Libertarian party) are not simultaneously anarchistic on matters of public service and law-and-order-minded on the police and military preparedness. Their antigovernment philosophy is wholly consistent. As such, they enjoy the distinction of having been attacked, the same month, by both the conservative *Na-*

---

*At which this author spoke—on the subject of the New Right.

tional Review and the liberal *Nation*—and praised, a few months later, by *Hustler*. The Libertarian party, wrote publisher Larry Flynt, deserves support for advocating "a return to a free-market economy and *genuine* civil liberties (which means getting the government out of victimless crime)."

While the libertarians detest and fear the New Right, and find the John Birch Society somewhat comical (a disdain which is returned), there are striking similarities between the two groups. Both the Birchers and the libertarians, so characteristic of the attitudes of the New Old West, are deeply suspicious of the federal government and of politics in general. The John Birch Society resolutely refused to endorse political candidates (though members sometimes seek offices), and it does not contribute, as an organization, to political candidates. The libertarians are similarly antipolitical. Although they now have a political party, which seeks to elect candidates from the local level of school boards to the national level of president, the function of those candidates is to spread the libertarian gospel and, if elected, to abolish the state. Libertarianism, seeing little legitimacy in public control of any kind, therefore denies the necessity or worth of political action and seeks an end to politics. Significantly, the only major daily newspaper with a libertarian philosophy, the *Santa Ana Register,* refuses to endorse political candidates on the ground that political elections are basically futile. The libertarians, like the Birchers, have no registered lobby. Both groups are individualists to the bitter end, yearning to get the federal agencies off their backs, the United States out of the U.N., and Uncle Sam's hand out of their pockets and away from their gun holsters.* These California-style variations of the right-wing revolt are, in their own way, the John Waynes of the Right, wanting only to be left alone to fend for themselves on the frontiers of the New Old West.

---

*The libertarians, while nonmilitaristic, believe that gun registration or confiscation is an unwarranted abridgement of individual freedom and an unjustifiable extension of state power over private behavior.

Unwitting allies, they usually end up voting in what must be, for them, a distressingly similar manner, against the liberals. Both groups love Howard Jarvis, and, when it comes time to put aside discussions of ideology and enter the voting booth to choose between the candidates before them, they reject liberalism and function as supporters (grudgingly or otherwise) of the New Right.

THE NEW JOHN WAYNES

The New Old West style, expected by New Rightists of its cult figures and leaders, explains not only the rightist John Wayne cult but also the appeal of Howard Jarvis (the creator of Proposition 13) and other no-holds-barred scrappers.

One of the roughest customers to lend his gravelly voice to the national debate, Howard Jarvis, consistent to the end to New Right principles, talks about free-enterprise economics and practices it as well, with a vengeance. To the considerable annoyance of more established right-wing professionals, Jarvis has engaged in competitive fund-raising schemes with other right-wing organizations, some of whose leaders have questioned the propriety of his competition. The logic of his position appears to escape them. Single-minded, Jarvis is obsessed with "lower taxes and less government"; he campaigned for measures like Proposition 13 sixteen years before California voters heard his message and voted his way. Garrulous, coarse, and a self-described "rugged bastard who's had his head kicked in a thousand times by government," Jarvis seems to have been placed by Central Casting as a New Right populist from the New Old West come to do battle with the effete liberals of the East—bellicose, dedicated, articulate, utterly unconcerned that others find him unrefined and argumentative. "We never knew whether he was a messiah or a maniac," an aide to one of the Los Angeles city supervisors said in *Time*. "He was surly, arrogant, and when the mikes were turned off he just raised his voice so you never knew the microphone was dead. Many times they had to call the sergeant at arms to persuade him to sit down." Intolerant of critics, Jarvis once threatened a lawsuit against a junior high school boy when the youthful journalist referred to him in the school paper as a big real estate owner.

Jarvis has a flair for flamboyant social protest. "We have a new revolution," he said of Proposition 13. "We are telling the government, 'Screw you!' " He tells lots of people, "Screw you!" No longer a member of the Republican party, he has called Republicans "the stupidest people in the world, except for businessmen, who have a genius for stupidity." The League of Women Voters, he said, are "a bunch of nosy broads who front for the big spenders," and he has variously described his political opponents as "liars," "dummies," "goons," "cannibals," and "big mouths" whose arguments are "a crock of manure."

The son of a Utah state supreme court judge, Jarvis attended Utah State University and, upon graduation, persuaded a local bank to loan him the money to purchase the then ailing *Magnus* (Utah) *Times* newspaper. By the time he was thirty he owned eleven newspapers; with the profits of his newspaper chain he started a chemical firm in Oakland, California, and ran a chain of home appliance factories, retiring in 1962. He ran for public office three times, losing each time: He sought the 1962 Republican nomination for U.S. Senate, the 1972 race for the State Board of Equalization, and the 1977 Los Angeles mayoral primary. A political activist and businessman, Jarvis in 1965 formed, with two associates, the National Freedom to Work Committee from the language of the existing right-wing National Right to Work Committee's charter substituting only the word "freedom" in its name. Reed Larson, of the National Right to Work Committee, who investigated the Jarvis organization, concluded in a private memo to right-to-work associates that the telephone solicitation raised $250,-000, much of it from businessmen who thought they were contributing to the National Right to Work Committee. "As far as we can determine," Larson wrote, "they do not appear to have an organizational set-up for any activity other than solicitation of funds"; he charged that the group's letterhead of the advisory board listed "fictitious names." Under subsequent pressures from Larson's group, the U.S. Post Office, and the Better Business Bureau, the competitive committee closed its doors in 1966.

Early in 1964 Jarvis and others had announced Businessmen for Goldwater, soliciting thousands of dollars by telephone from Los Angeles. "Before [a] suit could be brought to trial," Larson wrote in his 1965 report on Jarvis's activities, "this group had collected $115,000, the bulk of which ($88,000) was shown as having been paid over to [William] Morrison and [Norton H.] Nathan for PR fee and contract labor." Not a cent was turned over to Goldwater and could not be, since committees operating without the consent of the candidate were prohibited from giving directly to candidates by California law. After the Republican National Committee filed suit to stop its activities in 1964, "Businessmen for Goldwater" dissolved.

In 1976 Jarvis turned up as chairman of the Friends for Hayakawa, which operated to raise money for the Senate campaign of maverick Republican S. I. Hayakawa, admired by the Right for his resistance to leftist students in his post as president of San Francisco State College. The group raised $57,453, according to FEC records, yet campaign records show that the Hayakawa campaign never got any of the money. A competing group, Friends of Hayakawa, the official campaign organization, sued, forcing an out-of-court settlement that dissolved the Jarvis group, which soon folded. Jarvis, who in 1979 acknowledged to reporters his involvement in the enterprise, denied having received any of this money and explained that funds had gone for promotion.

Similar qualities of "gutsiness," belligerency, and aggressiveness are admired by the New Right in another cult figure, former Los Angeles Police Chief Ed Davis. Davis, a real-life lawman, endeared himself to New Rightists by being, in the words of *Conservative Digest,* "the meanest police chief in America." He left the force to pursue a political career, running unsuccessfully for the 1978 Republican gubernatorial nomination in California, with Richard A. Viguerie as fund-raiser. A portly but athletic, authoritative but good-humored man, Davis has been a controversial figure in California for some years. The breakdown in American morality, he once declared, is the result of "swinging mommies." In a letter to the *Los Angeles Times,* he called that newspaper the "Paul Revere of the oncoming avalanche of libertine behavior." He has attacked the "Beverly Hills and Bel-Air swimming pool Communists, who see to it that the revolutionaries trying to destroy us don't lack for money." When Governor Jerry Brown signed into law a bill reducing the penalties for marijuana possession, Davis declared: "It is obvious that Mickey Mouse and Goofy and all the other characters are alive and well in Disneyland North." The cause of many of the state's problems can be traced to the "funny little people" with "socialistic ideas" appointed by Brown to government jobs. Militant homosexuals and migrant workers, he said, should unite to form the "United Fruit Workers of America." Portable gal-lows should be constructed to execute captured hijackers on the spot. To federal charges that he did not recruit enough women and blacks to the Los Angeles Police Department he replied: "I always felt the government really was out to force me to hire 4-foot-11 transvestite morons."

Davis left the Democratic party in 1975 after party chair-man Robert Strauss announced the Democrats' decision to hold their 1976 nominating convention in New York City instead of Los Angeles because of the party's concern about possible police "over-reaction" to demonstrators. Decentraliz-ing authority and rewarding officers for reducing the crime rate, Davis could boast that under his leadership major crime fell five percent, with major crime in the ghetto dropping a full forty percent. "I eliminated all the Brooks Brothers, button-down-collar boys who were community-relations types, and I made every uniformed cop a crime fighter with a whole bunch of partners, the people," he said with obvious pride. Even the hostile *Los Angeles Times* has acknowledged Los Angeles po-lice incorruptibility.

It was Davis's militant aggressiveness and his vigilante frontier image, his defiance of liberals and liberalism that excited the New Right. To the surprise of many, he lost in the 1978 GOP primary to Evelle Younger, whom he described as "about as exciting as a mashed potato sandwich." Viguerie conducted an intensive direct-mail campaign for Davis with little television, a mistaken strategy, one knowledgeable political professional told me, in a state where television is preeminent.

While Davis's defeat for the Republican gubernatorial nomination removed him from the political scene, he is an ambitious individual who is not likely to remain out of the fray. He relishes the battle in true New Right fashion and can be counted on to return to the political arena. Upbeat and optimistic, in addition to being deeply concerned about law enforcement issues, Davis may have been defeated for elective office—but he will not be so easily silenced.

A cult figure of the New Right (as of many conservatives), in the field of education, and one of the few Easterners the Right admires, is Dr. Howard Hurwitz, principal of Long Island City High School in New York. Hurwitz was recommended by the conservative *Richmond News-Leader* as "Man of the Year" in education, "a throwback, if not an educational reactionary. He happens to be a disciplinarian in an age of permissiveness." Hurwitz has framed a clipping calling him AMERICA'S TOUGHEST PRINCIPAL. A frequent contributor to *Human Events,* Hurwitz first came to widespread attention in 1976 when he suspended a black girl he said was a discipline problem disrupting the progress of other students. His superiors at the board of education ordered him to readmit the girl, he refused, and a court order was obtained to evict Hurwitz from the school. A number of parents and students in the working-class community rushed to his defense, barricaded the school, closing it for three days while Hurwitz slept in his office refusing to budge. One angry mother said, "The middle-class community is finally standing up. We pay all the taxes. It's our school." "Without Dr. Hurwitz this place would be a jungle," said a student. The New Right was undisturbed by his defiance of a court order and by an act of civil disobedience they would have condemned in a liberal.

After prolonged negotiations, the board reinstated Hurwitz. The *Richmond News-Leader* summed up the right-wingers' interpretation of the events:

> In saner times, the girl's parents would have taken her to the woodshed. But this is 1976, so they took her to a local anti-poverty agency called Qualicap—no doubt financed by generous infusions of federal cash. The agency provided a lawyer for the suspended girl, and he claimed that Hurwitz had violated her rights by kicking her out of school.
>
> Also in saner times, the city school board would have given Hurwitz a pay increase and its firm support for his wholly justifiable action in trying to maintain order in his school—but, no. The board suspended him—first with pay, then without pay. The school board might have tossed him to the anti-poverty wolves, but Hurwitz received instant support from his teachers, his 3,000 students and their parents.

A technicality not noted by those who view the episode as a great victory for Hurwitz is the fact that the girl was readmitted to the school.

Hurwitz is praised by many as an intelligent, decent, and reasonable gentleman, a dedicated and effective administrator, with overwhelming support of his community and the loyalty and devotion of his students. But it was his anger, his courage, and his consistent record in defiance of school officials and educational bureaucrats, his emphasis on discipline and his toughness in resistance to liberal educational theories that aroused his New Right fans. In 1970, the board had asked that he distribute a students' rights handbook and he refused; in 1973, he was asked to distribute an ethnic census and again refused; in 1975 he censored a student article in the school newspaper because he considered it irresponsible. The girl who had been expelled said she did not believe the incident was racially motivated. "No, I think he'd do it to anybody. He doesn't care what color you are."

PROTECTING THE FRONTIER

The New Right's politics is *macho* politics, interested in those issues that affect the sense of national prestige in foreign policy and law and order in domestic policy. Appalled by the very idea that the United States would "surrender" the Panama Canal, they evoked Teddy Roosevelt and embarked on a nationwide crusade to save the territory from the fate that awaited it—and the loss of national prestige they believed ratification of the treaties entailed. Announcing that "There is No Panama Canal, There is an American Canal At Panama," the American Conservative Union and other organizations sponsored a "Truth Squad" of Republican senators and congressmen who alerted Americans to the crisis in key cities across the nation. At a cost of $381,470, the American Conservative Union produced a television documentary bringing the message to 270 stations in forty-five states and began work on another film with a similar theme—"Soviet Might/American Myth."

Determined to keep America's security forces safe from liberal—and, some suspected, pacifist—influences, the American Conservative Union worked closely with the weekly *Human Events* in 1977 to block the appointment of Theodore Sorensen as director of the Central Intelligence Agency in the Carter Administration.

The National Right to Work Committee has taken on the task of protecting hapless Americans from what the committee's publicists consider the bully-boy tactics of labor union organizers, placing advertisements in such publications as *Commentary* and *The New Republic* which purport to tell the inspiring stories of individuals, often rugged-looking young men or brave women who stood up to the abuse and violence of what the New Right considers "union bosses." Reed Larson himself stood up to the federal courts in June 1977, when his "respectful noncompliance" with a court order to disclose the names of committee and foundation contributors led Federal

District Judge Charles R. Richey to rule that he would henceforth have to assume that most of the funds come from employers with a "concrete interest" in the legal defense foundation's lawsuits and that the group is primarily an "interested employer association" or "agent and conduit for employers" with an interest in weakening the labor movement. "Reed Larson is devoted to the destruction of the trade union movement," says Joseph Rauh, who took the committee to court. Larson insists that he is interested only in the "human rights" issue of forced association with labor unions. The foundation's newsletters nevertheless goes beyond right-to-work issues, with headlines such as "NEA Counsel Says Teachers Are Beasts" and "AFL-CIO Caught in Postcard Fraud." Similar *macho* attitudes are suggested by the activities of the Public Service Research Council, the group that fights public sector unions as a way to protect Americans from danger to their homes and families should, for example, striking firemen allow their homes to burn. Donald Denholm, its executive director, told *Conservative Digest* that he sees his role as "working night and day to fight the abuses of power-hungry union bosses."

Some organizations are devoted solely to such *macho* concerns. The New Right arms of the gun lobby, for example, display he-man attitudes in their publications, talking tough and acting tough. In August 1978, the Citizens Committee for the Right to Keep and Bear Arms called on all Roman Catholic gun owners to boycott their churches' collection plates as a protest against the position of the American Catholic bishops in favor of gun control legislation. The policy, the committee charged, denied "means of self-defense" to the poor by opposing the sale of cheap hand-guns. If the bishops did not reverse their position, the Citizens Committee said, they would urge their members to "yank" their children out of parochial schools.

That year, the group took credit for persuading the Xerox Corporation to withdraw its support from an educational program the Citizens Committee considered hostile to Second Amendment guarantees. Another victory for the fiesty gun

lobby: It convinced the Internal Revenue Service to withdraw from the National Coalition to Ban Handguns the tax-
exempt status the anti-gun group maintained through its association with the United Methodist Church.

The Americans for Effective Law Enforcement manifests
similar attitudes. This organization routinely takes a pro-police
stand on public policy questions, attempting to diminish the
restrictions under which modern-day lawmen must do their
jobs. Executive director Frank Carrington has said he considers
it "ridiculous" for police to be compelled to go to court before
they can infiltrate political organizations, though he denies
that his group is a "police—right or wrong" organization. According to one of the group's brochures:

> We recognize the fact that there are a minority of law enforce-
> ment officers who do engage in willful and wanton conduct,
> and that they should be held accountable. On the other hand,
> AELE has taken the firm position accepted by the courts that
> policemen should not be punished for their good faith efforts
> to carry out their primary function of protecting the public.

A spokesman for the Chicago ACLU disagrees:

> The [Americans for Effective Law Enforcement] has a predi-
> lection, which I guess is fair to call a bias, in favor of police—.
> If the police are doing it, it must be right and legal. And if it
> isn't legal, then certainly right.

The origins of the hawkish American Security Council,
formed to protect the American people from threats foreign
and domestic, is also revealing. Its founder, William F. Carroll,
was a former FBI agent; and the organization in its early days
functioned, according to author Richard Dudman, "to operate
a private loyalty-security blacklist where employers could check
their employees and job applications for indications of left-
wing connections." Its letterhead is dominated by military
figures—including retired Major General John K. Singlaub,

relieved of his responsibilities in 1977 for criticizing President
Carter's foreign policy decisions. One reporter, writing in the
radical magazine *Seven Days,* joked that the group "has
grabbed all the former military brass it can get except for the
Pentagon plumbing system." Though its concern today is less
with internal subversion—it gained great publicity in 1978
with formation of the Coalition for Peace Through Strength,
headed by Senator Robert Dole of Kansas—reds-under-beds is
still a lingering concern, apparently, among the organization's
officialdom: In 1979, it added to its staff former Communist-
turned-right-winger Phillip Abbot Luce, editor of *The Pink
Sheet on the Left* newsletter and author of a book on the
campus radicals, *Road to Revolution.*

Affecting the style of their idealized sheriffs of the New Old
West, these *macho* New Rightists—nostalgic for a world in
which they exercised genuine leadership—swagger about the
national political scene, protecting the townspeople from the
liberal outlaws, eager for High Noon.

4

Good Guys and Bad Guys

What is power? It is the ability to tell others what the issues are, what the issues mean, and identify who the good guys and bad guys are. That is power.
   —HOWARD PHILLIPS of Conservative Caucus

Some weeks before the New Hampshire presidential primary of 1976, New Right fundraiser Richard A. Viguerie and a handful of key advisers flew to Texas to meet with former Texas Governor John B. Connally. Gerald Ford was in the White House, but barely, and Ronald Reagan—the overwhelming favorite of the conservatives—had made known his intention to challenge the incumbent for the nomination. Reagan, with the support of William Loeb's *Manchester Union-Leader,* could be strong in the Granite State and possibly finish off Ford then and there. The purpose of the call on Connally, however, was to forestall the Reagan campaign by persuading the Texas political leader, once a Democrat, to enter the New Hampshire primary, too—as a Republican. When Connally turned down the offer, the Viguerie faction scouted around for other options. An effort by the New Right to knock Ford *and* Reagan out of the race may sound bizarre, but it is wholly consistent with its rationale.

The New Right divides people into Good Guys and Bad Guys. It has a hero complex and a villain complex. Yesterday's Good Guy may become today's Bad Guy. The New Right imposes severe standards and thus is often disillusioned. Failure to live up to these severe standards is considered betrayal, and meets with hostility bordering on hatred. The New Rightists have been enthusiastic, in turn, about Barry Goldwater, George Wallace, Ronald Reagan, and John Connally. Despite early enthusiasm for Connally, who courted New Right leaders, the New Right nevertheless showed early signs of disillusion, abandoning yet another hero. There is a logic in what looks like madness. The logic is an obsession with political style, a militant "agin-ism" over any coherent political program or philosophy, a hard-line intolerance of political compromise tempered only by the cynicism of some self-serving New Right leaders. These New Rightists, it seems clear, will forgive or overlook deep flaws in their political leaders if their style is sufficiently bellicose—or if such forgiveness or selective vision serves the opportunists' immediate ends.

The New Right Good Guys are aggressive and tough customers eager to do battle with what they see as the corrupt forces of liberalism and liberalism's agents. The New Right ideologues, as opposed to the New Right opportunists, refuse to compromise and, therefore, they reject the dynamics and art of politics itself. The Good Guys are those individuals who are untainted by liberalism or moderation; they oppose it to the last corral, shooting it out like some Wild West sheriff holding off the outlaws of liberalism—like Senator Edward Kennedy of Massachusetts, "the most dangerous man who can do this country great damage," according to the Reverend Jerry Falwell of Moral Majority. The ideal of the New Right, as noted, is the lonesome lawman, sitting tall in the saddle—one brave man against a corrupt and lawless Old West. The New Rightists show their greatest contempt not for liberals but for individuals who are reluctant to ride the plains alone, who have adjusted to national politics. It is the old range war all over again— independent cattle ranchers against the settled farmers.

GOOD GUYS TURNED BAD GUYS

Convinced that the political system is corrupt, the New Rightists distrust and resent those who have chosen to work within it, since those who do must of necessity make deals, negotiate. Compromise means cooperation with the liberal outlaws, and a loss of integrity. By this logic, those who succeed in the political world and attain real influence are corrupt and can no longer be trusted to advance the true cause. Only the loners who refuse to play the game of the System are to be trusted. Consequently, any right-of-center politician or spokesman who achieves truly national stature is automatically suspect. Such a Catch-22 situation is well described by M. Stanton Evans in an adage about right-wing politicians. He firmly believes: "By the time they get into a position where they can help us, they are no longer one of us." Ironically, self-described liberals are often treated with less hostility than are conservative Republicans who stain their reputations by compromising with liberals, not unlike the Communists' traditional hatred of socialists and liberals. The New Right sees such compromises as "soft" or "squishy," the equivalent (in the vernacular of the Old West) of being yellow-bellied. In 1962, future New Right leaders like William Rusher and Lee Edwards were active in the draft-Goldwater movement, which succeeded in nominating the Arizona senator for president in 1964; both, by 1976, had turned against their former mentor because he endorsed the moderate-to-conservative Gerald Ford, and thus weakened Ronald Reagan's challenge for the GOP nomination. Yet by that same year, Edwards, the author of the 1968 campaign biography, *Reagan: A Political Biography,* had decided that Reagan himself was too Establishment and, as he told me, now preferred George Wallace as president.

In fact, Reagan's challenge to incumbent President Ford provided the pretext for the political mugging of Barry Goldwater, once a symbol of courage and conviction—the man who offered "A Choice Not An Echo"—to American right-wingers. The statue was knocked off its pedestal, beginning with a fascinating attack by Viguerie and Edwards in *Conservative Digest* in 1975. Lamenting the fact that the "news media and millions of Americans are still looking to Senator Goldwater to point the way conservatives will go," Viguerie wrote in his magazine:

> We can't afford to expect more of any man than he is able to give. We must separate reality from myth, fact from fiction.
> If we have reached the point where a new generation of conservative leaders is needed (and I believe we have), it's important for the rank and file of U.S. conservatism to know that.

Goldwater had come to represent "a serious problem for conservatives," Edwards and Viguerie wrote. "His image continues to be used and misused by others, in and out of the media." The national press corps "use Goldwater's still unique reputation for their own uses, quoting him when it suits their purposes." When Goldwater urged President Nixon to come clean on Watergate in 1973, the *Conservative Digest*'s publisher was dismayed that "the news media gave his remarks front page play." When he urged that Reagan reassess his decision to seek the Republican nomination, "Goldwater's enormous prestige was used by the media in an obvious effort to undercut Reagan." The "liberal" captivity of the Republican party was blamed on Goldwater's reluctance in 1975 to support the "conservative" candidate, Dean Burch, of California, for the GOP chairmanship: "As a result, conservatives lost control of the Republican National Committee and the Republican party." The Goldwater whom the Right had come to know and love for his presidential bid in 1964 simply was no more—and perhaps had never been. The real Goldwater never wanted to be president and "does not want to be a national leader" today. Rather, he "is a man who will stay in his office operating his shortwave radio while there is a roll call vote on the floor." If the issue before the Senate "is busing, gun control or some similar domestic issue, Goldwater will almost invariably be gone if a vote comes at suppertime." Goldwater is becoming increasingly lazy, "content to vote conservative, but not to lead any conservative opposition or counterattack."

The object of the assault was twofold. First, those in the *Conservative Digest* circle—Viguerie, Paul Weyrich, Howard Phillips, and other New Rightists—wanted to undercut whatever allegiance Goldwater may still have commanded from conservative voters, lest these voters support Ford over a challenge from the Right. Second, the New Right sought to assert its own leadership as the "new generation" of right-wing leaders. The audience for the article was as much the national news media as conservatives in the hinterlands. The objective was to establish, if only by implication, that the New Rightists—and not Goldwater Republicans—were the new spokesmen for true conservatives.

When Goldwater began to campaign for Ford in 1976 and criticize Reagan, others on the Right joined in the anti-Goldwater chorus. In his syndicated column, William Rusher expressed amazement that Goldwater had found good things to say about his old rival Nelson Rockefeller, speculating "that Goldwater's grip on conservative principles just isn't (and perhaps never was) the absolutely dependable thing we believed it to be." A month later, David Brudnoy, a conservative-libertarian commentator from Boston, followed up with a column of his own called "The Trouble with Barry." Noting Goldwater's support for Ford, Brudnoy accused Goldwater of putting "expediency before principle," concluding that "whatever happens to Ford and Reagan, Barry Goldwater is through as Mr. Conservative. The conservatives never retrieve their wounded, and to conservative eyes the image of Barry, Barry burning bright, has become a mirage, a figment of past imagination." Even Young Americans for Freedom cast aside their characteristic deference and timidity toward their elders, issuing a press release that pronounced Goldwater's intemperate remarks about Reagan "disappointing":

> Senator Goldwater's unfair and insensitive statement that Reagan's positions reflect "a surprisingly dangerous state of mind" indicate to young conservatives that Goldwater has either abandoned the conservative philosophy for which he is known or the sportsmanship and sense of fair play that have endeared him to millions.

Moreover, the organization's monthly magazine, *New Guard*, concluded: "As much as it hurts to admit it, the facts about Barry Goldwater are clear: Whatever his motivations, he has let conservatives down.

And he leaves young conservatives no alternative but to look elsewhere for leadership, inspiration and guidance."*

All in all, reaction to the mugging was favorable. Rusher, in a lengthy (and published) letter to Viguerie and Edwards, praised their "thoughtful and courageous" article, predicting that Goldwater would officially endorse Ford over Reagan, "and that would be a great tragedy, not only for the Republican party but for the cause of conservatism and the future of America." William Loeb of the *Manchester Union Leader,* in another published letter wrote to say he was "delighted" with the article, especially given "the kind and polite" way the infidel Goldwater had been savaged. Kevin Phillips in his column noted, "After all, Reagan is running against the Washing-

---

*The current author's own role in this fiasco should not go unremarked. I was then editor of *New Guard* and wrote both the press release and the *New Guard* article.

ton 'buddy system' and Goldwater is part of it—a man quite comfortable with the mixture of top administration officials, cronies and business lobbyists summed up in capital parlance as the 'Burning Tree' (country club) set." He said, "Goldwater has been a lazy failure" as a leader for at least six years and the Right "will not allow" him to pretend to national leadership ever again. Letters began to arrive at *Conservative Digest*'s offices backing the publisher. One reader from Waverly, Ohio, lamented that Goldwater "simply has lost his 'backbone' and all the 'vinegar' has simply gone away." A Wilton, California, reader wrote, "I have been aware for over two years that Goldwater was turning soft." (Several months before, one *Conservative Digest* reader wrote to protest the appearance of Goldwater's name in a poll of "favorite conservatives." "In checking your list of favorite conservatives," he wrote, "I feel that Barry Goldwater should be removed from the list. At one time he was a conservative. He is favoring Rockefeller and in other things leans toward the liberal side.")

In July, columnist John Lofton wrote, "I have read Sen. Barry Goldwater's endorsement of President Ford . . . and, not knowing precisely what motivated the senator, I'm inclined to give Mr. Goldwater the benefit of the doubt on this one. It is obvious that Sen. Goldwater's letter to all GOP convention delegates was written at a time when he was, well, not himself, perhaps during the postoperative period [for a hip condition] when he was still in an ether fog. . . . Possessed of all his faculties, he would never say the things he is saying about Reagan."

Oddly enough, the New Rightists were already in the process of deciding that Reagan as the GOP nominee or as president would be worse than Ford. As early as 1975, conservative columnist James J. Kilpatrick had issued a warning about the Right's absolutism:

> Reagan's difficult task is to project an image of moderate conservatism. The very notion will outrage rock-ribbed one hundred percenters who now cheer his every word. To them mod-

eration is seldom a virtue; extremism rarely a vice. If Reagan
ever appears to be waffling toward the Left, they will turn on
him with cries of "Judas!" But Reagan will never make it to the
White House if he is perceived, as Goldwater was perceived,
as a monster who would abandon the old folks and atomize
little girls.

One conservative activist, then becoming disenchanted with
the activities of the New Rightists, told me of a "Kingston"
meeting at which Weyrich of the Committee for the Survival of a Free Congress surveyed the other participants—
many of them still Reagan loyalists—and announced: "I
don't know about you guys, but I'm not for Reagan. If he
gets in, we're out. We'd have no input in that administration." Reagan's decision to retain the fund-raising services
of Bruce W. Eberle & Associates, instead of those of Viguerie, reportedly disappointed many New Rightists—and
angered Viguerie—thus increasing tensions between the
New Rightists and the Reagan camp, which was viewed as
dominated by Republican party professionals and not right-
wing ideologues.

These tensions exploded at the 1976 Republican convention after Reagan selected as his vice-presidential running
mate Richard Schweiker of Pennsylvania, a man with a liberal voting record. Viguerie and his friends announced
plans to attend the American Independent party convention coming up in Chicago, and Illinois Congressman
Philip Crane was especially angered, since he expected Reagan to name him—and not his next-door neighbor in
McLean, Virginia.

William F. Buckley, who had remained aloof from the internecine warfare at the GOP convention, observed in his
newspaper column that, perhaps, the explosion over Schweiker
was premature; that he was, in fact, a perfectly acceptable
choice upon which a "New Majority" coalition could be built:
Schweiker, after all, enjoyed strong support from labor unions
and had consistently voted with the New Right on the "social

issues" such as busing, gun control, abortion, and the death penalty. What is more, he was skeptical about the Helsinki human rights accords and, generally, opposed détente with the Soviet Union. As David Keene, a Reagan aide instrumental in the Schweiker gambit, told me: "They didn't understand this because they are not sophisticated enough to see that far into it. These are not, you must understand, the most, well, reflective people. . . ." Another American Conservative Union activist told me the Schweiker explosion pointed up yet another serious problem with the New Right: "They didn't know their own program. They talk a great deal about compromise to attract support from those who do not ordinarily identify themselves as conservatives, but they denounce the slightest variation from long-held right-wing dogma."

Many Reagan supporters had become convinced that Reagan's national campaign was infiltrated by liberals—chief among them Reagan's campaign manager, John Sears III, who worked for Nixon in 1968 and Reagan in 1976. It was Sears, after all, who orchestrated the Schweiker move; and Reagan's political action committee, Citizens for the Republic, reluctant to anger party regulars, had refused, in 1978, to contribute to conservative Republicans who were challenging GOP incumbents. Sears, for his part, was convinced that his candidate's most serious liability was the public's perception of him as a right-wing ideologue. "Events may erase that impression," Sears said, announcing in 1979 that Reagan was seriously considering dropping his long-held opposition to full diplomatic ties to Communist China; Reagan promptly denied it, but the damage had been done. Before Reagan's denial, the *New York Times* reported that the move gave the impression that Reagan was ready to embrace a "more flexible attitude toward international Communism." By February 1980, Reagan replaced Sears—to the great jubilation of supporters, conservative and New Right.

Reagan did seem to be softening his reputation as a crypto-Social Darwinist. "I know I'm supposed to be a terrible right-wing person," *The Wall Street Journal* quoted him as saying

early in 1978 to a group of Chicago businessmen. "But I just
wish people who think that would look at my record in California." There, he boasted, he had initiated "conjugal visits" in
state prisons, made the income tax "more progressive," and
increased welfare benefits to the "truly needy." Such breath-
taking reversals—as seen by the New Right—caused a number
of rightists to conclude that, however genuine his commitment
to conservative principles, Reagan is through as an intraparty
ideologue. They began to take aim against him in 1978 as they
had earlier in 1975 against Goldwater. Kevin Phillips wrote in
his syndicated column that, in addition to marking "the transformation of [Citizens for the Republic] into a vehicle of party,
not principle," the behavior of the Reagan camp might well
signify the Californian's effective retirement from relevant political struggles:

> Gone is the would-be charismatic insurgent of several years ago,
> the crusader who called for a politics of bold ideological colors,
> not pale pastels. Now we have in his place a 67-year-old party
> regular preaching unity while aides hint that he'd serve only
> one term . . . leaving the Republican ideological–factional fu-
> ture up for grabs.
>   Advisors who encourage Reagan to shed his ideology may be
> misreading the intensity of his strength on the right, though.
> Among the rightwing activists, a considerable number see Rea-
> gan as an aging figure from another era, an easygoing man who
> could easily be ineffective—or worse—as president. To the
> extent that he retains his ideological vim and credibility, Rea-
> gan defuses those private critics. But to the extent that he
> becomes just another faithful Republican, he gives doubters
> the reinforcement they require.

Die-hard rightists might indeed be disappointed with a Reagan presidency, or very likely by any presidency, although they
long to achieve that pinnacle. Reagan's record is an illustration
of the seeming inability of any mainstream politician, once in
office, to live up to the expectations of the New Right. When
Reagan first ran for governor in California, he promised

a quarter-billion-dollar cut in his first-year budget, but the budget increased from $4.6 billion to $5.7 billion and, by the time he left office eight years later, it had swelled to $10.2 billion. The average yearly increase in the state budget was 12.2 percent; the state sales tax rose from 4 to 6 percent; corporate income taxes from 5.5 to 9 percent and top personal income taxes from 7 to 11 percent. The number of state employees increased by 5.7 percent, while the total number of federal civilian employees during that period declined by more than 3 percent. Though Reagan had been critical of public spending for education, state funding for public elementary and high schools under his administration rose 105 percent—while enrollment increased by only 5 percent—and state support for junior colleges soared 323 percent. Grants and loans to college students, highly criticized by conservatives as well as New Rightists as a scandal-ridden federal program, shot up 900 percent.

Despite attacks on government interference, Reagan sponsored what has been described as one of the toughest water pollution control laws in the United States and stepped up state control over auto repair, home insurance, real estate, retail businesses, doctors, and dentists. He increased inheritance taxes, provided tax credits for renters, reduced the oil depletion allowance, and stiffened the capital gains tax. A frequent critic of gun control, Reagan signed into law the Mulford Act, which provided a penalty of one year's imprisonment or a $1,000 fine for anyone found with a loaded gun in his possession on a public highway, unless he could prove that he was in immediate danger. Despite a reputation as a hardliner on foreign policy, Reagan strongly implied that even in the event of a Soviet invasion of Western Europe he could not conceive of using nuclear weapons—a statement for which he was taken to task in 1976 by even the liberal *New Republic.*

While conservative writers in *Human Events* relentlessly attacked the liberal drift of the Nixon years, Reagan—true to his accommodating, genial nature—was silent, even on détente and wage and price controls. A Nixon loyalist, Reagan actually defended the second-story men of the Committee to Re-Elect the President when they were caught burglarizing the Democratic headquarters at the Watergate. They were "well-meaning individuals," Reagan said, who were "not criminals at heart." Many disgruntled Reagan supporters, in fact, believed he could have easily defeated Ford for the nomination had he only gone on the attack, casting aside the Eleventh Commandment—"Thou Shalt Speak No Ill of Another Republican"—which made his early primary challenges to Ford in 1975 seem half-hearted and unnecessary.

Would the soft-spoken Reagan compromise with liberals? "He talked about the California state legislature in the harshest terms," wrote Newspaper Enterprise Association columnist Ray Cromley, "but personally negotiated privately at greater length with legislative leaders than any previous governor. He introduced more compromise bills and legislative compromises on major as well as minor points—perhaps more than any other California executive within my memory. . . ." Did he have the commitment, the stomach, to wage the political warfare the New Right believes is necessary? Probably not. A governor who worked from nine to five, he delegated authority; interested only in broad policy decisions, he left the details to others. A framed photograph of Reagan in cowboy clothes at his ranch hangs on the wall of former aide Lyn Nofziger's office. "Lyn," it is inscribed, "Why can't I be like this more often?"

Though he starred in numerous Western movies, Reagan never was cast in the role of the tough, lonely sheriff, which did not fit his image; he was the nice guy, the amiable and easygoing fellow who did not like to spook the herd, an image that followed him through most of his films. He is, in fact, a more moderate politician than even his most ardent admirers would like to believe. He is, in short, a politician. To the extent that his rightist followers have made him out to be something other than he is, he cannot be held responsible for their sense of betrayal when he acts according to what he is, not what they think he is—or should be. He could be more—but not less—likely to disappoint those with unrealistic expectations of the office and the man than anyone else the rightists might choose to follow.

GOOD GUYS WHO ARE STILL GOOD GUYS

The New Right has embraced almost uncritically such rhetorically belligerent symbols of bipartisan reaction as George Wallace, former New Hampshire Governor Meldrim Thomson, North Carolina Senator Jesse Helms, and Georgia Congressman Larry McDonald. These choices display no significant strain of political or philosophical conservatism; they have been singled out by the New Right for reasons other than political or philosophical consistency—for political style—a style of redneck reaction. Wallace, perhaps more than any other contemporary political figure, represents to the New Right those cherished qualities found in the mythic Old West sheriff come to town to do battle with the liberal outlaws; tough, brave, and willing to take on all comers, these leaders, Wallace, Thomson, Helms, McDonald, Republicans and Democrats—symbolize to New Rightists the qualities necessary to rout the effete Eastern liberals and "turn this country around." The New Rightists looked with favor also on debonair Illinois Congressman Philip Crane, but he is of a different mold; neither primitive nor raging, he is not a redneck reactionary. Their support for him confounded their preferred style and it proved to be a passing fancy. They also turned, with some reservations, to a new-style lawman, Big John Connally, who combines the vigor of the Old West with the slick aplomb of a riverboat gambler. He had inherited the sheriff's star they once awarded to George Wallace.

Wallace is a Good Guy who has survived New Right disillusionment, in large part because, since being shot in 1972, he is a figure from the past, viewed with a certain nostalgia. Traditional conservatives, of course, dissociated themselves from Wallace. *National Review* dismissed the former Alabama governor as "an undesirable, a flagitious demagogue who, when in office, combined a skillful appeal to populist emotions with egregious welfare statism." James J. Kilpatrick, in *Conservative Digest*, stated categorically that Wallace is "no conservative," but "a political Bobby Riggs, a hustler, a showman, a master of the trick shot."

New Right activists, eager to forge a "New Majority" alliance between right-wing Democrats and disaffected GOP Reaganites, possibly under the banner of a new political party, talked throughout 1975 and 1976 of Wallace, almost to the exclusion of Reagan, even before Reagan made plain his decision to stay within the GOP. Patrick Buchanan wrote approvingly in his book, *Conservative Votes, Liberal Victories,* of a Wallace–Reagan third-party ticket; and William Rusher, in his own book, *The Making of the New Majority Party,* considered Wallace crucial to any alliance with blue-collar Democrats; Kevin Phillips proposed a Reagan–Wallace "Right Deal" for America in a guest column for *Newsweek.* Some compromise would be in order, all seemed to concede, if the Wallace constituency were to be corralled, a compromise that would have to originate in the Reagan camp.

Much would have to be overlooked, or simply left unaddressed, if the New Right was to throw their support to Wallace. As Alabama governor from 1962 to 1966 and from 1970 to 1976, he was a fairly orthodox New Deal Democrat who expanded the size and scope of state government. The payroll in Alabama increased more than 100 percent—double the rate of growth for the federal bureaucracy during the same period. The number of civilian government employees added to state payrolls increased 113.3 percent during the Wallace years, compared to 17 percent on the federal level. The state budget went up twice as fast as the federal budget—356.9 percent compared to 176.7 percent—while the federal debt increased 63 percent compared to an almost 400 percent increase in the state debt under Governor Wallace.

A legislative report card issued by the Alabama Chamber of Commerce during the years in which Wallace was a state legislator graded him a "Radical," and today a state administrator recalls Wallace then as "the leading liberal in the legislature, no doubt about that. He was regarded as a dangerous left-winger. A lot of people even looked on him as downright pink." One political crony, quoted by Marshall Frady in his book *Wallace* (1968), said his "economic programs surpassed the fondest dreams of every liberal in the state." In *National Review* in 1968, Ohio Congressman John Ashbrook, then national chairman of the American Conservative Union, expressed surprise "that many people consider Wallace a fiscal conservative, for his record shows that he is a big spender—of other people's money." In 1952 and 1956 Wallace supported Adlai Stevenson at the Democratic national conventions, and in 1956 he delivered one of the seconding speeches for John Kennedy for vice-president. Four years later he supported Kennedy for president.

New Rightists, nevertheless, hailed George Wallace in 1976 as the savior of the conservative cause, in part because of his shift from racial moderation to segregation. "American conservatives should make no mistake about it," Ashbrook wrote in *National Review,* "The only thing Wallace has against Washington is its racial policy. In all his other attitudes he is one of the biggest centralizers of them all.

> In one campaign [Wallace] ran as a racial moderate, accusing his opponent of espousing the principles of the Klan. When he lost, he turned around and ran the next time (in 1962) as a segregationist. . . .
>
> As a conservative I don't stand for enforced segregation. I stand for freedom and I think the Constitution does too. But George Wallace's slogan only recently was "segregation forever," and whatever he says now this has been the source of his appeal. In my view, this separates him decisively from the conservative position.

Ashbrook was speaking for classic conservatism.

Wallace's emphasis on the race issue was not his primary source of appeal to the New Right, however. His appeal went beyond race into his overall "agin-ism." The phrase, an invention of author Kirkpatrick Sale, is vividly described in *Power Shift* (1975), Sale's book on the rise of the Sun Belt:

> Wallace . . . plumbs to, rubs, and inflames the fears of those uneasy with the present and wistful for . . . some imagined past —the uncertain few who see themselves as the little against the big, the white against the black, the uneducated against the intellectual, the powerless against the powerful, the frightened against the secure, the looked-down-on against the lookers-down. Racism is a part of it, though somewhat muted in recent days . . . but more potent still is a broad *adversarianism,* a being-against. Wallace has no real policies, plans or platforms, and no one expects them of him; it is sufficient that he is *agin* and gathers unto him others who are *agin, agin* the blacks, the intellectuals, the bureaucrats, the students, the journalists, the liberals, the outsiders, the Communists, the *changers,* above all, *agin* the yankee Establishment: when he berates the "pointy-headed professors," the "filthy rich on Wall Street," the "federal judges playin' God," "the brief-case totin' bureaucrats," and the "socialist, beatnik crowd running the government,". . . when he says, "We're sick and tired of the average citizen being taxed to death while those billionaires like the Rockefellers and the Fords and the Mellons go without paying taxes" . . . and when he excoriates the two major parties for having moved "away from the people," and says, "there's not a dime's worth of difference in any of 'em, national Democrats or national Republicans" . . . then George Wallace is sounding that . . . chord that resonates so richly throughout the Southern Rim.

The Good Guys of the New Right represent, in varying degrees, this adversarianism or "agin-ism," a character trait the New Rightists themselves view as essential in their leaders. Buchanan, for example, praised Wallace as

> the authentic voice of the Forgotten American, the angry, white working man, North and South, heard raucously and continuously since 1964. Unlike those synthetic "new populists" created out of press clippings, whose strongest precincts are the

dormitories of the Ivy League, Wallace was the genuine article, the favorite son of the hard hats and the wool hats ... in 1966, 1968 and 1972 Wallace's appeal broadened; he came to represent for millions of Americans something other than defense of a dying past.

He stirred the embers of patriotism and nationalism in a country whose elite had marched into Vietnam and lacked the capacity to see it through. . . . Had he not been cut down in the Laurel shopping center, George Wallace could have been the catalyst for a new alignment in American politics.

Social protest and not governing is the real interest of the New Rightists; thus, the fact that Wallace's policies on centralization of government and public spending were not unlike those of the hated liberals was not primary. Deep down, Rightists were convinced, "he's one of us." New Rightists, therefore, were genuinely shocked and angered when Wallace endorsed fellow Southerner and Democrat Jimmy Carter in 1976 after losing the Florida primary, rejecting suggestions by New Right activists that he lead a third-party effort. Outraged, syndicated columnist John Lofton considered Wallace's endorsement of Carter a betrayal: "It's very sad, sad to have to say that at the end of his national political career, when the real crunch came, George Wallace put party above principle." His political career over, Wallace has been elevated, in the eyes of the New Rightists, to the somewhat unique status of Elder Statesman of Redneck Reaction; when he endorses the candidate of the Democratic party every four years, as he no doubt will, New Rightists will think nothing of it. Such endorsements are customary and, carrying little weight, can do little to hurt the New Rightists. He is viewed with affection and nostalgia but he does not figure in their future plans.

Another favorite of the New Right, Meldrim Thomson of New Hampshire, is also out of office, but the New Right hopes he can make a comeback. A political power in the Northeast, Thomson is, like all of the other New Right angry heroes, Wallace, Helms, and McDonald, a Southerner; he was born in

Georgia. He attended law school in Georgia and, later, transplanted to New England, ran for governor of the Granite State and lost, as an American party candidate. He then won as a Republican in 1972. He was so suspicious of his political opponents that one of his first official acts was to change the State House locks. He sent one of his top aides to examine the confidential tax records of his political opponents, an act the state supreme court promptly ruled unconstitutional. Thomson denounced the ruling; he would continue to enforce the Constitution as he saw fit, "and not as it is understood by others." Defeated in 1978 for election to an unprecedented third term as governor, Thomson promptly joined the national council of the John Birch Society. His support is more eclectic than this last move would suggest; he has admirers in more respectable circles as well. Still, he is at the core a Wallace-type primitive. "Consciously controversial, the governor comes close to being a populist of the right," Patrick Buchanan has written, "with the same flair for bizarre behavior that marked the fiery and famous populist of the left, Huey Long." When Governor Thomson—a dapper and garrulous extrovert with a toothy grin —showed up as a Reagan supporter at the 1976 Republican convention in Kansas City, wary Reagan aides assigned a special agent to follow him everywhere to make sure he did not say anything troublesome within earshot of reporters. The agent's code name: The Muzzle.

Thomson, like other New Right politicians, is obsessed by symbolic acts of social protest. One of his favorite rituals was the lowering of state flags to half-mast whenever he did not like actions taken in Washington, which was quite often. Flags were at mourning at the signing of the Panama Canal treaties. When he ordered the State House flags at half-mast on Good Friday to "memorialize the death of Christ," the New Hampshire Civil Liberties Union protested, while courts kept the flags "going up and down like yo-yos," according to a *Washington Post* account. The Supreme Court eventually upheld a lower court ruling against the governor. When President Ford called for a program of amnesty for Vietnam draft evaders,

Thomson declared Anti-Amnesty Day. On United Nations Day, he revived an ageless right-wing slogan and announced "Get the U.S. Out of the U.N. Week." He threatened to cut off funds for the University of New Hampshire at the first sign of any gay liberation organization on campus and, when confronted by priests seeking his endorsement of their boycott of Gallo wines, Thomson hied off to the local liquor store and, gathering reporters around him, purchased a jug.

Thomson gained great support nationally from the New Right for his "tough" treatment of protesters at the Seabrook nuclear power plant. Budget-conscious Republicans in the state stressed the cost of jailing and prosecuting the thousands of demonstrators, but the New Right was delighted. He ordered early antinuclear power activists arrested for attempting to collect signatures on petitions in parking lots of state liquor stores in which he had placed pro-Seabrook petitions. He sought to bar state employees from criticizing his policy. He "cracked down hard," as *Human Events* put it, on the "militant environmentalists," ordering state police to make mass arrests. After suggesting that the New Hampshire National Guard be trained in the use of nuclear weapons, the governor asked the state legislature to fund a giant fallout shelter for himself and the state's top 100 officials. The project's total cost: $750,000.

Oddly enough, it was the tax issue that brought Thomson down in 1978. In the only state in the union without either an income tax or sales tax, Thomson had built his entire political career on promises not to raise taxes. New Hampshire had become the fastest growing state in one of the most economically depressed regions of the country; 250 new industries came into the state, and existing industries added 60,000 jobs, with a state unemployment rate of only 3 percent, half of that in surrounding states. More than 100,000 refugees from "Taxachusetts" migrated across the border from 1970 to 1976. But Thomson was defeated by rising electric bills. The Public Service Co., of New Hampshire, Seabrook's principal developer, had won permission from the public utility commission to add a construction surcharge to its bills. Democratic legislators blocked the surcharge and Thomson vetoed it. Holding a utility bill in one hand, the Democratic candidate Hugh Gallen would charge, "It's the first time Mel Thomson imposed a tax on the average family in this state and they're not going to forget it." A lesser issue, suggesting that Thomson was not minding the store, was his eagerness to travel around the world, often in association with right-wing groups and causes. As governor, and as chairman of Conservative Caucus, Thomson toured Taiwan, South Africa, Israel, Panama, Germany, and Great Britain.

In his concession speech in 1978, Thomson vowed to "return to the fray," prompting speculation that he would run for the U.S. Senate or try for the State House again. He toyed with running as a Republican favorite son candidate in the nation's earliest presidential primary, a move that "would be devastating to other conservative candidates," *Human Events* had quoted former Governor Walter Peterson as saying. Thomson, like many New Rightists, had come to the feverish conclusion that Congressman Philip Crane was weakened by his willingness to accept federal campaign funds. Thomson has made public his refusal to support Reagan as long as John Sears, who denied Thomson control of the New Hampshire Reagan campaign in 1976, remained as Reagan's campaign manager. With Thomson no longer governor, Sears virtually ignored him. Having endorsed a third-party movement in America, Thomson said later, in 1979, that he would seek the presidency on an independent "Constitution" party ticket.

An equally blatant New Rightist from the South is Senator Jesse Helms of North Carolina, also said to have presidential ambitions, the first Republican to represent the Tarheel State in the Senate in this century. He is as doctrinaire and hard-right as anyone in Washington but with a reputation as a genuinely decent person and a dedicated, hard-working senator. He is loathed by the liberal press, singled out by the editors of *The Nation* as an "ultra-and-arch-reactionary." The son of a former police chief of Monroe, North Carolina, Helms first came to public attention as an outspoken radio editorialist. Like Connally, he was originally a Democrat, joining the Republican party in 1970 and elected to the Senate as a Republican two years later. Tall, courtly, and soft-spoken, he takes delight in fighting lost causes and sacrificing all (save election) to matters of principle. Admirers on the Right call him a "Totally Principled Politician," but his liberal critics dub him "Senator No." In 1977 he made much of the information that New York banks like Midland Marine and Chase Manhattan had investments in Panama—with the implication that renegotiation of the Panama Canal treaties was somehow a "bailout." He introduced a constitutional amendment that would have denied abortion even in cases in which the mother's health is endangered.

Helms's record is more flexible on certain matters close to home. In his denunciations of federal spending, he offered, according to *The Wall Street Journal,* "a spirited defense of the Agriculture Department's tobacco loan program," a position clearly at odds with his principled commitment to free enterprise; however, he voted against an agricultural appropriations bill with a $3 million provision for a tobacco research program in his own state because the bill included funds for the food stamp program. In his 1978 campaign he ignored his reputation as one of the Senate's most vigorous opponents of irresponsible expenditure of other people's money and waged the most expensive campaign fund-raising in history, with almost half of the $6.7 million raised going to firms controlled by Viguerie. Helms's campaign attacks on labor unions were, at the least, misleading: His fund-raising letters, for example, charged that "union bosses" were out to get him and that his opponent, state insurance commissioner John Ingram, had been endorsed by North Carolina's "largest and most powerful union, the AFL-CIO." The facts were not exactly as presented. North Carolina is one of the least unionized states in the country, and the AFL-CIO is weak and ineffectual there. The union's endorsement of Ingram was lukewarm. Ingram had been offered—but he returned—a $5,000 contribution from the AFL-CIO's Committee on Political Education, having vowed not to accept out-of-state money from what he considered special interests. Helms's campaign depended on a campaign bureaucracy the candidate would have condemned in Washington, staffed by 150 workers, with a budget of $4,000 for bookkeeping alone. He outspent Ingram by thirty to one, and when the campaign was over, appealed to major contributors one last time, with the news that his re-election effort was still roughly $200,000 in debt.

The favorite senator of the far-out white supremacy groups, Helms does not go out of his way for the votes of black citizens in North Carolina and, unlike South Carolina Senator Strom Thurmond, he refused to support the District of Columbia voting rights amendment in 1979. Like many New Right leaders, he consented to a lengthy interview in the John Birch Society's *Review of the News* and has been praised by *American Opinion*, one of whose frequent contributors described him as "this man who stands perfectly for everything which the sons of the Bolsheviks in Moscow and their alleged antagonists in Wall Street are trying to destroy in America." He is a force within right-wing politics. As a former Democrat in a state where Democrats outnumber Republicans three to one, Helms is seen as a key figure in forging a New Right alliance between Southern Democrats and GOP Reaganites. Under his leadership, the state Republican party registration increased more than 20 percent. M. Stanton Evans believes Helms to be potentially "the pivotal figure in our politics," equipped to speak effectively "to what has been called 'the new majority' in the American electorate. . . . As a southerner Helms has a natural kinship for the conservative Democrats of the once-solid South. In fact, Helms's Democratic supporters are so numerous that the North Carolina press has given them a special name—'Jessecrats.' "

A major figure in drafting the conservative platform at the 1976 Republican convention, Helms was also instrumental, along with Congressman Crane, in convincing Senator James L. Buckley of New York to offer his name to the convention as a "compromise" candidate for president—a move interpreted by many knowledgeable Washington conservatives as an attempt to punish Reagan for naming Senator Schweiker of Pennsylvania as his running mate. Buckley backed out before the trouble could begin. Helms, apparently ambitious for higher office, allowed North Carolina backers to mail several letters to Republicans who were potential delegates to the 1980 Republican convention, asking them to support Helms for the vice-presidential nomination. Helms, however, is known to be sympathetic to third-party movements and might lead such an effort should his disaffection with the Republican party—"a party of discount Democrats," Helms has called it—become intense enough.

A three-term congressman from Georgia, Larry McDonald, is a special favorite of the New Right bipartisans because he is a Democrat and active supporter of such organizations as the Conservative Caucus, the American Conservative Union, the Committee for the Survival of a Free Congress, the American Security Council, Gun Owners of America, the National Rifle Association, and the Young Americans for Freedom. He is also a member of the national council of the John Birch Society, an affiliation his office literature boasts of. Tall and broad-shouldered, McDonald appears fit for his war with the Democratic establishment; he told me that because of his views he is the victim of "marked bias" and "discrimination within the Democratic caucus." This, he said, "is the price you pay for trying to reclaim your party." Both major parties, he said, are "dominated by the same forces, internationalist forces that are downplaying national sovereignty" and "phasing out classical American concepts like the Bill of Rights and the Declaration of Independence" in favor of "international concepts." Who are these "internationalist forces"? The "key leadership in the [Council on Foreign Relations], the Trilateral Commission and the Bilderbergers . . . the American liberal internationalist establishment," McDonald told me, are "Eastern" and are promoting "international sellout." The situation seems so bleak, by McDonald's description, that there appears little that could be done to remedy it, but "to do away with parties altogether" might be a step in the right direction. "I am totally at a loss as to the value of maintaining a political party. Neither stands for anything," he said. He is not encouraged by the emergence of articulate neoconservative Democrats like Senator Daniel Patrick Moynihan of New York, whom he considers "a creature of the press," the "most powerful branch of government." Even the conservative community is suspect, having been infiltrated, in his view, by imposters like journalist William F. Buckley, Jr., who begins "frothing at the mouth at any mention of conspiracy" and went "out of his way to crush an ally"—John Birch Society founder Robert Welch. McDonald used to admire *Human Events,* but he believes that from 1965 on, the journal has "vacillated" and is no longer truly effective, because it is careful never to mention the sinister forces promoting "international sellout." He attributes this posture to the weekly's conservative editor, Thomas Winter, who knows it would be "socially unacceptable" to tell the truth about the conspiracy that is controlling American policy: "Put it like this. *National Review,* Bill Buckley, to a degree the American Conservative Union and *Battleline,* are 'respectable conservatives.'" Translated, that means, "impotent," that they are "no real threat." Liberals, he explained, are happy to have these "respectable conservatives" on hand, because they represent no danger to their monopoly on power. They pretend to disdain groups like the John Birch Society precisely because "they are a threat."

McDonald's Capitol Hill office is decorated with photographs of Joe McCarthy and General Pinochet, Chile's right-wing dictator—an appropriate base of operations from which to fill the *Congressional Record* with record-setting numbers of pages of statements and remarks, many of them dealing with international Communism. He has endeared himself to the New Right not only by virtue of his considerable disregard for the ridicule he receives from the Eastern press but also by virtue of his solidly New Right voting record and his willingness to introduce measures, in 1978, calling for the impeachment of Andrew Young as United Nations ambassador and, in 1979, demanding "a sense of Congress" that homosexuals will not receive "protected status" from the government. Larry McDonald is an unreconstructed Georgia primitive with no interest in appearing to be anything else, and the New Right loves him for it.

THE McLUHAN-ERA MATT DILLONS

The enthusiasm of some New Right leaders for Congressman Philip Crane—and, to a lesser extent, for John Connally—suggests a new sophistication, a desire to be represented by political candidates who can be successfully packaged and marketed in a media age. Both are presentable and both can make a striking impression on television. They are handsome men with an ability to communicate. Crane presents the right-wing platform in a manner that sounds moderate and plausible, sometimes deceptively so. A four-term Republican from the Chicago suburbs, he came to a sort of national attention when in January 1979 he became the first declared candidate for the Republican presidential nomination. For a time he seemed likely to become the New Right's favorite candidate. He is a gregarious and articulate former professor of American history at Indiana University and Bradley University—in his case, intellectual achievement is acceptable because he is not an East Coast Ivy-Leaguer. He is an enthusiastic campaigner who, over his eight years in Congress, has traveled tirelessly, speaking before conservative and New Right audiences and making numerous television appearances. From the beginning of his presidential campaign, he had the blessing of fundraiser Richard A. Viguerie, who stood by his side when he announced his intention to seek the Republican nomination. For roughly ten months, Viguerie raised money for the Crane campaign. The forces motivating Crane to run were murky. He is ambitious and was angry at Reagan for choosing Schweiker as his running mate, an honor Crane himself expected, as noted in the preceding section; and he regarded Reagan as vulnerable because of his age (thus did Crane refer to the necessity of "physical strength" in a chief executive, leading one conservative wag to suggest—"Arnold Schwartzenegger for President").

The Crane campaign was low comedy from the start,* though a profitable one for fund-raising. The *Manchester Union Leader* publisher promptly fired off a scathing front-page editorial accusing Crane of "an exercise in egotism and vanity," and doing an "about-face." Publisher William Loeb, a Reagan supporter, said Crane had, in 1979, told him Reagan was the one man in America capable of handling the problems facing this country. "To divide the strength of the conservative element at this time," Loeb summed up, "is nothing except insanity." Insanity or not, the campaign was off and running. Reagan aides said benignly that they would profit from having a candidate "to the right of" Reagan in the race. Crane took great umbrage at this; he was not, he insisted, "to the right of" Reagan—there were no differences at all between the two candidates. Why was he running then? Neither he nor his aides were ever able to answer. When I asked campaign manager Richard Williamson why Crane was in the race if he had no quarrel with Reagan, Williamson accused me of trying to pick a fight between the two Republicans. The Crane camp did pick up a number of former Reagan supporters, even key state organizers, impatient with Reagan's characteristic reluctance to get into the fray.

Human Events relentlessly probed the internal difficulties within the national headquarters, leading to a walkout of Crane's entire staff. Still more devastating, however, was a lengthy investigation by Loeb's *Union Leader*, which interviewed some thirty former aides and associates of Crane and charged that the candidate who offered to lead the right-wing crusade of moral righteousness was a hard-drinking gadabout

---

*In June of 1978, this author was approached by the Crane campaign committee and asked to write a biography of Crane to be published by Green Hill Books of Ottowa, Illinois. I discussed the project with Crane himself at some length, but turned down the offer after a representative of the candidate sent me a contract for the book.

who has told friends he wants to bed down "1,000 different women" in his lifetime. His defenders responded that they had never seen him drunk or unruly. Through Viguerie's direct mail, Crane had raised $1.7 million by March 31, 1979; the campaign had spent $2 million and was $880,000 in debt, $461,000 to Viguerie, and Crane, it was said by disgruntled New Rightists, was not spending enough time talking about "the social issues," and was emphasizing instead economic concerns of interest only to orthodox Republicans.

Despite a photogenic face, Crane is bland and sometimes obtuse, preferring to lecture his audiences on economic policy in a somewhat pedantic manner. An ineffective legislator, he has a spotty attendance record (especially in House committee meetings) and is a remarkably poor administrator, plagued by staff turnover. Associates and former aides, many of whom approve of his solidly right-of-center voting record, describe him as a shallow and vain man more interested in the limelight than in serious political concerns—all of which accounts, to some degree, for the lack of seriousness with which his campaign was taken by his Republican opponents and, eventually, by the New Right itself. Even early supporters like Viguerie seem to have realized that, however acceptable his views, he is not the courageous and dedicated lawman they desire and is at best a Hollywood imitation in a rhinestone-studded cowboy hat.

"The Crane campaign from here on out has nothing to do with political reality," one conservative fund-raising specialist told me in May 1979. "It must be viewed, instead, as a direct-mail proposition only. That is, it will continue whether it is politically relevant or not. The only question is how long it will remain profitable. . . . It will continue to live, and Crane will continue to be a candidate, as long as it makes money for Viguerie, and when it ceases, it will die."

Viguerie raised money for Crane until his campaign qualified for $1 million in federal matching funds, and then the two parted company. The matching funds would be more than enough to cover the debt.

One emerging Republican politician who combined both a

commanding media magnetism and an image of the tough sheriff was John Connally—and the New Rightists took note. As early as 1975, columnist Kevin Phillips called him "the most charismatic and articulate of the New Conservatives" and "the most competent, dynamic and able political leader who might be in a position to go as a third party candidate." Viguerie in 1975 called him "a man on a white horse, a strong leader, a gladiator and that's what the country needs." In 1979, when Reagan was leading all Republicans in public opinion polls seeking presidential preferences, William Rusher praised Connally as "a strong, energetic leader, and that may be what this country needs now to re-assert its prestige in the world." (Ordinarily, Rusher told me, he does not, as a matter of principle, favor "strong, energetic" presidents.) When Connally declined the offer to enter the New Hampshire primary as a Republican, Viguerie—acting on a 1976 Supreme Court ruling allowing unlimited individual spending on behalf of a candidate, provided the money does not pass through the candidate's campaign treasury and there is no communication between the candidate's committee and the independent effort—spent between $35,000 and $50,000 of his own money to back Connally as a write-in candidate on the Democratic line in the 1976 New Hampshire primary. According to Federal Election Commission reports, Viguerie took out ads in ten state newspapers with a total circulation of 202,000 and mailed almost 13,000 letters to right-wingers in the state. Warned by *Human Events* editor Tom Winter that the Connally effort would draw votes away from Reagan, Viguerie dismissed the warning and went ahead with the project. The write-in campaign gained little support, costing its sponsor about $1 a vote. And in 1979, when the presidential campaign of Crane began to founder, Viguerie took over Connally's direct-mail fund-raising effort. New Right disaffection with the Crane candidacy and the movement by Viguerie and others into the Connally camp provoked a bemused response throughout conservative political circles, since New Right leaders like Weyrich implied that Crane, by playing down such volatile social issues as abortion, prayer in the schools, and busing, was insufficiently conservative.

There was certainly nothing like unanimity on the Right when Viguerie and Connally joined forces. Indeed, traditional conservatives and some New Rightists had expressed deep disagreements with Connally almost as soon as Viguerie, Phillips, and others began to speak highly of him. In almost every significant case, the conservatives pointed out, Connally's positions are more liberal than Reagan's or, more recently, Crane's.

Connally, for example, refused to support a constitutional amendment prohibiting abortion ("I just don't think we ought to legislate what ought to be done," he told *Conservative Digest* in 1975), and he supported certain forms of gun control, leading Citizens Committee spokesman John Snyder to tell me, "Connally's support of gun control legislation indicates to us that he is not in agreement with traditional American values and is, in effect, one of many typical whores on the American political scene." Connally, indeed, has denied that he is a conservative.

"It is hard for people to put me into a category," Connally told the delegates to the 1977 Young Republican National Federation convention, "for sometimes I am a conservative and on some issues I am a liberal; it is impossible to put me into a stratified position. I take the broad, middle ground." He has supported the foreign policy of Henry Kissinger and détente, "if by détente we mean the opening and continuity of conversation with the People's Republic of China and the Soviet Union." And he has shown nothing but disgust at protests over Soviet grain sales: "The idea that you get a bunch of longshoremen out there that are going to dictate the foreign policy of the country . . . because they are not going to load ships is ridiculous on its face." Because of these and other positions—notably, his defense of the Nixon Administration's wage and price controls—*Human Events* was appropriately outraged at Viguerie's support for Connally. Connally, the weekly noted, supported creation of a costly Consumer Protection Agency and liberalized abortion laws—"anathema" to most conservatives. Even the more conservative elements in the Ripon Society, a Republican policy group long associated with the Rockefeller wing of the party, were also opposed. "What makes us moderates and progressives most uncomfortable about Connally is very much like that which bothers *Human Events* and the conservatives," Ripon Society president John Topping told me. "To the extent that we . . . view ourselves as proponents of limited government, we fear Connally as having too strong a preference for using state power. We sense that he is a statist, a man too far ready to use the power of the federal government, whether it is for conservative or liberal ends." Cited by both liberal and conservative critics is the Youth Service Project, a Connally proposal of 1974 to make it mandatory for every young person who reaches the age of eighteen to serve the government for one year. As Connally explained in an interview with Lofton, the program would accomplish a number of objectives. First, "you teach young people that they have an obligation to become interested in their government." Second, "you provide a discipline for these young people, which we desperately need in this country." Third, it would reduce unemployment by creating public sector jobs. Young people would be compelled, under Connally's plan, to work for local police departments, rebuild highway roadbeds or "clean up the highways, since the young are the ones, by and large, who litter." A bonus, he told Lofton, is that forced association with government would familiarize young Americans with "bureaucratic inefficiency" so they would "never want the government to run anything"! Conservative economist Milton Friedman, for one, was not impressed, calling the Connally plan "totalitarian" and a warmed-over version of "Adolf Hitler's youth movement." And columnist Nicholas von Hoffman, a liberal deeply influenced by Friedman's economics, has dismissed the idea as an "imbecilic bit of totalitarianism." Connally advocated (before the editorial board of *The Wall Street Journal,* no less!) a version of the Townsend plan he calls the "national dividend program," under which the federal government would split up all corporate tax money among the nation's voters, thus increasing the voter registration rolls.

Certainly Connally's past is well known to the New Right, and there is little in it that suggests a genuine commitment to philosophical or political conservatism—nor to the routing of liberals. Brought into government by Lyndon Johnson, he served under Kennedy's New Frontier and Johnson's Great Society, and, by 1972 a Republican, sold hated wage and price controls to the country as treasury secretary under Richard Nixon. Only on questions of foreign policy did Connally seem to be in line with New Right ideology, representing an aggressive, almost jingoistic interventionism. New Rightists, weary of Jimmy Carter's inability (they believe) to negotiate effectively with the Soviets over arms limitation, saw Connally—a self-described "horse-trader"—as a shrewd wheeler-dealer up to the task of dealing with the crafty Commies. But his association with the new wealth of the Sun Belt, as opposed to the settled wealth of the effete East, was suspect: Between July and September of 1979, Connally received campaign contributions from David Rockefeller, chairman of Chase Manhattan Bank, and his brother Laurance; Andrew Heiskell of Time Inc.; and other bastions of big business.

By fall of 1979, there were indications that some New Rightists were not prepared to back Connally, as Viguerie was; at a meeting with right-wing leaders in Washington, Connally by no means won over all of the participants. One New Right leader, quoted by columnists Rowland Evans and Robert Novak, reported afterward that Connally was "LBJ with charisma!" To the extent that he continued to command some allegiance from them, it was because, though slicker than George Wallace, he represented a similar political style. Appearing on the cover of *Conservative Digest* as the Texas cattle-rancher in his cowboy garb, Connally represented the familiar sheriff from the Old West, in whose animosity to citified ways the New Right saw hope that he would shoot it out with the city slickers of the Eastern seaboard—or, as the riverboat gambler, take their money in a poker game. Like Wallace, he seemed out of sorts with the social and cultural—if not economic—policies of the McGovern liberals. Deep down, and despite his flaws, Connally, too, is "one of us."

In March 1980, after suffering a series of primary defeats at the hands of Reagan, Connally dropped out of the presidential race. This left many New Rightists once again disappointed and presented the possibility that, lacking any other alternative, they would close ranks—however reluctantly—behind their one-time hero Ronald Reagan. The likelihood was increased, certainly, when Reagan dropped as campaign manager their *bête noire*, John Sears.

As the American historian Richard Hofstadter has written, the ideologues (as opposed to the opportunists) of the American Right suffer not so much from the policies of this or that administration but from a deep-seated distrust of all constituted authority. Entertaining "expectations that cannot be realized," being "uncomfortable with

> the thought of any leadership that falls short of perfect, the extreme right is also incapable of analyzing the world with enough common sense to establish any adequate and realistic criterion for leadership. One of the fundamental qualities, then, of the right-wing mentality of our time is its implicit utopianism. I can think of no more economical way of expressing its fundamental difference from the spirit of genuine conservatism.

Always searching for leaders who will not disappoint them, they are constantly betrayed by those who engage in the practical necessities of electoral politics. Tolerating no compromise, accepting no half measures, and understanding no defeats, "they stand outside the mainstream of normal democratic politics," Utopians to the bitter end. The last major office-holder in this country whom the New Right claims to be one of their own was Spiro Agnew, who was allowed by Richard Nixon to make right-wing speeches. And even Agnew was never really one of them at all. It remains one of the great secrets of

conservative trivia that in 1966 an American Conservative
Union survey of the fifty governors ranked Agnew among the
most "liberal," cheek-by-jowl with Romney and Rockefeller.
Only after the Baltimore County riots of 1970 did the Right
take Agnew to its heart, only, that is, after he talked back to
black leaders and, in 1969, the "effete" press, thus manifesting
signs of *adversarianism,* of being-against, of right-wing social
protest.

5

Protecting Hearth and Home: The Woman's Place

As long as we've got schools in this country we're
going to have to realize that there are people who
are trying to destroy our basic concepts. We've got
to be on guard from now on.
—WEST VIRGINIA TEXTBOOK PROTESTOR,
quoted in *Conservative Digest*, June 1975

While the men of the New Right symbolically guard the
frontier from external threats, exercising their energies on
macho issues like gun ownership, national defense, law and
order, and "free-market" economics, the women—with some
help from sympathetic male politicians and preachers—protect hearth and home from threats to their way of life. Like
the women of the Old West, they work with the school and
church to safeguard the home and neighborhood. Their
struggles over textbook selection, busing, abortion, gay rights,
and the Equal Rights Amendment have produced charis-

matic political leaders and cult figures like Phyllis Schlafly,
Anita Bryant, and the Reverend Jerry Falwell. They have become a political force of awesome power, with a potential of
becoming more powerful still, given their zeal and numbers.

At stake, as they see it, is nothing less than the future of
society itself and the values that will prevail in it. On one
side, threatening traditional values, are the feminists, the liberals, the university communities, minorities, residents of the
urban centers, and the media. On the other—the side of the
angels—are the "pro-family" forces, the leadership of the
New Right and its disgruntled constituents, plus a growing
political movement of fundamentalist evangelical ministers
speaking from their television and radio pulpits in support of
right-wing politics. Both sides are competing for the soul of
America.

The wave of "permissiveness" that is sweeping America
has convinced many of these people that the very foundations of their society are beginning to shake—a belief that
has gained credence outside right-wing circles. There is an
array of data to support their fears and a renewed defense of
traditional morality and the institution of the family by neoconservatives and, on the left, by radicals like Christopher
Lasch. Divorce rates are soaring, venereal disease has reached
"epidemic" proportions, teen-age pregnancies (despite great
emphasis on sex education and the availability of contracep-
tives) are increasing, abortions in some cities have outstripped
live births, homosexuality is on the rise, more and more
women are having children out of wedlock. Drug abuse and
teen-age alcoholism are reaching into the high schools, where
violence and crime increase—and test scores plummet. Middle Americans, alarmed over these developments, are convinced that their morality, indeed their way of life, is under
attack by upper-class liberalism, and that the time has come
to fight back, to protect it from the enemies within.

CONTROL OF THE CULTURE

The New Right women, with the help of the fundamentalist ministers, are determined to reassert control of the culture, to further not only specific political goals, but to assure that the values they believe in are allowed to survive—and prevail. No better summary of their fear exists, perhaps, than this fund-raising letter from Christian Voice, a fundamentalist political lobby:

THIS LETTER WILL MAKE YOU ANGRY!
But I'm Going To Tell
You The Truth About . . .
. . . Militant gays
. . . Liberal Educators
. . . Cruel Atheists
. . . And Godless Politicians

Dear Friend:
I am rushing you this urgent letter because the children in your neighborhood are in danger.
How would you feel if tomorrow your child . . .
. . . was taught by a practicing homosexual?
. . . was bused 20 to 30 miles away to school every morning?
. . . was forced to attend classes in a school where all religion is banned?
If you think this could never happen . . .
. . . you are in for a shock!

The rest of the letter, signed by the Reverend Robert G. Grant, head of Christian Voice, said that the drive for homosexual rights, busing, the ban on prayer in public schools, and other related issues are *"just a fraction of a master plan to destroy everything that is good and moral here in America."*

This "master plan" is orchestrated by "godless militant gays, liberal educators and vicious atheists" who—unless stopped—

"will tell you how your children will be educated." They will, that is, determine America's future by shaping the minds and hearts of youth, by undermining the values instilled in the home.

According to the New Right, this attempt to undermine the home influence was at the root of the effort in 1979 to create a cabinet-level Department of Education. *The Right Woman,* a newsletter for committed female activists, stated that the effort was part of a broader offensive, which included increased funding for day care centers and stepped-up regulation of private schools.

> There is an underlying assumption in all three—that the care and education of children is the primary responsibility of the State. . . . This view [is] contrary to the Judeo-Christian tradition which has always maintained that the education and care of children is the primary responsibility of parents. God has not only blessed parents with children. He has given the responsibility for nurturing children to parents. To interfere, or to attempt to interfere, with a parent's right is a violation of First Amendment Rights.

Busing is also seen as part of this offensive against the family. In his book *Clear and Present Dangers* (1975), M. Stanton Evans argues, for example, that the real rationale for busing is that busing removes the child from his home for as many hours as possible, before and after school. This, Evans wrote, "maximizes the amount of time a child is away from his home," and minimizes the influence of his parents. Busing also entails a form of race-mixing, by providing for integration of the schools, thereby choosing for parents the kind of communities in which their children will be raised.

The issue of textbook selection—and the removal from school libraries of books considered objectionable by parents— is also intended to protect the family and, by extension, the neighborhood and its values. Textbook protesters invariably see themselves as upholding the values of the local community against the alien influences of school administrators, who are often from other regions or, at least, have been infected at their colleges or universities by pernicious outside influences, thus becoming "progressive" influences hostile to "traditional" values.

The Equal Rights Amendment perhaps most of all is viewed by the New Right women as an attempt to undermine the family by withdrawing privileges that keep the family together by protecting the woman in her traditional role within the family, and without which the family—they believe—would disintegrate.

The revolt of the New Right women is, clearly, a rear-guard action to arrest the society's growing acceptance of views more liberal than their own. It is, in this sense, a status revolt, growing out of deep anxieties on the part of those Americans who, in Ben Wattenberg's words, are "unyoung, unpoor and unblack," "middle-aged, middle-income and middle-minded," who fear that the culture is being controlled, more and more, by "new morality" liberals. These Americans resent the fact that many of the relevant social questions are being resolved by others. They sense a loss of their own social status, resulting in attitudes which Friedrich Nietzsche described in the late nineteenth century as *ressentiment,* a term now used to explain the social behavior of persons frustrated by their roles in society.

David R. Schweitzer, author of *Status Frustration and Conservatism in Comparative Perspective,* a contemporary study of the concept, believes that "what is at stake for increasing numbers of Americans and Europeans alike is not so much economic survival as achieving or maintaining high social status." Status frustration, Schweitzer says, afflicts those who see their prestige in the society threatened by the upward mobility of groups—such as American blacks—traditionally below them on the social ladder. For Americans, this insecurity is increased by the lack of respect shown to them and their values by upper-class "prestige-givers." This can explain the resistance to busing and affirmative action of many lower-middle-class whites.

Status resentment frequently results in the appearance of right-wing backlash groups which attempt to reestablish, through formal political processes, the social support that the group's values once commanded. Thus, the Ku Klux Klan or the John Birch Society, extreme examples, are responses to perceived threats. Analyzing the constituencies of Barry Goldwater in 1964 and George Wallace in 1968, the political scientist James McEvoy III, in *Radicals or Conservatives? The Contemporary American Right* (1971), concluded that both these movements surfaced, at least in part, in response to feelings that society had withdrawn its approval from the values the groups upheld.

McEvoy observes that for both groups interest in politics was largely symbolic. Symbolic politics is "the politics of groups that enjoy relatively greater representation than newly challenging groups but which are somewhat marginal with respect to their relations with the dominant segments of the society. In the case of declining groups, the target of their hostility and criticism is the society at large."

The New Right is such a symbolic movement, a movement of social protest whose preferred issues—the "hearth and home" issues of the New Right women—are often nonpolitical, fringe issues at best. They seek through victory to regain lost status, to embarrass or humiliate their enemies in the Eastern liberal establishment, and to regain control of the culture. It is a politics that is almost wholly reactionary.

THE DEFENSE OF WOMEN'S PRIVILEGE

New Right women hope to stave off the liberal challenge and assure the survival of their way of life by defeating the Equal Rights Amendment. It is clear from the writings of anti-ERA activist Phyllis Schlafly that the New Right women do not want equality but preferential treatment, which Schlafly calls "rights." In *The Phyllis Schlafly Report,* she has written:

Wives have traditionally had in this country a great variety of extensive rights based on their marital status, as a result of our public policy to respect the family as the basic unit of society, and as a statutory and common-law balance to the biological fact that only women have babies. These rights, which vary from state to state, include the wife's right of financial support in an ongoing marriage, the right of separate maintenance and payment of attorney's fees during divorce litigation, the right to alimony after divorce, the right to a presumption of custody of her children, rights against her husband's alienation of his property during his life or by will, and a variety of special benefits accorded to widows.

She calls such a system "benign discrimination."

A skillful organizer with an ability to create fierce loyalties ("There are women who would kill for Phyllis," a conservative woman told me), Schlafly has been remarkably successful in her efforts to block ratification of the ERA, which in 1980 seemed permanently stalled, despite backing by the White House and a congressional extension for ratification. Her nationwide grass-roots organization has posted monitors in each of 59 legislative districts in her native Illinois. Her national 50,000-member organization has two names, Eagle Forum and Stop-ERA. How are the leaders of local and state affiliates chosen, I asked her? "I pick them," Schlafly said. A neatly coiffured woman with an attractive but hard face, Schlafly is ambitious, intense, seemingly tireless—and powerful. "I really think I have more power right here—with this organization—than I would as a senator," she has said. In 1978, when Illinois Republican Daniel Crane was seeking the Twenty-second Congressional seat, his campaign organizers turned over one of their district offices to Schlafly volunteers. Working a phone bank at Crane head-quarters was Schlafly Eagle Jeannette Boone—a Republican precinct committeewoman who was once a member of the John Birch Society and who had resigned from the Birchers to join Eagle Forum. The Eagles, she told me, "are far more effective at getting things done." She decided to perform vol-unteer work for Crane, she said, because of his opposition to the Equal Rights Amendment. Judy Mack, wife of a factory supervisor and a Schlafly supporter, worked for Crane because "he is a family man and a Christian man," she told me.

The self-assertion of women of the Right has manifested itself in some open criticism of Schlafly. One of these women is Maureen Reagan, the articulate daughter of Ronald Reagan and with a varied career as an actress, a talk show personality, and a Republican campaign consultant.

Reagan stated in an interview conducted for the *New Guard* in 1976, that, in her opinion, Schlafly thinks the Equal Rights Amendment is a "Communist plot" to require same-sex bathrooms. Critical of Schlafly for focusing on this single issue and blaming on it many of the problems facing this society today, Reagan said that she would not be surprised if the anti-ERA activist blamed the amendment for the fact that the Soviet Union has "more submarines" than the United States does.

Reagan supports the Equal Rights Amendment, believing it to be a conservative measure that would diminish the power of the federal government. Saying she regrets the "bigoted" position conservatives have taken toward the women's movement, she is at a loss to explain their position. She calls the ERA another step toward releasing the individual from governmental control, which—she notes—"is what my father says he wants to do." Reagan compared the ERA to consenting-adults laws denounced by the right as a "Homosexuals' Bill of Rights." On the contrary, she believes that such legislation liberates heterosexuals as well by decreeing that the bedroom is no place for governmental interference. Who supports a family—the husband or the wife—is similarly a matter to be determined by the husband and the wife—and not by the government.

Juanita Bartnett, a Republican activist from Illinois once employed by the American Legislative Exchange Council, told me that the secret of Schlafly's success is the conservative men "who have given Schlafly a platform and let her be the spokesman on this issue. Phyllis can say things that no man could get away with saying. She serves their cause, and they use her in full knowledge of what they are doing. She is the biggest tool that conservative men, who want their women barefoot and pregnant, have."

Schlafly scoffs at the notion that, as a political activist, author, and lecturer, she embodies the kind of self-assertion that she claims to loathe in feminists.

> Look, I've never argued that women should not have careers. . . . And it is true that I have everything that the women's libbers wish they had—a rewarding career, a wonderful husband, and a beautiful family.

When Anita Bryant led the crusade against a "gay rights" ordinance in Dade County, Florida, in 1977, she touched off a nationwide controversy. She activated hundreds of New Right women who view the rise of homosexuality, like the Equal Rights Amendment, as a threat to the family and the way of life that the family represents. The maintenance of traditional sexual roles, they believe, is essential to the survival of the traditional family. Because they demand traditional role models for young children in the schools, they especially oppose the employment of homosexual teachers. The "born again" Christian entertainer started a mini-movement, dedicated to locking the closet door on homosexuals. It took political form in a nationwide organization called Save Our Children, Inc.* In the wake of Bryant's victory in Dade County came six other anti-gay-rights victories, although a second measure put to Florida voters lost. In April 1978, voters in St. Paul, Minnesota, by a margin of two to one, repealed by initiative a gay rights ordinance. In May, voters in Wichita, Kansas, repealed by a five-to-one margin an existing gay rights ordinance and, later that month, voters in Eugene, Oregon, repealed by referendum another ordinance, this time by a vote of two to one. Only in California—where a ballot measure,

---

*It was first called Save Our Children, then changed to Protect America's Children to avoid confusion with the Save the Children Federation.

Proposition 6, was opposed by conservatives like William F. Buckley, Jr., and Ronald Reagan—did the anti-gay-rights forces lose. Save Our Children, Inc. was involved in each of the controversies.

Seventeen full-time staff members were working with the Bryant organization in 1979. At that time, the leaders planned to branch out into production of television and radio specials to publicize "God, family and country" rallies. Executive director Ed Rowe, a fundamentalist minister, told me that Senator Jesse Helms of North Carolina was a "very helpful friend" whose "wise counsel" was very important in the organization's early stages. According to Mike Thompson, a Florida public relations specialist active in right-wing politics who worked closely with Bryant in Dade County, a "kind of cooperation" existed between Save Our Children, Inc. and Phyllis Schlafly's Stop-ERA. He told *Conservative Digest:*

> For example, several Florida state senators voted against the ERA because our campaign indirectly alerted them to the homosexual implications of ERA. In fact, some political observers say the two people who did most to turn around the Florida Senate on ERA were Phyllis Schlafly and Anita Bryant.

Those who supported Bryant in Florida are a broad-based group, and Thompson points with pride to the fact that the majority of black, Catholic, and Jewish voters—most of whom ordinarily are Democrats—voted against the gay rights ordinance; twenty-seven of thirty-one Dade County rabbis who took a position on the issue sided with Bryant. Two other key leaders in the fight were liberal Democrat Bob Daly, who once worked for Congressman Claude Pepper of Florida, and Bob Skiddell, a Democrat, who is president of the Miami Beach Lodge of B'nai B'rith. Once the political struggles of 1977 and 1978 subsided, Bryant's organization directed its energies into a new organization, Anita Bryant Ministries, a nondenominational operation dedicated to counseling "people oppressed by moral problems," Rowe said. Those "oppressed by moral problems" are usually homosexuals, thousands of whom, Rowe said, approached Bryant after the Dade County controversy, seeking spiritual guidance. A counseling center was established in Miami, and "in excess of 1,000" homosexuals have since been treated, he told me.*

Through a direct-mail fund-raising campaign in which Bryant asked for a "gift of love," Rowe estimates that the organization raised "upwards of $1 million" in 1977 alone.

Although it is an important part of the "pro-family" coalition, the National Right-to-Life movement—a successful, broad-based, and well-organized coalition—functions as part of the constituency of the New Right but does not share some of its views on issues other than abortion. Nevertheless, with the Right-to-Life movement's proven ability to motivate citizens to cast their votes on the basis of a single issue, its members —in one sense, at least—epitomize the New Right at its maximum strength and intensity. Their more generalized concern for "the family" and their opposition to "social engineering" of "liberals" suggests that they have much in common with the New Right. Nevertheless, it is the strength of the right-to-lifers that they have not diluted their single-minded constituency by trying to make common cause with, say, the gun lobby; as a result of their single-minded zeal they may be one of the most powerful political forces in the country. The right-to-lifers, with much justification, are proud of the way their movement cuts across ideological lines, drawing huge support, for example, from New Deal Democrats of the industrial Northeast.

---

*One homosexual who went to the counseling center intending to write a "scathing story" reported in *The Advocate* that he found "friendliness" instead of a "bunch of religious fanatics" who would try to "brainwash him":

> Not once was I made to feel uncomfortable by the men and women working in Bryant's offices. If they knew I was "queer," and I'm sure they did, it didn't seem to bother them. . . . I met some decent people . . . who are dedicated and sincere in their religious beliefs and their love of God and their fellow man.

They seem wary, therefore, of attempts to influence them by professional right-wingers who are associated with what appears to be a much narrower constituency. In 1979, one right-to-life lobbyist, Thea Rossi Barron, a Washington attorney, resigned from the committee after she saw signs that it had "started to ally [itself] with other conservative groups." In 1978, she said, antiabortionists had joined forces with New Right groups in an unsuccessful effort to block extension of the time period for approving the Equal Rights Amendment. "You need the votes of moderates and liberals," she said. "A conservative alliance is bad for the right-to-life movement." However, there is little evidence that the right-to-lifers generally share the same overriding anxieties as the New Right activists. Mrs. McCormack, for example, favors gun registration, day care centers for the poor, détente with the Soviets, and abolition of capital punishment—all positions that strike the New Right as dangerously liberal.

SUBVERSION IN THE SCHOOLS

Broad concern about the condition of the public schools has given rise to a booming private school movement and to increased involvement by New Right women in the day-to-day functioning of the schools, a traditional female role. Noting increasing violence in the schools, and declining test scores, right-wing parents trace these problems to liberal attitudes of teachers and administrators, seeking to minimize their influence by playing greater roles in textbook selection, even by removing from school libraries books they consider objectionable. They have been so effective in their efforts to monitor books that a study by the National Council of Teachers of English in 1978 showed that censorship of books, school newspapers, and other curriculum materials in public schools had increased in the last fifteen years by 78 percent. Parents were most concerned, the study found, by texts and library books that presented attitudes and lifestyles of those of different cultural backgrounds.

> It appears that the most common objection was to the language of the books [but this] is ambiguous; it sometimes refers to the grammar or dialect, or it may refer to profanity, or to so-called obscenity. . . . Next in frequency were objections to sex, or erotic qualities in the books. . . . It is noteworthy that relatively few objections of an ideological sort appear.

Alice Moore is an articulate and soft-spoken young mother of four school-aged children in Charleston, West Virginia, the wife of a fundamentalist minister, who came to national attention in 1974 as leader of the textbook protests of Kanawha County. Alarmed over the nature of the textbooks in the public schools, she set out to do something about them. She won election to the school board after objecting to the school system's sex education program. In the school board election of 1978, her back-to-basics ticket swept to power and now controlled the Kanawha County school board. It was a fierce battle. When the controversy peaked in 1975, wildcat strikes by members of the United Mine Workers erupted. A school building was bombed, and the Reverend Marvin Horan, an independent fundamentalist minister in nearby Cabin Creek, was convicted of conspiring to bomb the school building and sentenced to three years in prison. Even the Ku Klux Klan showed up to offer its services—which were rebuffed by Moore and her allies. "What is at issue here, what we are fighting for," she told me, "is simply who is going to have control over the schools, the parents and the taxpayers and the people who live here or the educational specialists, the administrators, the people from other places who have been trying to tell us what is best for our children. We think we are competent to make those decisions for ourselves." As Curtis Selzer, writing in the liberal *Nation*, observed, perusal of the books (which included works by Eldridge Cleaver, Germaine Greer, and Lawrence Ferlinghetti), reveal that white, working-class parents from coal fields and Southern mountains do have legitimate grounds for complaint. The editing reflects a value system that runs counter to most of what they cherish. The supplementary books, in particular, play out the alienation felt by urban intellectuals and university militants of the 1960s, who seem to the protesters to have taken over the publishing houses in New York. Some of the selections were unpatriotic, sacrilegious and pro-minorities, and they would, as the parents predicted, legitimize different values and raise heretofore taboo questions. Equally important was the almost total exclusion of people like themselves from the "multi-cultural" texts. The editors had not thought that coal miners, or country folk, or Appalachians or working people were either distinguishable groups or important enough to include. Paradoxically, the board's attempt to broaden the English curriculum had shifted the spectrum away from the majority of citizens in the country.

Mrs. Moore was successful in her efforts, in part because of help provided by the husband-and-wife team of Mel and Norma Gabler, for several years involved in textbook struggles in their native Texas, and by James T. McKenna, a lawyer sent to act as counsel for the protesting parents by the Heritage Foundation.

The Heritage Foundation in 1975 formed the National Congress for Educational Excellence to unite the widely scattered parents' groups—estimated to number roughly 200. The effort was only modestly successful. Jil Wilson, a Wisconsin housewife active in Kenoshans Concerned for their Schools and People of America Responding to Educational Needs in Today's Society (PARENTS), reports

> that efforts to form a nationwide organization to coordinate the activities of the textbook protesters met with little success, its meeting between the leaders erupting in quarrels that prevented genuine unity. Nevertheless, these meetings provided an opportunity for the activists to meet one another—and many remain in close contact on an informal basis.

As might be expected, these are shoestring operations. PAR-ENTS, the group with which Mrs. Wilson is affiliated, exists on $5 donations to cover postage for its mimeographed news-letter.

Protesting parents won a major victory in 1979 when federal Judge George C. Pratt of Long Island upheld the 1975 decision of the Island Trees, Long Island, board of education to ban from its libraries books by Kurt Vonnegut, Bernard Malamud, and Langston Hughes. The Island Trees story began when three board members attended a state conference held by People of New York-United (PONY-U), a right-wing parents' group; at the conference they obtained a list of thirty-two "objectionable" books, and promptly discovered nine of the thirty-two on the shelves of the district's high school library. A tenth book was found in the junior high school library and an eleventh on the reading list for a literature course for high school seniors. The school board banned them all, calling them "anti-American, anti-Christian, anti-Semitic, and just plain filthy." "While removal of such books from a school library may, indeed in this Court's view does, reflect a misguided educational philosophy," Pratt said, the board has the right to remove the books because "one of the principal functions of public education is indoctrinative, to transmit the basic values of the community. . . . A constitutionally required 'book ten-ure' principle would infringe upon an elected school board's discretion in determining what community values were to be transmitted."

HIJACKING THE SCHOOL BUS

The antibusing forces, a far-flung collection of what appear to be ad hoc local organizations, are convinced, like the textbook protesters, that the federal government is out to destroy their way of life, substituting its own alien values for theirs. "Social engineering," they believe, is again at work, with busing being used to achieve ends believed desirable by liberals in Washington and in the judiciary—but by few parents, black or white. While there appears to be no national organization to oppose busing, New Right leaders have been involved in antibusing efforts when local controversies have arisen. In Massachusetts, for example, Howard Phillips worked closely with the antibusing protesters of South Boston and still maintains close contact with the activists of the South Boston Information Center, organizing regular luncheon meetings. And in Los Angeles, former Young Americans for Freedom activist Arnold Steinberg organized the BUS-STOP group, and raised money for its antibusing activities through a sophisticated direct-mail fundraising campaign. Although busing is a "hearth and home" issue concerning children and the schools, it has been commandeered for the most part by men of the New Right—perhaps because of the involvement of blacks and the threat of violence, from both of which New Right men want to protect their womenfolk.

ONWARD, CHRISTIAN SOLDIERS!

Important allies of the New Right women in protecting hearth and home, school and community from the liberal onslaught are certain fundamentalist ministers who are becoming increasingly involved in right-wing politics.

Their following is immense, and the power they wield from the television and radio pulpits may well make them a political force of enormous impact in the 1980s. Benefiting from the growth of the fundamentalist churches and the decline in membership in liberal Protestant churches—the Southern Baptist Convention alone gained almost two million members, from 10.77 million in 1965 to 12.51 million in 1974—these ministers represent a revolt against the move toward "relevance" and "secularism" in the churches. As the Reverend Jerry Falwell, the most prominent of the new right-wing evangelists, said of his own militancy: "Jesus was not a pacifist. He was not a sissy." Falwell, a fundamentalist from Lynchburg,

Virginia, services his growing flock from his Old Time Gospel Hour, which airs on 325 television stations and 300 radio stations each week, netting roughly $1 million to the coffers of his Thomas Road Baptist Church in Lynchburg and its affiliated colleges and schools. During the days of the civil rights movement, Falwell spoke out against clergymen who were involved in politics, a position he has since reversed, on the grounds that the church is now being "assaulted" and "attacked." The result is his far-reaching "Clean Up America Crusade" and a political organization, Moral Majority. As Falwell explained in a Capitol Hill rally in April 1979, the time has come to "fight the pornography, obscenity, vulgarity, profanity that under the guise of sex education and 'values clarification' literally pervades the literature" that children read in the public schools. Falwell is alarmed also by homosexuality and bids his followers to send their dollars to fight these and related evils. "We are very much trying to create emotional involvement in these issues," he said. . . . "We are going to single out those people in government who are against what we consider to be the Bible, moralist position, and we're going to inform the public. . . ." Falwell announced his intention in 1979, for example, to oppose the presidential candidacy of Senator Edward Kennedy of Massachusetts.

In 1977, Falwell shared his pulpit with his close friend Anita Bryant. He once called for a speedy return to the "McCarthy era" where all Communists should be registered, and "we should stamp it on their foreheads and send them back to Russia." In September 1979, he drew criticism when, addressing an "I Love America" rally on the Capitol grounds in Richmond, Virginia, he admonished his supporters not to be anti-Semitic. The only reason some of them do not like Jews, he said, is because they "can make more money accidentally than you can on purpose." He later said the statement was made "in jest," that he is "a Zionist and very pro-Israel and have always come down pretty hard on anti-Semitics." He has not come down hard, however, on racists, and for several years the school he ran in Lynchburg was all white.

Other right-wing fundamentalist ministers also owe much to "the electronic church," the vast radio and television operations run by the fundamentalists. It is immense, with thirty-six wholly religious television channels, 1,300 religious radio stations, and dozens of gospel television shows that buy time on commercial stations, reaching an estimated 100 million Americans each week. The flagship of the new evangelical talkshows is the "700 Club" of the Christian Broadcasting Network, which operates out of a $20 million facility in Virginia Beach. "700 Club" host Pat Robertson, a genial graduate of Yale Law School and son of a U.S. senator, in 1979 spoke out against "the humanistic/atheistic/hedonistic influence on American government," which he said was the result of control by the "Trilateral Commission and the Council on Foreign Relations," also a bogeyman of the John Birch Society. Of growing stature is the Reverend James Robison, a fiery Dallas evangelist who was dropped from a local commercial station in Dallas but reinstated after 12,000 fans turned out to express their support for a controversial sermon against homosexuality which had temporarily cost Robison his air-time.

Their constituency is estimated to consist of roughly 50 million "born-again" Christians, mostly Protestant, plus 30 million "morally conservative" Roman Catholics and a few million Mormons and Jews. As Pat Robertson put it, "We have enough votes to run the country. And when the people say, 'We've had enough,' we are going to take over." This takeover is to be mounted through Falwell's Moral Majority, Inc., a political organization formed in 1979 that plans, so *Conservative Digest* has reported, "to mobilize at least two million Americans to work for pro-God, pro-family policies in government." Its executive director is the Reverend Bob Billings, who in 1978 described himself to me as "the liaison between Congress and the Christian community." A fundamentalist from Maryland, Billings already works closely with his own organization, Christian Voice, a Pasadena-based political lobby with access to the same mailing list used by Moral Majority. Christian Voice plans to rate legislators on a "morality scale," according to their stands on homosexuality, abortion, pornography, prayer in the schools, and other issues.

Like Carl McIntyre and other right-wing evangelists of the 1950s and 1960s, the "electronic churchmen" of the 1970s and 1980s are stressing political concerns, determined, as Falwell put it, to "turn this into a Christian nation." One manifestation of the close association between the fundamentalists' and the right-wingers' shared anxieties over school busing and textbooks is the emergence of hundreds of Christian private schools, estimated by *The Wall Street Journal* to be a $2-billion-a-year industry. Supporters include Senators Helms of North Carolina, Paul Laxalt of Nevada, Gordon Humphrey of New Hampshire, and Congressman Robert K. Dornan of California—all of whom attended Falwell's Capitol Hill rally.

The growing political clout of the "born-again" lobby was felt in 1978, as the "moral majority" constituency claimed credit for blocking the Equal Rights Amendment, for denying election to liberal Iowa Senator Dick Clark, and for repealing, by referenda, gay rights ordinances. Politicians are beginning to pay heed. In mid 1979, Republican presidential hopeful John Connally held a private meeting at his ranch with top religious broadcasters and activists, including Falwell and Billings, and, as one participant told *U.S. News and World Report,* "At the end of the meeting, some of those guys were ready to carry Connally out of there on their shoulders." A second presidential aspirant, Illinois Congressman Philip Crane, a "born-again" Christian, was asked to appear on the "700 Club."

In October 1979, fundraiser Richard Viguerie in his magazine *Conservative Digest* called for a national day "of fasting and prayer" to "devote completely to prayer, meditation, thanks and repentance for our sins."

The New Right is encouraged by the growing alliance between the "pro-family" forces and the "born-again" ministers, but some traditional conservatives are troubled by the trend. "Fundamentalist ministers on television like Jerry Falwell may claim to be politically conservative, but they betray true conservative principles when they lobby for legislation that would intrude the government into individuals' private lives—as Falwell has done in his various anti-gay campaigns in Florida and California," said Jere Real, a conservative writer and teacher in Lynchburg, Virginia, who has followed Falwell's career for several years.

The potential political muscle of this alliance is bolstered by zeal and dedication. *Campaigning Reports,* a newsletter of political tactics, noted that the "zealous participant multiplies his minority status through activism." A study by the National Right to Life Committee in 1979 revealed, for example, that its members show no hesitation about total political participation; more than 70 percent of those interviewed had voted in a primary or general election in 1978. Another 50 percent donated from $25 to $50 to at least one pro-life campaign. A high 55 percent said they would vote against a candidate solely on the issue of right-to-life, even if they agreed with him on virtually every other important issue of the race. More than 35 percent were prepared, they said, to cross party lines to vote for an antiabortion candidate. This is especially significant when voter turnout is low, as it increasingly has been. When voter participation is down, single-issue minorities who get their supporters to the polls can exercise power out of all proportion to their numbers. As Maurice Rosenblatt of the Committee for the Study of the American Electorate told *The New York Times,* the nation may be "losing the votes of the broadly concerned citizen, leaving the field to those motivated by narrow, parochial, and emotional interests."

Judging by their zeal alone, the New Right women have the potential to become a significant—and perhaps enormous—political force in the 1980s. Their self-assertion, already impressive, no doubt comes as a surprise to American liberals who assume that conservative women believe their place is in the home, with the children, and not in the rough-and-tumble world of politics, and that their opposition to the Equal Rights Amendment suggests that they are somehow fighting against their own best interests. Nothing could be further from the

truth. As Maryland Congresswoman Marjorie Holt, a right-
wing Republican, explained:

> I believe that we have a special responsibility, that women have
> to be very careful because we have been cast in the role of
> child-bearers and I think we have the responsibility to preserve
> the family.

Jo Ann Gasper, editor of the Washington-based *The Right
Woman,* said: "These women are concerned about family issues. . . . They see it as a threat to the way they live their lives
and that's why they are getting involved now."

As the women of the New Right see it, they are fulfilling
traditional roles women have always played, safeguarding the
home from unhealthy influences while their men are out making a living and protecting the frontier from external threats,
like the hardy pioneer women without whose influence settling
and civilizing the Old West would have been impossible.

6

Antielitism and the New Class Warfare

Organize discontent. That is our strategy.
—HOWARD PHILLIPS of Conservative Caucus

Clinton Rossiter in the second edition of his book *Conservatism in America* wrote in 1962 that throughout recent history conservatives had been "skeptical of popular government," drawing support from men "who have a sizable stake in the established order." The Left, he said, in contrast, is made up of those who "demand wider popular participation in government" and "draw particular support from the disinherited, dislocated and disgruntled." In little more than a decade his description has been turned on its head. Rossiter's 1962 description of leftists would apply in the early 1980s more to the

New Right than to the Left. Howard Phillips told me that the goal of the Right is "to organize discontent," that is, to mobilize the disinherited, dislocated, and disgruntled. Paul Weyrich of the Committee for the Survival of a Free Congress said the New Right is a "middle-class" revolt against an "elitist upper class." The new enemy to these angry Middle Americans, and to the practical politicians, journalists, and pundits who articulate their anger, is the elite, the established, the affluent, the cultivated intellectual. In a rather remarkable turnabout the Right has shifted from conservatism to right-wing populism. The one force they *do* trust is popular government.

In the struggle between the "hardhats," "Archie Bunkers," "provincials," "rednecks," "primitives," "Middle Americans," and "reactionaries" and the "goo-goos," "radical chic," "limousine liberals," "do-gooders," and "Eastern establishment liberals," the New Right is firmly on the side of the "hardhats." As the New Rightists see it, these members of the "silent majority" have been oppressed and exploited by "elitists" who repaid them for past loyalties by labeling them "bigots" and worse.

CONSERVATISM AND "THE MASSES"

True conservatism has always been concerned with the conserving of values. Thoughtful intellectuals—balanced, rational, aristocratic, elitist—placed such confidence in the capacity of the common man to conserve. Conservatives from Edmund Burke to Henry Adams to Irving Babbitt to T.S. Eliot to George Will have expressed a cautious disdain for the masses. The masses to them are impulsive, irrational, emotional, unappreciative of the heritage of culture that only the elite could have preserved.

Yet the tumultuous circumstances of the years from the end of the Second World War to the present reshaped the face of American conservatism. They disarranged the established order, questioned established values. The rapaciousness of the populist New Right in the 1970s is one result.

George Nash in *The Conservative Intellectual Movement in America Since 1945* (1976) notes that "a series of Supreme Court decisions . . . aroused not just conservative intellectuals but broad segments of the populace, which right-wingers could now, at long last, cultivate."

> These [Nash wrote] included policemen and law enforcement officials enraged by court decisions which protected the "rights" of criminals, millions of Americans who could not understand why the "rights" of atheists should prevent the voluntary reading of the Lord's Prayer and the Bible in public schools; Americans angry about "permissiveness" and Court rulings on pornography; politicians astounded by the Court's reapportionment decisions; and anti-Communists alarmed at the Court's continual blows at congressional investigations and cold war legislation.

Campus unrest and the rise of the New Left in the 1960s and early 1970s also alarmed many American parents, who blamed the disorder on liberal college professors and administrators who, having nourished rebellious ideas in their young charges, lacked the will to resist when the students carried their rebellious teaching to the logical extension of chaos. The failure of liberal intellectual leadership to cope effectively with rapid social change was, in part, to blame, but so was the conservative leadership that failed to participate and to safeguard against the populist revolt.

THE ELITE IS THE ENEMY

New Right strategists like Kevin Phillips and Patrick Buchanan in the 1970s began to realize that they need no longer be bound by the conservative image of "bluestocking Republicanism," the country club, and inherited wealth—so destructive to potential coalitions with blue-collar Americans. Indeed, they would demolish the structure by reversing it. Their new image would be antielitism. They would ride into power on the wave of class hostility by appealing to the resentments of the "forgotten Americans" who felt exploited by those in power.

Seizing on Frank Meyer's references in 1970 to the "producing majority," William Rusher in his book *The Making of the New Majority Party* (1975) produced a theory about American politics that envisioned a new alliance of "producers" (including "businessmen, manufacturers, hard-hats, blue-collar workers and farmers") against "nonproducers"—chiefly members of the knowledge industry, the major news media, the educational establishment, the federal bureaucracy, the foundations and research centers—and a semipermanent welfare constituency."

The conservative periodicals began to bristle with references to "verbalists," "elitists," and "bureaucrats." The editors at *Conservative Digest* took pains to publicize local antibusing and antitextbook revolts against "liberal elitists." *Conservative Digest* was concerned, above all, to raise the class consciousness of "the little people," whose identity was never carefully defined but appeared to be mostly white and lower-middle-class Americans. (Rightist leader Phyllis Schlafly was once referred to in its pages as a woman successful in politics despite her lack of "tie-ins to the Power Elite," in a phrase lifted from the work of Marxist sociologist C. Wright Mills.) At least one conservative—Hamilton Rogers, writing in *The New Guard*—attacked this strategy as "fundamentally anti-intellectual."

> It is not that "pointy-headed" intellectuals are not to be encouraged or kept by government: all intellectuals [the New Right contends] have "pointy-heads." The lunchbox is glorified while the briefcase disdained. Ridicule of the sociocultural style of the Northeast is an important means through which the New Right can coalesce the alienated elements of the New Deal coalition into a pattern of political support. Constant attacks on Washington, the foundations, the media, and research institutions are the *bon mots* of Phillips' New Right.

>The New Right is, however, more than populist; it is "McLuhan-era marxism."

The New Right has urged the political uprising of one class against its oppressors that is much akin to an uprising described by Peter Viereck in his essay "The Revolt against the Elite." Viereck had analyzed McCarthyism as less concerned with the threat of Communism and Communists—real or imagined—than with an effort to embarrass Eastern liberal intellectuals in the universities and the government. It was a revolt of angry Americans who, through the exploits of the Wisconsin senator, acted out their own feelings of inferiority and resentment of those better educated and more prestigious than they. As Viereck might put it: Ex-Marxists plus status-resenting know-nothings equals right-wing populism.

Both McCarthyism and the New Right caricature of Marxism are vengeful rear-guard actions by Americans who feel dispossessed or overlooked. These Americans may have legitimate grievances, lacking adequate roles in the governing process. Whatever the legitimacy, their anxieties represent genuine potentials for social unrest. The New Right counsels them to reject constituted authorities. To traditional conservatives who look for inspiration to such giants as Edmund Burke, any political activity deliberately designed to fuel fires of social discord must be considered fundamentally anticonservative and, even more, revolutionary. The New Right is light-years away from the conservative stabilizing tradition of Disraeli and Churchill.

New Right pundits have drawn much ammunition in their polemical war against the elite from the works of neoconservative writers and scholars like Irving Kristol and Daniel Bell who, in an unwitting assist, have focused on the concept of "the New Class." The idea originated with Milovan Djilas, who argued in *The New Class* (1957) that Communist societies are increasingly ruled by "those who have special privileges and economic preference because of the administrative monopoly they hold." The New Right has transposed the term to apply to American society, maintaining that a ruling class similar to that which Djilas identified has emerged, composed of bureaucrats and managers assigned by corporate capitalism to administer the welfare state and defense establishment. As the focus of the economy has evolved from production of goods to the distribution of services, with the burgeoning of the white-collar class and the decline of farm workers, manual and even skilled labor, new skills—mainly intellectual—have become increasingly essential. This professional technical elite, the New Right argues, wields power and prestige undemocratically.

The revulsion at the New Class had led the New Right into its populist attachment to the masses—an identification reinforced by certain conservative intellectuals once on the Left who'turned anti-Eastern as well as antielite. Whittaker Chambers, an ex-Communist, noted, for example, that "the plain men and women of this nation" stood by him in his great struggle against the Eastern establishment. James Burnham, after a cross-country tour in the late 1940s, returned refreshed and full of hope for the common American who rejected the defeatism of the "ingrown" East. The political scientist Willmoore Kendall wrote of the "native good sense of the American people," and Willi Schlamm wrote with pride that Senator Joseph McCarthy was a product of the presumably robust "heartland of America."

At a small party on Capitol Hill shortly after the 1978 elections, one young right-wing activist who had studied at a university in his native Western state before completing his undergraduate work in the East said of "Ivy Leaguers": "They think they're better than anybody else. They think their shit don't stink."

Encountering a well-known right-wing activist at a Harvard buffet some months back, I introduced myself, and he immediately confessed he was surprised to be invited, explaining: "I don't get to attend many of these Ivy League cocktail parties." Rightists talk frequently of "cocktail parties" in a suspicious tone, though they, too, give parties. It seems to be assumed that at "liberal cocktail parties" plots against the republic are hatched.

Accompanying such talk is often an inference that the life-styles of Easterners are somewhat racier than the rightists' own, and that this decadence explains liberal political attitudes. At a dinner party in 1977, I recall how, to my considerable shock, a bright and able aide to one right-wing Southern senator expressed his disdain for columnist James J. Kilpatrick on the grounds that he was "a limousine liberal—just like all the rest." Kilpatrick, in truth, is a hopelessly square conservative who lives in the mountains of Virginia.

Kendall as early as 1942 had written of his outrage at "the most gigantic and unpardonable *trahison des clercs* of which History offers any record. To think of it makes me sick at heart." He once planned to write a book that would constitute "a declaration of war on the intellectuals." Burnham attributed the riots of the 1960s to "a collapse of the morale of the governing elite"; Will Herberg wrote of the "defection" of an uprooted intelligentsia whose "self-extrusion" from bourgeois society was leading it to war against its own society. The historian Stephen Tonsor has referred to "the last hours of the great liberal ascendancy." Jeffrey Hart, a Dartmouth scholar who writes for *National Review,* assaulted the "habitually antago-nistic, and sometimes even treasonous, relationship" of the intellectuals "to their surrounding society." Hart observed that the "adversary writers" who once railed against "respectable" society had, in an inversion, become a *"mass* intelligentsia" and "mass adversary culture." In other words, the Right hadn't changed; its enemy *had.*

The New Right has identified as members of the New Class: professors and educational administrators, research scientists working on government grants, federal bureaucrats, planners in the public and private sectors, consultants and public relations experts, national newscasters and network journalists, writers and critics. These are "pointy-heads" in the contemptuous view of the "practical" men of the New Right who boast that they, in contrast, know how to meet a payroll. Right-of-center outbursts like the movements that supported Wallace in 1968 and Agnew in 1972 are in large degree manifestations of this anti-intellectualism. Speeches by Wallace bristled with phrases such as "pointy-head professors" and "brief-case totin' bureaucrats." Agnew spoke out for "the great silent majority" when he blasted journalists as "an effete corps of impudent snobs who characterize themselves as intellectuals." President Nixon's popularity was at its peak in the days immediately after his "great silent majority" speech.

When, alerted by their spokesmen to the liberal taint in professional educators, conservative parents began to do battle with elementary and secondary school administrators on textbooks, curricula, and library books they were rising in anger not only at "arrogant educational specialists" who seemed to believe they knew better what values their children should be taught, but at educational "specialists" who were "outsiders," educated at prestigious universities, "invading" the communities to "impose *their* values" on the natives. Innovative programs were to blame; the "back to basics" movement gained new allies, ironically enough, joining the protest from black ghetto parents disgusted with decreased academic quality in their children's schools.

The revolt against the values of the New Class expanded its sights from schools to the national news media. Charges of biased press coverage of the Vietnam War, of the student riots and the presidential campaigns of the late 1960s and early 1970s, were pressed with fervor and effectiveness by Agnew and Nixon. But their dissatisfaction was only a boiling over of the resentments that had been simmering in conservative Republicanism for several decades. Just as Robert Taft had lashed out against the Eastern newspapers for what he, with much reason, considered unfair coverage, so President Dwight Eisenhower, who had been the beneficiary of that coverage earlier—at the 1964 convention that nominated Barry Goldwater—ripped into "sensation-seeking columnists and commentators." Entire books were written subsequently on the treatment of Goldwater by the news media; and in *The Future of Conservatism* (1968), rightist journalist M. Stanton Evans criticized the major television networks for preoccupation with the New Left and blindness to numerically larger conservatism. In the late 1960s and early 1970s a number of published studies seemed to give support to such charges of media bias. Edith Efron's *The News Twisters* documented what she said was negative coverage of the Nixon 1968 campaign. Ernest Lefever of Georgetown University published a hard-hitting analysis of press coverage of the Vietnam War, widely publicized in right-of-center circles. Howard K. Smith, Daniel Patrick Moynihan, Irving Kristol, and Theodore White supported similar conclusions. As Kristol wrote in *The Public Interest,* "ideological bias on television newscasting" was not "a malicious invention" of Spiro Agnew.

Despite the symbiotic relationship of the New Right to the neoconservatives, the New Right's deep distrust of intellectuals and the university world, as well as its resentment of the East, has made for little sympathy or cooperation between the two groups. The New Right is incapable, moreover, of accepting the "conservatism" of anyone who claims that description yet who has not proven that he is an "authentic conservative" by embracing the "movement," its personalities, and its practices. The New Right, therefore, remains suspicious of the neoconservatives. "I do think we are better off with those people as adversaries," Patrick Buchanan said of the informal cluster of writers and scholars like Kristol, Daniel Patrick Moynihan, Daniel Bell, Nathan Glazer, Seymour Martin Lipset, and Norman Podhoretz who make up the neoconservative movement. Genuine intellectuals, these academics and editors have, in recent years, moved from liberal and even leftist views to relatively conservative ones, highly critical of the presumptions of the Great Society and a decade of détente. They have promoted in publications like *The Public Interest, Commentary,* and *The American Spectator* traditional views of the family, abortion, homosexuality, and other social questions. On many issues they have come to conclusions similar to those reached by the New Right, although they disagree on the means by which their goals should be advanced.

Neoconservatives agree that a more hawkish posture should be adopted in dealings with the Soviet Union, but they disagree with the New Right on matters of domestic and economic policy. "The [American Right] refused in the 1930s to join in the national mandate for the welfare state," Podhoretz told me, to explain the major difference between the political positions of the New Right and the neoconservatives. Though skeptical of government's capacity to solve many social ills, the neoconservatives nevertheless find nothing objectionable per se in the existence and maintenance of the welfare state, while the New Right seeks to dismantle much social welfare legislation. *Public Interest* editor Kristol, one of the few Republican neoconservatives and a supporter of New York Congressman Jack Kemp (a conservative favorite about whom the New Right is unenthusiastic), said of Kemp: "Jack has no interest in repealing or railing against the welfare state. He grew up under it, and he has no particular animosity to its existence at all. In fact, he believes that with sufficient tax cuts we could simultaneously maintain and even increase current levels of public spending and public services, by increasing production and expanding the tax base." This attitude is rejected to a large extent by New Rightists, who still favor vast reductions in government services. The neoconservatives are also more interested than is the New Right in the correctness of procedure with which political goals are pursued. The New Right seeks immediate gratification of its political desires, exhibiting disdain for traditional procedures of representative government. "Unlike the New Right, we have no interest in, and little sympathy for, methods of direct democracy like initiatives and referenda," Kristol explained.

But deeper resentments lurk beneath the surface. New Rightists consider the neoconservatives as elitists—which certainly they are—and, therefore, as not to be trusted. They do not look kindly on an unabashed intellectualism that takes a greater interest in disseminating ideas than in gathering votes. The neoconservatives, Kevin Phillips has written, are "chiefs without Indians," ultimately irrelevant eggheads who must "seem reassuring" to Establishment liberals on a number of cultural/ political grounds:

1. Disproportionate eastern, even New York City, origins
2. Close identification with the intelligentsia and elite publications such as *Commentary* and *The Public Interest*
3. Strong antipopulism and lack of grass-roots political organization or interest
4. Disproportionately Jewish antecedents and strong support for Israel
5. Strong previous identification with the Democratic party
6. Support for the elitist-internationalist-institutionalist side of conservatism rather than the populist or nationalistic variety
7. Long-standing insider involvement in Washington affairs.

Ironically, the backgrounds of certain important New Right theorists are tonier than those of neoconservatives. Buchanan studied philosophy at Georgetown, M. Stanton Evans, economics at Yale. Kevin Phillips studied at Harvard and the London School of Economics. William Rusher, a New Yorker since his childhood, received his law degree from Yale. The neoconservatives, on the other hand, tend to come from lower-middle-class backgrounds, educated at schools like the City College of New York. Moynihan was a Times Square shoeshine boy who spent many summers of his childhood on an Indiana farm. Podhoretz was a street kid from Brooklyn, a polemical brawler who fought his way up the New York literary and intellectual ranks. That these writers came to be associated with the academic and publishing worlds, however, put them beyond the pale for New Rightists, whose deep alienation from such worlds (perhaps gained from their own experiences as right-wingers in liberal schools) suggests that the New Right cannot abide potential allies who in important respects are not, in their terms, trustworthy. Neoconservatives must be watched at all times, lest they sabotage the cause.

HATE OBJECTS OF THE NEW RIGHT

So deep is the New Right's antipathy for intellectual elitists that it has prompted them to turn their guns also on genuine conservatives who, by their cultural styles, appear to New Right primitives as enemies.

The most frequent target of such abuse is, of course, William F. Buckley, Jr., whose learning, cultivation, and wealth invite suspicion.

Member of a rich and distinguished family, Buckley exemplifies much of what the New Rightists despise: Educated in England and at Yale, he is cultured and erudite, speaking with what many New Rightists suspect is an accent he has affected. Cosmopolitan in his attitudes, he has been an iconoclastic journalist, controversial and unflappable. He plays the harpsichord and paints, has been known to swear on television, and writes in a prose style that is highly individualistic and often obtuse. He prefers to use the correct word, even if it is unlikely to be understood immediately by many of his readers. He has what he calls "transideological friendships" with economist John Kenneth Galbraith, historian Arthur M. Schlesinger, Jr., and journalist Murray Kempton. A member of fashionable New York society, he attends novelist Truman Capote's annual ball. Buckley's periodic deviations to the left—an endorsement of liberal Democrat Allard Lowenstein for Congress, support for the Carter administration's Panama Canal treaties, decriminalization of marijuana use—are often explained by vexed right-wingers as contamination by Buckley's liberal friends. "Buckley spends too much time skiing with that Galbraith," a conservative newspaper publisher once told me. Another favorite theory, this to explain Buckley's support for the Panama Canal treaties, is that the writer and debater "is under Kissinger's influence," as though mesmerized, a reference to his friendship with the former secretary of state.

Time was when *National Review,* under Buckley's guidance,

was the publication most responsible for drawing together the disparate elements of the political right, actively promoting the presidential candidacy of Barry Goldwater in 1964, and covering the events and personalities of the burgeoning "conservative movement" of the early 1960s. As Buckley became more involved in other pursuits during the mid- and late-1970s— writing novels, serving as a member of the United States delegation to the United Nations—his influence on the conservative community declined, making way for the new breed. "I suppose there is that feeling that I have been on the scene an awfully long time," Buckley told me, "and maybe it is that people are just tired of the same old face. I can understand that feeling. Maybe they are looking for new faces."

Owing, perhaps, to Buckley's own growing weariness with right-wing politics, *National Review* has in recent years become increasingly indifferent to the Washington hurly-burly that is the focus of New Right money and attention. As a political force, one hears on Capitol Hill, *National Review* has become "irrelevant." It has chosen to turn its interests elsewhere, Kevin Phillips said, a "nominal rightist" publication that has elected "to prance off harmlessly in pursuit of Oscar Wilde's prose, Château Lafite's wine and Otto von Hapsburg's relevance."

At a Capitol Hill Christmas party in 1978, I heard someone ask, "Why is Buckley taking all these 'liberal' positions?" "Because he's all messed up on drugs" came the reply. "He's been a liberal ever since." Probing this strange and baseless notion, I was reminded that Buckley once admitted smoking marijuana on his yacht outside the three-mile legal limit. The "addiction" —about which Buckley laughs—was, from all accounts, the creation of a fevered right-wing imagination.

Howard Phillips of the Conservative Caucus sums up the opinions of a growing number of activists on the Right that "Buckley, for all the good work that he has done, is simply not on the cutting edge of American politics anymore. His positions on legalizing marijuana and passage of the Panama Canal treaties were a great disappointment. He really isn't with us any more." Others note that he has mellowed in recent years, devoting more and more time to his novels and to introspective works like *Airborne* (1976).

A genuine hate object of the New Right is George F. Will, the conservative columnist of the *Washington Post,* whose elitism offends the neopopulists. Will, a frosty and somewhat aloof highbrow, is Midwest-born but the Oxford-educated son of a professor of philosophy. He first made contact with the Washington conservative community in 1968 when he took a job with Senator Gordon Allott of Oklahoma. He was almost instantaneously disliked by many right-wing activists, and when he was named Washington editor of *National Review,* they were outraged. "There is no question that George Will is the foremost conservative writing in America today. I identify very closely with the kind of conservatism he represents," an American Conservative Union activist told me. But he admits to ambivalence.

> When he began contributing those early pieces to the *Washington Post,* he demonstrated a really galling amount of opportunism. I was an aide to Senator Buckley at the time, and all too often it seemed to me that he used his credentials as *National Review* correspondent to trash whatever the conservatives on the Hill were doing, and I'm sure his editors at the *Post* loved him for it. Once he was established and began to write a regular column, he has been very solid and very good. But I can't help but fault him for the way he got there, and I don't blame some of the conservatives who still resent him for it and don't altogether trust him.

Some deny that Will is a conservative at all. His reluctance to support the 1976 candidacy of Ronald Reagan, for example, aroused much rightist hostility. "When George Will Writes, Should Conservatives Heed?" *Human Events* asked in 1977, and answered: No. "He is frequently palmed off as a conservative by the liberal media," yet a less than laudatory column about Reagan "revealed—despite his once having written for

National Review—that he is about as conservative as, well, Nelson Rockefeller, whom Will used to trumpet as being in the 'conservative' tradition until he thought it opportune to knife him." Will is less critical of federal government power and spending than *Human Events* wanted him to be, and that "should lay to rest any suspicions about the genuineness of his conservative faith." Especially dastardly, he is "a stout champion of liberal Republicans." His "liberal positions are legion." "Do we think George Will is a conservative?" asked *Battleline*. "Let's put it this way: If he is, then every other conservative we know isn't." Will, however philosophically conservative, is "not really one of us"—to quote a favorite line of right-wing activists.

The New Right's discomfort with William Safire—who has proved to be one of the best investigative reporters in the business, and certainly the only one on the conservative side— is the result, to some extent, of the role he performed in modifying the Nixon Administration's ideology. *Human Events* attacked him shortly after publication of his memoirs of those years, *Before the Fall* (1975), for he frequently clashed with Patrick Buchanan, who was pushing Nixon to the Right. Safire, adhering to the notion that "the political center is the place to be," prevailed with Nixon; *Human Events* wrote that "for helping to turn the President leftward, one supposes, Safire wound up as a columnist for the *New York Times.* Curiously, the *Times* sells Safire's column to other publications as representative of 'conservative' opinion."

"As flacks go, Safire is one of the best," wrote Kevin Phillips. How Safire came to the *New York Times* is amusing and informative. Publisher Punch Sulzberger says he was hired as a 'conservative spokesman.' . . .*The New York Times* does not want a 'genuine conservative,' of course; it wants a White House PR man to serve as half a fig leaf."

Safire, in fairness to his critics, but also to himself, was never associated with the right wing of the Republican party; when he went to the White House, he was known as a Rockefeller partisan. But the attacks on Safire give one the definite impression that his association with *The New York Times* is in itself part of the problem.

The New Right's rejection of Buckley, Will, and Safire as authentic spokesmen for conservative values demonstrates the corrosive character of its antielitist, anti-intellectual stance. It feeds on resentment and, to some degree, on envy, and smacks of an egalitarianism that is the exact opposite of all that true conservatives stand for. Its vengeful attitude reflects the deep alienation that the New Rightists feel toward both those below them on the socioeconomic level and those above them. It is the ideology of the insecure who want to salve those insecurities by a leveling process. Their intent is the fomenting of class warfare.

The Journalist
as Machiavelli

*I suppose you can't play every instrument in the
orchestra—you can't be a philosophicker and a
politicker at the same time. That has always been
a favourite theory of mine and I believe 'tis true.*
—ALBERT JAY NOCK

No single incident has dramatized the changing players and
personalities of right-wing journalism quite like the much-
publicized debate, in 1978, between William F. Buckley, Jr.,
speaking for the affirmative, and Ronald Reagan, speaking for
the negative, on ratification of the Carter Administration's
Panama Canal treaties. The scene at the televised confrontation between Buckley and Reagan at Duke University featured
the *National Review* editor and long-time conservative debater
at one table, the two-term California governor and presidential
candidate Reagan at the other. At Buckley's side, to help

prepare the affirmative argument, sat George F. Will, the *Washington Post* columnist. At Reagan's, to bolster the opposition, sat Patrick J. Buchanan, the Nixon Administration speechwriter and New Right polemicist. Buckley squared off against the most eloquent political spokesman of the American Right over an issue that had been proclaimed by New Right activists to be a "litmus test" of one's political faith. And Buckley, to the dismay of some of his most ardent admirers on the Right, had gone into battle against them, needlessly, some thought. By then, he had, in effect, already abdicated to a new dynasty of journalists and commentators without his brilliance, who now speak for the united front of the New Right, while Buckley—they have told me—speaks only for himself.

The New Right pundits who stepped into the vacuum created by Buckley's increasing absence were not only less astute—they were also more involved in the activities and personalities they were to discuss and, thus, too easily compromised. They lacked, that is, a sufficient sense of the journalistic calling and, at their worst, were little more than "movement" apologists and flacks. They operated on Red Alert; their publications, lacking the toniness of *National Review* or *The Freeman* (under the editorial direction of Albert Jay Nock in the 1940s), tended to be house organs, more concerned with advancing political careers than with independent journalism. The few who have worked their turf without over-concern with the immediate political impact are viewed on the Right with suspicion and distrust. George Will of the *Washington Post* and William Safire of the *New York Times* have met such a fate. They are not "authentic conservatives," in the argot of the movement.

THE NEW RIGHT'S GRAND STRATEGIST

By far the most influential of the New Right theoreticians is Kevin P. Phillips, a Bronx-born voting-trends analyst and former congressional aide, who, in 1969, wrote *The Emerging*

Republican Majority, the book credited with formulating the Nixon Administration's successful "Southern strategy." Despite the author's insistence that his book "was not and is not a 'strategy,'" Phillips provided the initial historical and philosophical underpinnings of the political strategy of the New Right. Pugnacious and argumentative, he may well be the only articulate spokesman for unreconstructed right-wing populism in America. The theme of his strategy was that "the national GOP was shifting to a southern and western base, and that such a coalition would triumph over northeastern liberalism in upcoming elections," that the heyday of the Northeast, which has so long dominated American politics, is dying and power moving to Middle America and the "Sunbelt" states.

> The great political upheaval of the Nineteen-Sixties is not that of Senator Eugene McCarthy's relatively small group of upper-middle-class and intellectual supporters, but a populist revolt of the American masses who have been elevated by prosperity to middle-class status and conservatism. *Their* revolt is against the caste, policies and taxation of the mandarins of Establishment liberalism.

The political alliances dating back to the New Deal and the industrial revolution, Kevin Phillips announced, are no longer relevant. With an elaborate array of statistical support, he argued that the New Deal coalition of "have-nots" in the South and West pitted against the "haves" of the moneyed (and Republican) Northeast has completely reversed itself politically, with the Republican party now drawing its greatest support in presidential elections from the South and West. Thus Phillips has become the political theorist–strategist of the New Old West and the antielitists of the New Right.

A King Features Syndicate columnist and CBS Spectrum radio commentator for several years in the mid-1970s, Phillips is a Harvard graduate of lower-middle-class origin whose articles drip with scorn for "Eastern elitists" and glowing tributes to the wisdom of Middle Americans. Once an aide to Republican Congressman Paul Fino of New York, Phillips was a Republican partisan who worked as voting-trends analyst for Richard Nixon's 1968 presidential campaign.

Phillips dedicated his book to this "new majority and its two principal architects: President Richard M. Nixon and Attorney General John N. Mitchell." He had taken the rough draft of the manuscript to the 1968 Nixon presidential campaign staff and, as a result, was signed on, eventually becoming special assistant to Nixon campaign manager Mitchell. Though the book was "in no sense cleared or censored by the Nixon Administration," galley proofs "were made available" to officials of the Republican National Committee. "I knew that I would be in the new GOP administration; and not unreasonably, I had been advised to keep away from policy matters and to make no policy recommendations," he wrote. "Nor did I feel free to criticize the Republican party." During the fall campaign, "elements of my book were distilled into strategy memos." Phillips was acknowledged to have pointed the way to the Republican sweep of the South.

In 1969, Phillips left the White House to become a syndicated columnist. In 1975, he published *Mediacracy: American Parties and Politics in the Communications Age.* The growth of the "knowledge industry" has resulted in a "massive shift in the locus of American wealth, culture and power," throwing old party loyalties "into a tizzy," he wrote. "In New York City, the blue-collar workers and bus drivers of Queens keynote conservative animosity toward the liberal post-industrial upper-middle class of midtown Manhattan, a reversal of industrial era ideological conflict."

Thus Phillips refined the New Old West's anti–New York City syndrome. He pinpointed the source of infection, not middle-class Queens, but midtown East Side Manhattan, home of the mass media and "the multi-billion dollar social engineering industry" that have given rise to a new communications elite, replacing the once conservative business "elite." He found that the infection had spread to "many of the nation's chic residential districts, formerly the strongholds of conservative businessmen" but "now strongly liberal"—Back Bay, Boston; Scarsdale, New York; Shaker Heights, Ohio; suburban San Francisco. In these urban and suburban centers, "educators, consultants and media executives" had replaced "yesteryear's population of bankers, railroad vice-presidents and merchants." Liberal educators, government planners, social workers, and network newscasters replaced "yesterday's millowners and railroad barons as the focal point of popular indigestion." Conservatism, Phillips said, "musters its greatest support in the Southern and Western areas of historic *populist–radical* proclivities." A "middle-class Counter-Revolution" is brewing on the frontier; the future belongs to political leaders in the tradition of Andrew Jackson "who represent the raw insurgent forces of the South and West."

These themes became outright political recommendations in Phillips's columns and magazine articles. He proposed a presidential ticket of Ronald Reagan and George Wallace in 1975 in a "My Turn" guest column for *Newsweek*. He has called for abolishing the Electoral College as an impediment to new parties and therefore to neopopulist revolt; for restrictions on the press's exercise of the First Amendment; and for federal spending programs to benefit the anti-egghead constituency rather than the poor, expressing an enthusiasm for what his conservative critics have called "middle-class welfarism."

Perhaps the most stinging indictment of the Kevin Phillips thesis has come from Hamilton Rogers, a pseudonym for a traditionalist conservative who was once, like Phillips, in the Nixon Administration. Reviewing *Mediacracy* in *New Guard*, the magazine of Young Americans for Freedom, "Rogers" took issue with Phillips's notion that American history is little more than one great conflict between the masses and a "highly educated" elite. Phillips's notion that "the elite is the enemy," "Rogers" wrote, reverses traditional concepts of American conservatism: "Whether the leadership is Alexander Hamilton, Mark Hanna, Robert Taft or Thomas Dewey, they consistently contrast with the political leadership of Andrew Jackson, William Jennings Bryan, Franklin Roosevelt or Harry Truman. The latter represented the less-educated, the acultural and the non-elite." By the Kevin Phillips logic, the political genealogy of the American Right would run instead "from Jefferson, Jackson, Bryan, Roosevelt and Truman to Wallace and Connally." He saw Phillips and the New Right taking advantage of a political vacuum created by a change in the Democratic party which gave up "the populist anti-Northeast tradition of Jackson and Bryan in favor of an association with an elite." The political objective, "above all others, is the gaining and holding of power," "the exploitation of social alienation," and the spurning and "prudent actions to ameliorate social tensions." But what is the cost of power for conservatives? Possibly "our purpose for being and our integrity," the conservative critic wrote.

BUCKLEY'S HOUSE POPULIST

William A. Rusher, a New Right political strategist deeply influenced by Phillips, has been publisher of *National Review* since 1955, when he was hired by William F. Buckley, Jr. Despite his position, Rusher is something of an outsider at *National Review,* so populistic are his political attitudes. Rusher has written that Buckley "came to conservatism from the intellectual side, the journalistic side," while "I come from the political side. I was in the Young Republicans back in the 1950s; thereafter I was a conservative in Republican politics and, to a certain extent, a Republican in conservatism—and a spokesman for both." When offered the post at Buckley's magazine, he accepted, "a big decision, because I had to leave the career for which I had been trained." Although the dapper and self-possessed bachelor, member of wine-tasting societies and resident of New York's Murray Hill, moved from the Midwest to the East when he was nine years old and was educated at Yale, Rusher told me that even when he was a small child, "I had a sense that I was a Midwesterner in New

York"; and that feeling has endured through the years. The career he left to enter the world of journalism was the law. Rusher had been an attorney, briefly serving as associate counsel to the Senate Internal Security Subcommittee during the Pat McCarren-led investigations into Communist infiltration of the Treasury Department; he described himself as a "Senate red-hunter." A "backroom political operator," he was a key figure in the Draft Goldwater movement in 1961 and has worked to push the Republican party rightward during the intervening years. Frustrated by his efforts, he issued his political manifesto, *The Making of the New Majority Party,* in 1975.

Rusher argued that the Republican party, "being spectacularly unfitted to be the political vector" of a coming conservative revolt, should be unceremoniously dumped. The presence of Easterners associated with Rockefeller dominance, he said, is a plague that prevents the GOP from making common cause with the Wallace constituency in the South, West, and blue-collar urban centers of the Northeast. The nomination of Goldwater, in this analysis, became something of a triumph:

> It demonstrated, with mathematical finality, that a Republican candidate did not need the support of New York, Massachusetts or Pennsylvania to win the party's nomination. He didn't even need that mysterious entity called "Wall Street"; there were new concentrations of financial power—in Houston, Los Angeles and elsewhere—that had money, too, and were prepared to put it where their mouths were.

"Social conservatism," as a movement of the lower middle class, the Wallaceite constituency, is marked by a profound alienation from upper-class liberalism. The blue-collar workers of the South and Midwest, the urban ethnics of the industrial North, and labor union members all over the country, Rusher contends, are extremely traditional in their attitudes toward "social issues"; they are patriotic and often militaristic. They believe in the home and the traditional family. They adhere to the work ethic, and deplore welfare. They are angered by crime in the streets and resent busing. They may feel threatened by all large institutions, including the labor unions and certainly large corporations that are protected by government subsidies and regulations. The "social conservatives" can make common cause with "economic conservatives," who constitute the "long suffering backbone of the Republican party."

Scathing antielitist epithets spice Rusher's book: "upper-class WASPs and their fellow travelers"; a "Boston Brahmin [Henry Cabot Lodge] whose liberalism and ineffable Eastern-ness exceeded, if possible, even that of Nelson Rockefeller"; John Kennedy "of Massachusetts and Harvard and the interna-tional Jet Set."

Rusher did little to clarify apparent contradictions. He ac-knowledged that another survey found that most self-described "conservatives" identify not with right-wing political ideology but with a conservative lifestyle—personal deportment, social attitudes, moral values—and that the "most likely beneficia-ries" of this conservatism are political moderates—an admis-sion that would seem to damage his thesis. Indeed, in the 1964 presidential election, a large number of voters supported Lyn-don Johnson in the belief that he was the more "conservative" candidate; these Americans viewed Goldwater as dangerously radical.

In his 1975 book Rusher nevertheless plowed ahead, even giving the political party he wanted to create a name—the "Independence party." He offered the beginnings of a political platform that took the pragmatic position that "many glaring inequities, technically unjustified subsidies, and inherently un-sound tax practices" and probably "unbalanced budgets" would be political realities for some time to come. It was an admission that led one Republican liberal to tell me, with some amusement, that Rusher "is proposing for his new party the very same sell-outs, trade-offs, and compromises that he finds absolutely unconscionable within the GOP."

Another surprise was Rusher's advocacy of a possible inva-sion of Middle East oil fields; he maintained, in a swaggering Old West style, that such an invasion "would reaffirm America's will and cement its alliances, while administering a mighty setback to Soviet pretensions and influence all over the world." Even *National Review* was unmoved by its publisher's arguments. Its reviewer, Robert D. Novak, wrote:

> A few basic policy suggestions—a strong national defense and foreign policy, less government and less governmental interference, a return to the work ethic—might well attract the broad-based coalition he envisions.
>
> But the Rusher platform is chock-full to the brim of particularized positions; anti-abortion, pro-school prayer, restrictions on the press (which, in my view, clearly violate the First Amendment), and even a possible expeditionary force to seize Arab oil. The number of conservatives who could agree to all would constitute a cozy group indeed.

It is unlikely that one could muster much support for such a platform even among the staffers at *National Review,* and Rusher's influence on the magazine's editorial policy has declined in recent years, according to sources close to the *National Review* staff. (In 1979, the magazine published an editorial critical of the Reverend Sun Myung Moon's Unification Church, which prompted a letter to the editor from the publisher taking issue with the editorial. When the letter was published, so was a *second* editorial, reasserting the original editorial position and disagreeing with Rusher's letter!) While Buckley did not acknowledge to me any sense that he and Rusher are going their separate ways on matters of ideology, discussions of the New Right and neopopulism are extremely uncomfortable for the magazine's conservative editors, many of whom are in outright disagreement with the publisher.

Rusher based his manifesto on a Gallup Poll of 1974 that reported that 38 percent of the respondents would favor a "conservative party" if the American party system were to be realigned along ideological lines, while only 26 percent said they would favor the more liberal party; 36 percent were undecided. (Rusher did not address the fact that a Gallup Poll taken three years later found that a full 41 percent of the American people—not counting those who were undecided—would favor creation of a new "center party.")

THE RIGHT'S NEW PEGLER

Patrick J. Buchanan, the Nixon Administration speechwriter who came to national attention as a result of his cool performance before the Senate Watergate Committee, is a New Right tactician like Rusher and Phillips, credited with responsibility for Vice-President Spiro Agnew's blistering attack on the national news media—though he has denied it. Buchanan has been closely tied to Nixon since his college days when he caddied for Eisenhower's vice-president at the Burning Tree Country Club. He distinguished himself in Thomistic philosophy at Georgetown University, then became an editorial writer on the *St. Louis Globe-Democrat.* In 1967, Nixon, gearing up for another shot at the White House, hired Buchanan as a researcher in his New York City law firm. Buchanan went to the White House in 1968; after the Nixon Administration collapsed, he became a columnist for the New York Times News Service.

A colorful, sometimes brutal stylist, the contentious Buchanan appears to have been deeply influenced by the early Westbrook Pegler (before Pegler's anti-Semitism), whose blistering columns he read as a child. Typical of his earthy prose was his comment on the use of ACTION funds to pay for the abortions of Peace Corps volunteers, which he called "shelling out 50-grand a year to execute the unborn children of upper-middle-class bimbos whose idea of bringing the blessings of Western civilization to the Third World is to take a tumble in the hay with the local witchdoctor." (William Safire has written in *Before the Fall* that Buchanan, in his opinion, "spoke for Nixon's most elemental moods.")

Buchanan's 1975 book, *Conservative Votes, Liberal Victories: Why the Right Has Failed,* drew on his experience in the pragmatic Nixon White House, and attempts to explain why we have a liberal government when the American people are overwhelmingly "conservative." Despite conservative inclinations, President Nixon, once in office, adhered to a centrist line ("We are all Keynesians," he said) and, in Buchanan's opinion, did more than was necessary to appease the liberals, who disliked Nixon almost by instinct. And thus was lost the mandate of 1972. Foremost among the reasons for this, Buchanan believes, was the enormous power wielded in American politics by institutions like the federal bureaucracy, the federal courts, and the national news media—"an unelected oligarchy . . . guided by their own ideology and insulated from the electorate and the common man."

> The political pressure of millions dependent upon federal checks and federal benefits, and the entrenched and unresponsive power of the media, the bureaucracy and the courts, taken together, prevent implementation of a conservative mandate in American political life. This is why, as polls and surveys show, the nation is moving to the right, the government continues to move to the left.

Against this opposition, it is no wonder that "millions are coming to consider participation in the democratic process, through the ballot box, like playing poker for matchsticks— an instructive exercise, perhaps, but one that bores readily, as it is devoid of meaning." These angry masses must be mobilized, Buchanan argues, and they must "set as their central political objective" the capture of the White House. Only the presidency "has the discipline and resources to conduct siege warfare against the bureaucracy." Conservatives must turn that "mighty instrument of government . . . into a siege gun against the welfare state." Buchanan is a modern Western vigilante on the prowl. It is too late, he concludes, for the politics of "communication, conciliation, compromise and cooperation," promised by a reassuring but inept Gerald Ford. The time has come to "declare war on the Congress," to "seek out, not avoid, political conflict with liberals of both parties," to engage in "confrontation politics," Buchanan told me.

Buchanan's lack of interest in a coherent program for conservatives calls to mind a comment by the *New York Times* editorial writer, later U.S. ambassador to Ireland, William V. Shannon. Since Buchanan "makes clear his disapproval of Nixon's policies on welfare reform, civil rights, wage-price controls, unbalanced budgets, and detente," Shannon said in the *New York Times Book Review,* "one can only conclude that it is this shared resentment of intellectuals and various cultural establishments that bound them together."

JOURNALIST-ADVOCATE

This call for "confrontation politics" has been refined by M. Stanton Evans, a philosophical conservative whose political attitudes are decidedly New Right. M. Stanton Evans, who refers to himself as Stan, is a Mississippi native with Southern sympathies who was graduated from Yale University. Editor of the *Indianapolis News* until 1975, and national chairman of the American Conservative Union for six years, he is a columnist for the *Los Angeles Times* Syndicate and CBS "Spectrum" commentator.

Evans came up the conservative ladder rung by rung. His father is Medford Evans, a far-right journalist, with a doctoral degree from Yale, whose views are considerably farther to the right than his son's. A founder of Young Americans for Freedom, M. Stanton Evans was an activist in Young Republicans and a colleague of William F. Buckley, Jr., at Yale, and one of the brightest young stars on the right-wing horizon. At twenty-five he joined the staff of the *Indianapolis News,* and within a matter of months became the nation's youngest editor of a major metropolitan daily. His first book, *Revolt on the Campus* (1961), appeared two years later. A pale man with thinning, sandy hair, highly intelligent, well-read, with a dry yet wildly imaginative sense of humor, he does not fit the antielitist image the New Right cherishes, despite his expressed enthusiasm for lowbrow culture.

He has a thorough knowledge of public policy. However, the deep involvement in political struggles that cost him much of his credibility as a journalist has reassured his ideological constituency and helped him escape Buckley's fate at New Right hands. As a consequence of subordinating his journalism to his political activism, Evans has had an influence increasingly limited to the small circle of Washington political operatives and die-hard right-wing activists in which he moves.

Evans's book, *The Future of Conservatism,* while addressed to Republicans, is a Machiavellian blueprint for New Right politics. Responding to the popular notion that, in order to win elections, conservative Republicans should strive to appear more positive, devising alternatives to the liberal programs, Evans writes:

> To date there is no evidence that the constructive approach has done the party any good, and a great deal of evidence that it has worked the party harm. If constructiveness is pushed much further and becomes established deeply enough in the thinking of enough Republicans, it could easily cancel out the gains the GOP stands to inherit from the suburban revolution, the shift in American population, and the growth of popular resentments against the burgeoning costs of the welfare state.

Convinced that the "best established fact of political life is that people vote 'against' much more than they vote 'for,' " Evans urges the Right to dispense with the concept of "constructiveness" altogether. "The real job of stirring up the voters and winning elections depends chiefly upon the politician's effectiveness in mounting a negative attack against his opposition," i.e., moderate and liberal Republicans and Democrats. The Democrats have triumphed in the past several decades by conducting "a successful negative campaign

against Republicans as heartless ogres, tools of economic roy-
alists, witchhunters, Social Security destroyers and, of late,
nuclear irresponsibles." Conservatives can win, but "they will
have to make their negative presentation superior to that of
the Democrats; they must make their version of the bad
things that will happen to the country under Democratic rule
prevail over the Democrats' version of the bad things that
will happen to the country under Republican rule." His columns are nearly barren of criticism of others on the Right,
and he is willing to use them to advance the careers of right-
wing politicians in a way that subordinates journalism to politics. In 1977, for example, Evans was approached by a representative of Roger J. Stone, the young right-wing activist who
was involved in the "dirty tricks" campaign of the Committee to Re-Elect the President (CREEP), then conducting a
successful campaign for the chairmanship of the Young Republican National Federation. The Stone campaign needed
someone to write its side of the "dirty tricks" story, and
Evans referred vaguely to "allegations" and "late-blooming
charges" against the candidate. Stone's election to the youth
post, Evans told me, was important because Stone's opponent, a Reaganite, was, in fact, a "Rockefeller front-man."

Evans's position as national chairman of the American Conservative Union, he told me, "impeded my ability to advance
professionally." He had accepted the post "because I felt I
owed it to what I believe, although I was never quite comfortable, given my position as a journalist." In 1975, when the
organization under his leadership undertook an independent
effort on behalf of Ronald Reagan's campaign for the Republican presidential nomination, Evans contributed some of his
own money in the form of personal loans (never repaid). He
worked long hours to advance the effort and to be "point man,"
as he put it, for the Reagan campaign. "It caused real tensions.
I would be attending a press conference one day and holding
a press conference the next."

His political activism may have cost Evans his position at the

Indianapolis News. In 1975, he had spoken at the annual Conservative Political Action Conference urging formation of a new political party to replace the GOP. *Indianapolis News* publisher Eugene Pulliam responded with an editorial dissociating the newspaper from Evans's proposal. Evans harbors no animosity. The *News,* he says, was "very good to me" and "gave me a very free hand while I was there." Shortly thereafter he left the paper and came to Washington to write his column.

In 1978, Evans recorded a radio advertisement on behalf of Alex Seith, the Democratic candidate for the Illinois Senate seat held by Charles Percy, as part of an ad campaign devised by Tony Schwartz, best known for his agency's fierce campaign against Barry Goldwater during the 1964 presidential campaign. The Democratic candidate, Evans explained, was a "personal friend." He used his syndicated column to promote Seith's political career and signed a fund-raising letter for the Seith campaign. Though scrupulous about his personal finances—he accepted no payment from the American Conservative Union or any other political organization with which he is associated—he considers himself an "opinion journalist," an "advocate," and a "conservative spokesman," not a "reporter." He has been critical of the fund-raising tactics of some of the less scrupulous New Right organizations, and has used his influence in right-wing circles to minimize these practices. All the same, he has steadfastly refused to use the weapons at his disposal—his newspaper column or radio broadcast, for instance—to bring these facts to public attention.

Evans refrained from writing about fund-raising activities that he finds objectionable, he explained, because his long-time identification with the American Conservative Union might make such articles appear to be "internecine bickering." One conservative activist who shares Evans's objections to the New Right fund-raising activities told me that if Evans had used his column to expose the fundraisers, "he could have stopped them then and there. But Stan is such a decent and honorable guy that he simply will not use his column to pursue what might look like a vendetta against a personal enemy. And Stan *has* been feuding with some of these guys for some years now. The other problem, though, is that he has become so personally involved in the developments about which he is writing that it has hurt him, too."

Evans obeys an unwritten "movement" code that "there is no enemy to the Right."

"I know a great deal about politics and politicians that I do not choose to write about," Evans told me.

> There are many things I know precisely because I've been allowed to attend meetings in which someone who was only a journalist would not be allowed. And, as an ethical matter, I do not believe that I can exploit journalistically what I know as a result of attending these meetings.

PUNDITS AND PUBLICISTS

Another prominent right-wing journalist, John D. Lofton, Jr., was, during the late 1970s, on the payroll of the American Conservative Union, editing its monthly magazine *Battleline*. Once editor of the Republican National Committee's *First Monday*, Lofton is now a United Features Syndicate columnist, specializing in satiric assaults on the foibles of Republican and Democratic liberals. His favorite foil is the New Left. Interviewing Yippie Jerry Rubin at the 1972 Democratic National Convention, he attached the following headline to the story which appeared in *First Monday:*

McGOVERN BACKER NO LONGER
THINKS SONS, DAUGHTERS
SHOULD KILL PARENTS

He is a dependable right-wing apologist with few lapses. Shortly after Illinois Congressman Philip Crane was named to succeed Evans as chairman of the American Conservative Union, a column by Lofton extolled the virtues of his new boss with lengthy quotes from Crane's paperback book, *The Sum of Good Government* (published by Green Hill Books).

Crane's book was written by Allan C. Brownfeld, a long-time Crane ghostwriter, who now distributes his own column and services a number of South African newspapers as a Washington correspondent.

Brownfeld is not only close to domestic politicians and organizations—in 1977–1979 he worked for his South African newspapers from a desk in the congressional office of Oklahoma Congressman Mickey Edwards, a staunch New Rightist —but he is also close to other foreign governments. In April 1978, for example, he was hired by a representative of the Nicaraguan dictatorship of General Somoza. His assignment, as he told me, was to write a "research paper," a task that required him to tour Costa Rica, Nicaragua, and Panama at the expense of the Nicaraguan government. Brownfeld is a frequent contributor to *Human Events* and *Conservative Digest* and briefly edited the Young Americans for Freedom magazine, *New Guard*.

Then there is Lee Edwards, once a Young Americans for Freedom activist, the first editor of Viguerie's *Conservative Digest.* When the Justice Department brought suit against the American-Chilean Council in 1978, it came out that one of the organization's activities had been to plant material favorable to the Pinochet government of Chile with Edwards, then a Washington-based public relations man, who writes and distributes his own newspaper column. Edwards included the information in his newspaper articles. The accomplishment was reported back to the Chileans by the Washington officer of the American-Chilean Council, L. Francis Bouchey, another product of Young Americans for Freedom, who had shared office space with Edwards back in 1975 when Edwards was working closely with representatives of the Taiwan government.

THE PUBLICATIONS

In 1975, fundraiser Richard A. Viguerie founded the slick monthly *Conservative Digest* after he tried repeatedly and failed to buy *Human Events*. *Conservative Digest* (circulation roughly 130,000)—I know because I was its first assistant editor, serving from May to December of 1975—was designed to appeal to lower-middle-class Americans of the Wallace constituency, in addition to the traditionalist conservatives who already subscribed to *Human Events* and *National Review*. There would be no fancy prose or big words. The letters column, which I edited, reflected our success in communicating with the anti-intellectuals. For example, the magazine was praised by one reader because it appealed "not only to the elitist conservatives but to the lower-income . . . who make up the bulk of America." Two readers in one issue praised the prose as "easy to read." The editors did their part to contribute to this antielitist effort. A review of George Nash's *The Conservative Intellectual Movement in America Since 1945* cautioned the reader not to be "put off by the word 'intellectual' in the title; Nash has an easy-to-read style." The book review section later succumbed to the Philistines, replaced by something called the *CD* Reader Service, a commercial book club venture through which readers can buy books through the Richard A. Viguerie Company.

Acutely aware that there were untold Birchers among our loyal readers, we pandered to them as best we could, trying to please them by publishing at least one article alluding to the mysterious activities of the Bilderberger Conspiracy. We made valiant efforts to appeal to the working man also, including in the first issue, for example, an article written by George Meany (on détente). (Meany wrote to tell us it was the only article in the magazine with which he could agree.) We featured cover stories on George Wallace and placed a heavy emphasis on the "social issues" like busing and gun control. Edwards contributed an essay on the nature of populism, tracing the genealogy of the New Right, as represented by *Conservative Digest*, from Andrew Jackson through William Jennings Bryan to George Wallace.

The editorial chores were, without question, a collaborative New Right effort: Edwards once wrote an article which carried Viguerie's by-line; it had to be dispatched to Alaska to be approved by Howard Phillips of the Conservative Caucus before it could be printed. On another occasion, I was told to affix my own by-line to an article promoting something called the Ad Hoc Committee for a New Majority, headed by Rusher, Phillips, and Viguerie, the purpose of which was to publicize the third-party theory. It had been written, I was informed, by Morton Blackwell, who feared identification that might weaken his chance to be a delegate to the 1976 Republican National Convention. (The article quoted columnist Jeffrey St. John, who called the third-party concept "a gun pointed at the heads of the two major parties.")

Conservative Digest was to be "a fresh breath of air cutting through the liberal media," an advertisement promised in 1975, yet numerous articles were reprinted from such organs of the Eastern liberal establishment as the *Washington Post* and *The New York Times* simply because the editors could not find enough good material elsewhere, discovering, too, that such publications contained many excellent and unbiased stories relating to the Right and its activities.*

Against the competition, *Human Events*, an independent publication owned by its editors, has maintained its position of leadership, and, benefiting from the growing irrelevance of *National Review* as a political publication among the Right, *Human Events* has gained in impact. A tabloid-sized weekly, *Human Events* "enjoys an impact out of all proportion to its circulation," *Newsweek* said in 1969. At the height of the

---

*Concluding that *Conservative Digest* had come to be little more than an adjunct of the Viguerie fund-raising operation, functioning to promote "rising stars on the right" (many of whom were RAVCO clients) as well as to cover political developments, I accepted a position with Young Americans for Freedom to edit its publication, *New Guard*, and left *Conservative Digest*.

Nixon Administration, it was considered "must" reading at
the White House. It is the one conservative publication
that has improved since the days when *National Review*
was king, growing from a small newsletter into a full-fledged
newspaper of roughly 50,000 subscribers. An "indispensable
source of information," according to Patrick Buchanan, it is
owned and edited by Allan Ryskind—son of the Marx
Brothers' scriptwriter—and Tom Winter, a low-profile,
high-influence American Conservative Union activist, who
functions, in the words of one associate, "to moderate the
crazies."

This is not an easy task, since much of the readership of
Human Events consists of somewhat primitive right-wing
activists who must be appeased if the magazine is to remain
afloat. "It is a fair criticism to say that we don't go out of
our way to anger those people," Ryskind told me. The editors have, nevertheless, managed to alienate some of the za-
nies on the Far Right. Larry McDonald, the Georgia Democratic congressman who is on the national governing board
of the John Birch Society, for example, told me that he
thinks the weekly has declined in quality since it came
under the control of Winter and Ryskind, that it has
"vacillated" in recent years and is afflicted by a "heavy Republican bias." The Birchers think *Human Events* should
publicize the evil intent of the "International Banking Conspiracy," which forms the linchpin of Birchite ideology.
McDonald says that Winter is reluctant to tell the truth
about the conspiracy because it would mean that he would
no longer be invited "to the right cocktail parties."

Outspoken in its criticism of the Nixon Administration's
"pragmatism," the weekly has a leadership role in conservative
circles that cannot be underestimated, as even its enemies
concede. Winter's personal influence "is absolutely enormous," Viguerie has said.

> Why *Human Events* has been a kind of Bible for me for the
> past twenty years. And as its editor, Tom [Winter] is im-

mensely respected. We've had our differences, that's true, but there's no denying his importance among conservatives. I'm publisher of *Conservative Digest,* but quite frankly we don't have nearly the impact that *Human Events* does. I wish we had.

The differences to which Viguerie refers point, quite clearly, to what may be *Human Events'* greatest contribution in recent years: It has steadfastly—but cautiously and diplomatically—provided responsible leadership that has undercut the rise of the New Right zealots. *Human Events,* its conservative side prevailing, has debunked the new-party nonsense; it publicized the tactics of New Right fundraiser Viguerie; it backed Reagan when the New Right extremists were (as noted in Chapter 3) attacking him; and it exposed the record of John Connally as not conservative.

Human Events, at its worst, is strident and somewhat doctrinaire. Also, its editors could more carefully screen advertisements they publish. One classified advertisement I answered offered "Confederate and KKK memorabilia"; it brought me applications for Klan membership.

Newsletters have proliferated on the Right; Viguerie himself publishes *The New Right Report.* Edited by Morton Blackwell of the Committee for Responsible Youth Politics, until 1979, *The New Right Report* monitors political campaigns and imparts other items of interest to right-wing activists in a journalistic style.

In September 1978, *The New Right Report* predicted that President Carter "now intends to impose national wage and price controls in the next few days." Quoting a "highly placed source," it announced that the action had been planned to give the president "a quick way to look forceful and dynamic in some area of foreign policy." Even James J. Kilpatrick, a "faithful reader," felt obliged to inform the editor that the paper had misspelled the names of both Ramsey Clark and Clarence Kelley in one sentence: "This is probably not a record for a sentence of 25 words," commented the Sage of Scrabble, Virginia, "but it justifies a little marvelling all the same." "It's not journalism at all," former Heritage Foundation staffer John Sullivan has commented. "It's a shill."

An entertaining addition to the journalism of the Right is the *Washington Weekly,* which began as a supplement to the *Fairfax* (Virginia) *Globe,* one of more than forty newspapers owned by John P. McGoff's Panax Corporation. Out of a desire to bring a conservative voice to the nation's capital and, thereby, provide an ideological alternative to the liberal *Washington Post,* in 1974 and 1975, McGoff—owner of numerous weekly and daily papers in Michigan—tried to buy the *Washington Star.* He presented a bid of $26.5 million, but the bid was rejected, in part because the *Star*'s owners could not determine where McGoff was getting the money. In 1979 the South African government admitted that in 1974 it transferred $11.5 million from its Defense Department budget to a Swiss bank for purchase of the *Washington Star* as part of an effort to gain influence abroad. McGoff denied press reports that the money had been given to him for this purpose, calling them "utter nonsense." It was later learned that McGoff has part ownership in a ranch in South Africa and that his Panax Corporation had investments in a printing plant there. McGoff, moreover, had considered buying the *Citizen,* a pro-apartheid newspaper.

In 1978, McGoff played a key role in efforts by the South African government to control the short-lived *New York Trib,* started by Leonard Saffir, a former aide to Senator James L. Buckley. Saffir told me the *Trib* was offered secret financial backing from the South African government, with the middleman to be McGoff. Saffir and McGoff met to discuss the deal but nothing came of it, Saffir said, because of Saffir's unwillingness to surrender control of the newspaper, which he took to be a condition of the investment. Even Richard Mellon Scaife, a member of the Mellon family whose Scaife Foundation has been a contributor to conservative causes, got into the act, Saffir says. The meeting with McGoff took place at the suggestion of Scaife, who has subsequently assumed 50 percent interest in a California newspaper string that includes the *Sacramento Union,* owned by McGoff.

McGoff is a colorful character himself, having reportedly fired two of his Michigan newspaper editors in 1977 when they refused, on the grounds that the stories were unprofessional, to carry stories he had instructed them to publish. Written by a former contributor to the *National Enquirer* who specialized in stories on the occult, astrology, and Hollywood celebrities, one of the stories contended that President Carter condones sexual promiscuity on the part of his male staffers; the other story quoted a New York psychologist who said the chief executive is grooming wife Rosalynn for vice-president in 1984. Late in 1978, according to *Editor and Publisher*, McGoff was arrested on charges of third-degree assault, disorderly conduct, and reckless endangerment, in connection with an incident at an Aspen, Colorado, supperclub. The flagship Panax newspaper—the *Escanaba* (Michigan) *Daily Press*—carried its account of the incident with a two-column, thirty-six-point headline PUBLISHER IS FACING CHARGES, followed by a four-column, forty-eight-point headline, MCGOFF ISSUES STATEMENT. According to police, McGoff had become angry after a musical group performed a song that he described as "extolling drugs of all kinds," and tossed a glass at the stage. The glass hit a chandelier, which fell on a girl in the audience, who had to be taken to a local hospital for five stitches. McGoff pleaded guilty to the reckless endangerment charge and was allowed to serve sentence in a program of volunteer work at a drug rehabilitation program.

That behind him, McGoff finally landed a Washington outlet—by creating his own. Originally called *Politics and Religious News*, the supplement to the *Fairfax* (Virginia) *Globe*, the suburban Washington newspaper was edited by the Reverend Lester Kinsolving, an Episcopal priest. "The supplement often featured a sex-scandal story and other sensational items occasionally reflecting the alleged loose morals of religious leaders," one former *Globe* reporter told me. "It was a real embarrassment to the rest of us." McGoff and Kinsolving transformed the supplement into the tabloid-sized *Washington Weekly* in 1978, with a rip-snorting collection of columns by

Buchanan and other polemicists, and with original articles by Kinsolving attempting to demonstrate the liberal bias of the *Washington Post* and *Star.* McGoff no longer owns the tabloid, having sold it in 1979 to Kinsolving, a boyhood friend, who writes a political column for the McNaught Syndicate and reports for radio station WAVA in Arlington, Virginia.

In 1977, Kinsolving was voted out of the State Department Correspondents Association; his press credentials allowing access to the congressional press gallery were revoked when it was learned that he had accepted payments from the South African government. According to Kinsolving, he had agreed to attend meetings of the stockholders of corporations under fire for their activities in South Africa to respond to criticism of their government, for which he was paid $2,500. Kinsolving has compared the payments to "lecture fees."

Despite these and other troubles (White House press secretary Jody Powell once threw a rubber chicken at Kinsolving during a news briefing), the *Weekly* continues to be distributed widely on Capitol Hill, though with little influence. It remains, for the most part, a collection of reprinted syndicated columns and, more recently, voluminous articles by John Lofton, the weekly's new managing editor, who took on the task along with his job of editing the American Conservative Union's *Battleline.*

One legislative aide of a conservative Republican congressman told me:

> There's no question that the *Washington Post* has some very serious blind spots, so I would think a conservative paper in Washington would be very healthy. All the same, I don't think *Washington Weekly* is it. It is biased, and sensational, and altogether kind of shoddy. A lot of people seem to read it, but they don't take it seriously.

Washington Weekly cannot begin to compete with Accuracy In Media (AIM) when it comes to exposing the liberal prejudices of the press. Established in 1969, AIM intends "to provide a watchdog of the news media by promoting accuracy and fairness in reporting on critical issues facing America." AIM does an effective job of this despite its own right-of-center bias. The creation of the tenacious Reed Irvine, a former Fulbright Scholar and Federal Reserve Board economist, AIM keeps close watch on the national news media, publishing its findings in Irvine's syndicated column (distributed by AIM itself), and in a bimonthly newsletter *AIM Report*. Not content, as Evans has written, to "document and complain," Irvine and his cohorts have developed a *modus operandi* that can be maddening to business. They have purchased shares of stock in those major media outlets that are public corporations and have attended stockholders' meetings to badger, among others, Katharine Graham of the *Washington Post*. In May of 1978, for example, Irvine completed a study of the *Post*'s lack of coverage of the atrocities then being carried out by the new Cambodian regime, despite heavy coverage of "human rights" violations in Chile. He confronted Mrs. Graham with the results at a stockholders' meeting. When he received an explanation that seemed to him feeble, at best, he proceeded to show that the *Post*'s Havana correspondent had once been employed by the Castro government. He demanded to know what procedures the *Post* takes to ensure that the newspaper is not being infiltrated by the Soviet KGB. The *Post*, he learned, had no system whatever for screening applicants politically, though Graham agreed that the newspaper would be a prime target for KGB infiltration. After a series of skirmishes with Irvine, *Post* editor Ben Bradlee finally fired off a testy letter denouncing AIM's resident pest as a "miserable, carping, retromingent vigilante."

No single figure in American journalism has more convincingly proved his ability to make liberals reel aghast than William Loeb, publisher of the *Manchester Union Leader*, New Hampshire's only statewide daily. The septuagenarian Loeb carries great influence, especially every four years when presidential hopefuls gear up for the nation's first primary election. Loeb may be a rock-ribbed rightist, but it is his journalistic style rather than his politics that rile many liberals most, driving them to periodic denunciations of the *Union Leader*. The son

of an aide to Theodore Roosevelt, Loeb is married to the
Scripps-Howard heiress and lives in gentlemanly splendor
thirty miles north of Boston overlooking the sea. In print, he
is a Neanderthal, hammering out front-page editorials that
have denounced politicians Left and Right as "Jerry the Jerk"
(Gerald Ford), "a skunk's skunk's skunk" (Eugene McCarthy),
"a stinking hypocrite" (Dwight Eisenhower), and "the California flake" (Jerry Brown). The reaction against this name-calling
often leads Loeb's liberal critics to overestimate his influence.
In 1970, for example, Loeb's choice for governor, Democrat
Roger Crowley, was defeated.

Loeb is, in truth, more politically moderate than is suspected. A soft-spoken, gentle, and courteous man in person, he
is opposed to right-to-work laws and generally prolabor, favoring 100 percent inheritance taxes (the *Union Leader* will pass
into the hands of its employees upon Loeb's death). And he
has, he explained to me, reservations about the rise to prominence of Richard Viguerie and the zealous elements of the
New Right. One news service reporter, reviewing Kevin Cash's
biography of Loeb in Young Americans for Freedom's *New
Guard*, explained the New Hampshire Reaganite's fearsome
reputation like this: "He is a conservative, and the Establishment media likes to conjure up right-wing threats for their
liberal heroes to slay." His weakness for the colorful epithet
may, however, be responsible for a reputation for political
warfare. When he called Nelson Rockefeller a "wife swapper"
in 1964, the thrice-married Loeb explained to a reporter: "I
make no claim to excessive virtue, but I had to get Rockefeller
out of the picture. It was important that Goldwater win."

BUSTING UP "BIG MEDIA"

While the New Right pundits and publicists fire away at their
liberal enemies, the hostility of the New Rightists to what they
consider the liberal media continues unabated (at almost the
pitch it reached when Spiro Agnew lashed out at the press

during the Vietnam War), despite evidence of growing fairness to the conservative, if not New Right, viewpoint in the major newspapers, magazines, and on television. The rise to prominence of a number of conservative, though decidedly not New Right, commentators—Safire and Will, for example—and the continued visibility of William F. Buckley, Jr. and James J. Kilpatrick make it increasingly difficult to argue that the conservative position is not amply and ably represented. That these pundits are not "authentic conservatives," but "creatures of the liberal media" (in New Right jargon) only intensifies the anger of New Rightists who feel shut out from the major media. As this hostility grows, so does the impatience of the New Right pundits and politicians who, along with their new hostility to big business, have begun to view the national news media as a monopoly badly in need of government regulation, if only in the form of "trust-busting." Kevin Phillips has argued in the pages of *Human Events* that the First Amendment is "obsolescent" since it "cannot . . . cope with Big Media power," a situation that "invites—even obliges—the government to move in and in the name, of course, of the free press, correct the situation." If the First Amendment can't stop the adversary culture, Phillips writes, "we need a new socioprudential approach that *can* solve the problem before the government throws the baby of a free press out with the bathwater of Liberal Establishment bunk."

Such talk must surely cause distress to conservatives committed to the conservation of civil liberties, suggesting an area in which government regulation of the media could accomplish precisely what conservatives have warned occurs when government extends its tentacles to regulate private activity: Freedom is diminished. And, in the case of the press, it would occur where freedom is crucial to the survival of the society. Failure of the New Right journalists to understand this is in itself distressing.

8

The Rage Against Leviathan

King George is alive and well in Washington.
    —Former Los Angeles Police Chief Ed Davis

Our Enemy, the State
    —title of a book (1935) by Albert Jay Nock

The New Right, a political revolt of the insecure and resentful, is the result, at least in part, of the incapacity of its adherents to come to terms with modern society—with the corporate state, with large business institutions, and with the organized labor movement. Despite their talk of defending free enterprise and sympathizing with the working man, the New Right is deeply distrustful of the institutions that exist to support business and labor. Since the "free enterprise" they evoke is largely mythic and cannot be said to exist anywhere in the world—which Paul Weyrich of the Committee for the Survival of a Free Congress readily admits—their movement is utopian and, as such, precisely the contrary of true conservatism. The remedy they prescribe for complex economic and social problems is destruction of the welfare state, another utopian vision. Their apparently paradoxical defense of unbridled capitalism and, at the same time, of the blue-collar factory worker is not cynical, but a manifestation of a deep ideological confusion that is characterized, nevertheless, by a certain consistency. That consistency is a hostility to bigness, extending, it seems, to all social and political institutions except the defense establishment. The defense establishment, they believe, is necessary to ward off a far greater evil—the monstrous superstate of the Soviet Union.

"Bigness" in government and in labor unions has become "badness" to the New Right. And, having discovered that modern capitalism, with its international contracts and government subsidies, is a partner, not an enemy, of big government, the New Right now sees big business as ominous, as well. Business, unable to permit government to withdraw from its "intervention" in the marketplace, has come to welcome regulation, which, frequently, protects existing industries and discourages competitive newcomers, thus encouraging the enmity of the New Right. Until the New Deal, business was seen as a defender of individualism and as a bulwark against the rise of the welfare state. Now, business seems to the Right to be a collaborator. The proliferating federal bureaucracy has also come to symbolize for the New Right a vast, unresponsive state that oppresses lower-middle-class Americans, a slow-moving Goliath of unelected civil servants who are, more and more, assuming authority once vested in elected officials. Bureaucracy is distant from the people—faceless, anonymous, enormous—bumbling yet authoritarian, playing an ever-greater role in the everyday lives of the citizens. They see the bureaucracy, like the Supreme Court, as an intermediary institution that intervenes between the people and their elected representatives.

While many Americans see the rise of the "affirmative state," or the "service state," or the welfare state as a costly and inefficient, but generally benevolent, presence, the New Right sees a Leviathan so gigantic and all-powerful as to engulf the nation, sapping the soul of the society, and existing for the benefit of a small clique of leaders of big government, big business, big labor, and, recently, big media. This revolt against these "four bogeymen" is, however, a revolt not only against "bigness" but all institutions, all orderly stabilizing structures, in favor of amorphous, undefined, but emotional attachments, an antisocial, antipolitical, anticonservative impulse linked to the New Right's emerging preference (see Chapter 13) for methods of direct, rather than representative, democracy.

In December 1978, a story in *The New Right Report* suggested the New Right's view of the power of the federal bureaucracy. Under the headline

MRS. TED STEVENS: ANOTHER VICTIM OF BIG GOVERNMENT

it reported that, while "the bureaucrats at the Federal Election Commission intended no such result, the wife of Sen. Ted Stevens (R-Alaska) is dead because of a little power grab by the F.E.C." *The New Right Report* stated that Stevens had convinced his daughter to postpone her wedding because the F.E.C. had ruled that costs would be counted as campaign expenditures. "Had the long arm and small mind of the Federal bureaucracy not been involved, the wedding would have taken place in the fall, as intended, when the weather would have been better." (Alerted by the Senator's office that they had seriously botched the facts, the editors later printed a retraction.)

The New Right would like the federal bureaucracy dismantled—transferring, as Weyrich put it, much of the functions of the federal agencies "to the private sector."

THE TRADITIONAL MODEL

For most Americans, conservatism has perhaps best been understood as a political and economic philosophy rooted in big business and against big government and big labor, for the rich, against the poor. For decades, conservative Republican politicians did serve the interests of business.

Old Guard Republicanism and "Old Right" conservatism embraced a U.S. Chamber of Commerce—if not Chase Manhattan Bank—veneration of business interests, "disposable income," the role of profits, and the necessity of economic growth and technological progress. For conservatives concerned with social mobility and individual opportunity, "free enterprise" was the key to getting ahead. A song of Young Americans for Freedom was only partly in jest:

> *God bless free enterprise,*
> *System divine.*
> *Stand beside her, don't deride her,*
> *Just so long as the profits are mine.*

Even *that* individualist conservatism was a corruption of classic conservatism, which rejected what Peter Viereck called "the rival materialisms—Marxism and laissez-faire capitalism." Traditional American conservative thought, represented by Russell Kirk, understood that laissez-faire did not derive from conservatism, but from Gladstone and Manchester liberalism in England, and Jacobinism in France. As Viereck has written:

> Wherever the armies of the anti-conservative French Revolution went, one of their first thoughts was to abolish the allegedly "outworn" guilds and establish laissez faire. This was their means of establishing the middle class in power.

Traditionalists like Kirk and Viereck, dominant in England and on the European continent, placed the highest value on an orderly society—one that was often hierarchical—stressing community, stability, and social harmony, without which, they believed, a free society was impossible. Freedom could not be both ends and means. Conservatives like Disraeli sought to ameliorate the vast upheaval of the Industrial Revolution, while liberals like Gladstone celebrated its "progress." Milton Friedman, guru of free-enterprise philosophy, and an adviser in 1964 to Senator Barry Goldwater, freely acknowledges the liberal political origins of "free enterprise," in his book *Capitalism and Freedom* (1975), identifying the values he espouses as "liberalism":

> As it developed in the late eighteenth and early nineteenth centuries, the intellectual movement that went under the name of liberalism emphasized freedom as the ultimate goal and the individual as the ultimate entity in society. It supported laissez faire at home as a means of reducing the role of the state in economic affairs and thereby enlarging the role of the individual; it supported free trade abroad as a means of linking the nations of the world together peacefully and democratically. In political matters it supported the development of representative government and of parliamentary institutions, reduction in the arbitrary power of the state, and protection of the civil freedoms of individuals.

Thus, the chief spokesman for right-wing economics is a self-described "liberal." The traditional American conservatives like Kirk, however, feared the dynamism of unbridled capitalism. Kirk once said that the American economy might be "too efficient for life on a truly human scale," criticizing what Robert Nisbet called "the corrosive, antisocial laissez-faire of the nineteenth century. . . ." It has weakened social bonds, he said, and accelerated "the aggrandizement of the omnicompetent State," correctly noting that economic questions concern nothing short of the relationship of man to the state. Whittaker

Chambers once informed William F. Buckley, Jr., that if conservatives did not address the dynamism of the American economy, which he called "profoundly anticonservative," conservatism in America would be "foredoomed to futility and petulance." Later Buckley himself chastised Friedman for elevating the free-market system to a "dogmatic theology."

With champions like Barry Goldwater and Ronald Reagan, the individualist, libertarian impulse prevailed over the traditionalist school which, lacking a constituency, has survived if at all almost as an intellectual underground. It is from that individualist impulse extending beyond Goldwater and Reagan that the profoundly antipolitical nature of the New Right has derived, resulting in hostility to the government and to the political function itself.

REVOLT AGAINST THE MARKETPLACE

The New Right's growing hostility does have historical precedents. Midwestern GOP conservatives like Robert Taft traditionally expressed a gnawing antipathy for large business institutions associated with New York City, the Eastern seaboard, and the banks. Conservative Republicans, while generally sympathetic to business, grew resentful of the Rockefeller forces at Republican conventions, which, internationalist in their attitudes, opposed the Midwestern conservatives. They became increasingly suspicious of business as it adjusted profitably to the growth of big government.

Gregg Hilton, executive director of the Conservative Victory Fund and the son of a millionaire multinational businessman with offices in New York's Pan Am Building, has rejected his father's liberalism and his father's view of business and government. "The Establishment has changed," Hilton told me.

> It used to be conservative. It was pro-free enterprise, antigovernment. But today it is pro-government, anti-free enter-

prise. Business today, as my father practices it, is tied up with government, dependent on government for cooperation in its international dealings, subsidies, grants, you name it. As you might guess, my dad is a Rockefeller Republican and something of a liberal. But I'm not. I don't agree with this partnership of government and business, and I'm a conservative. I'm for competition, free enterprise. He's not.

This realization is coupled with the New Right's status concerns and their desire to bolster their ranks by appealing to Wallaceite Democrats and to blue-collar workers. As Republican activist Julian Gammon told me:

What you have to realize is that the New Right types don't like Big Business for reasons that don't have a great deal to do with economics or public policy. These people don't like business, generally, because it conjures up all kinds of associations they don't like—Ivy League educations, Wall Street, New York, banks, internationalism, old wealth as opposed to nouveau riche. Many of these New Right people, after all, seem to come from lower-middle-class backgrounds and these things make them kind of uncomfortable.

In a "bill of indictment," Patrick Buchanan in *Conservative Digest* summarized complaints against business. He cited "the obscene haste with which Big Business acts to meet Soviet requests for the latest in Western machinery or technology," quoting Alexander Solzhenitsyn's speeches in the United States that referred to the "alliance between our communist leaders and your capitalists." Conservatives, neoconservatives, and New Rightists alike have viewed with similar dismay the eagerness of American corporations to help build the Soviet war machine, and to trade with Mainland China and more recently Castro's Cuba. Reporting from Havana in 1978, Allan Ryskind, *Human Events'* Washington editor, described the business executives who participated with him in the East–West Trade Council excursion:

Like the Communist Lenin and the capitalist Schumpeter, the Cubans believe the businessmen will sell the rope for their own execution. And many of the capitalists I traveled with furnished little evidence to disabuse the Cubans of this notion. Whether they considered themselves "hard-headed," "anti-Communist" or "liberal," they were eagerly seeking profits, and most seemed particularly uncomfortable when politically sensitive subjects were raised, apparently on the grounds that it might queer any trade deal.

Business interests have failed Americans on the domestic front as well, Buchanan wrote, by their participation in a *ménage à trois* with "radical politics and hard-core pornography."

While conservative, probusiness publications like *National Review* are barely able to sustain themselves financially, Buchanan complained, many corporations whose existence the conservative publications defend pay millions of dollars each year to purchase advertisements in *Playboy, Penthouse, Rolling Stone,* and other publications, in effect, "subsidizing and contributing to the degradation of moral values" as well as providing a forum for opinions often hostile to capitalism. The October 1976 issue of *Penthouse,* he noted, featured full-page advertisements from major American businesses, along with an interview with radical activist Tom Hayden, who argued that Americans "must confront the concentration of economic power and wealth in this country" and smash "the system that gives rise to war." Another issue of the same magazine described Cesar Chavez of the United Farm Workers as "one of the few uncorrupted heroes we have left . . . a continuing inspiration to common people everywhere who are being ripped off . . . by mindless corporations." (Perhaps, Buchanan wrote, "mindless" is an accurate description of the producers of Jim Beam, Wild Turkey, Smirnoff Vodka, Benson and Hedges, and others who advertise in such publications.)

The worst fears of the New Rightists were confirmed in April 1979, when Joseph Coors's Colorado brewery purchased advertisements in *The Advocate,* a leading newspaper for homosexuals, informing readers that the company "does not discriminate on the basis of sexual preference" and "neither the Coors family nor the company has ever donated one dime to Anita Bryant or the Briggs Initiative or in any way supported these types of campaigns." Articles in the issue were devoted to "The Lesbian Legacy" and "Coming to Grips with Sadomasochism." Coors himself was promptly denounced by the Reverend Jerry Falwell and Briggs himself, whose comments were quoted in *The Spotlight,* the monthly newspaper of the far-right Liberty Lobby. "The fact that Coors would lend support to the homosexual community and solicit their economic participation degrades them in my opinion to the lowest echelon of their industry," Falwell told *The Spotlight.*

American business interests, in the view of the New Right, have aided and abetted a domestic enemy more awesome than the skin magazines or homosexual news-sheets, creating through their advertising dollars a monster institution oppressing the people: big media. "Conservative resentment of Big Business," according to Buchanan, is caused also by the fact that "our common adversary—the networks and the national press—are being subsidized by the advertising dollars of the Fortune 500." Right-wing animosity toward the networks is nothing new, but a common hostility toward business and the media is. Since most Americans—up to 75 percent, by some accounts—rely on the network news as their primary source of information about their government and society, they are, Buchanan believes, exposed to views that are "well to the left of the electorate," especially in the case of views toward business. New Right opinions get such short shrift on television, William Rusher argued in *The Making of the New Majority Party,* that the "fairness doctrine" (generally viewed by conservatives as an unwarranted example of meddlesome governmental regulation) should be "vigorously enforced" to redress the imbalance:

> Beyond that, the anti-trust laws already on the books can and should be used to prevent any single individual or corporation

from acquiring a monopoly position through multiple ownership of newspapers, radio and TV stations in a given area.

Rusher tends to support "busting up Big Media."

American corporations, the New Right believes, simply
lack the foresight and common sense to defend their own
interests. In addition to subsidizing the major networks and
the glossy publications like *Penthouse* and *Playboy*, they also
pour millions of dollars into the Corporation for Public
Broadcasting, although, as Buchanan said, "left-wing journalists have turned public television into their private pork bar-
rel." They subsidize American colleges and universities
"where America's past is derided in the history department as
racist and imperialist, and America's free enterprise system is
damned in the department of economics as exploitative and
unjust." In short, while "the conservative community and the
business community have long confronted a common foe, the
conservative, at considerable political cost, has been battling
that foe—while the businessman has been trying to buy him
off." This is nowhere so apparent as in the way corporations
and their affiliated political arms contribute to political candidates. Business interests, rather than spending their money to
elect probusiness candidates to public office, often invest in
incumbents regardless of their political records. In 1977,
Conservative Digest, relying on research by *The New Right
Report,* reported that a number of political action committees tied to business organizations gave an overwhelming percentage of their contributions to Democrats. The U.S.
League of Savings Associations, for instance, contributed
$129,190 to political candidates, 79.7 percent of whom were
Democrats—many of them liberals. The American Optomet-
ric Association contributed 85.6 percent of its $175,019 to
Democrats as well. As *The New Right Report* editor Morton
Blackwell wrote: "The shocking fact is that, with some notable exceptions, corporations and associations have compiled a
sorry record of inactivity, waste and self-destructive support
of their enemies. . . ."

Most of the existing business-oriented PACs put their money on "powers that be." Their pattern of giving shows they were lobbying, not trying to elect legislators with a pro-free enterprise philosophy.

Many of the corporate and association PACs gave most of their money to the same liberals who were receiving major support from big labor. In many cases, the pattern was pronounced: Those handing out the corporate and association PAC money were activist liberals, hostile to the maintenance of the free enterprise system.

The conclusion was inescapable: "The time has come," Buchanan wrote, "for conservatives to end their politically costly, all too often uncritical support for Big Business—and to draft new treaty terms for the old alliance." The Right can no longer afford to be perceived as "the obedient foot soldiers of the Fortune 500."

There was an undeniable hint of cynicism in all this, though much sincerity, too. "The time has come to get the Fortune 500 off our backs," Nevada Senator Paul Laxalt began telling audiences. "In the past we conservatives paraded all those Chamber of Commerce candidates with the Mobil Oil billboards strapped to their backs," Paul Weyrich told *Time,* and it didn't work. Buchanan, writing in his nationally syndicated newspaper column, observed that for years Republicans had fought as "volunteers" in business's battles—a pattern that would soon end.

Whether the adversary be organized labor or disorganized demonstrator, Naderite or radical, Socialist or environmentalist, Big Business could rely upon its Republican infantry to close ranks and march across that wheatfield up Cemetery Hill. Where has the alliance gotten the GOP? Indelibly identified as the party of the privileged, the party of the country club conservative, the party of Big Business. . . .

The oil companies came under increasing attack as profits soared in 1978 and 1979. Laxalt, national chairman of Ronald

Reagan's 1976 bid for the Republican presidential nomination, made headlines calling for independent audits of the major oil companies. Kevin Phillips noted that activists of the Right who attacked "multinational corporations, suing to block ambassadorial appointments for bank directors and doing a host of other things" are coming "surprisingly close to the tradition of the old Western GOP progressives—the Hiram Johnsons and William Borahs." Many of the new critics of big business were, like Laxalt, from Western states. Senator Orrin Hatch of Utah, for example, called business leaders "gutless wonders." "Too many of our top corporate leaders," he said, "are inheritors who have never known what it's like to put everything on the line, to meet a payroll."

Not a little disturbed by these developments was John Chamberlain, the respected conservative journalist and literary critic, who detected a "distinct whiff of a new right-wing Populism" at the 1977 Conservative Political Action Conference in Washington. The danger, Chamberlain wrote, is that "this campaign against Big Business will become indiscriminant." True conservatives, he warned, should take a long hard look at the system within which these reviled business leaders must operate or risk "untold damage to the free-wheeling atmosphere that has made American production the envy of the world." In the contemporary business world—that of the corporate state—the executive

> must answer to government for all his personnel policies—hiring, firing, promotion, wages, pensions and unionization. He must kowtow to the Security and Exchange Commission, the Federal Trade Commission and the Internal Revenue Service. He can't merge with another company or acquire a new subsidiary without consulting the Department of Justice. He must put up with OSHA [the Occupational Safety and Health Administration] and submit his advertising and sales practices to the FTC [Federal Trade Commission] for ratification. He is restricted in his use of land, and must bow to the environmentalists even when they are crazy. And he must raise capital in a

world that discriminates against profits and no longer supports
the sanctity of contracts.

The New Right, in other words, must come to terms with the
corporate state—with a world far more complex than most
New Rightists are accustomed to. As the American economy
has passed through the Industrial Age and into a postindustrial
one, it has long since ceased to be primarily entrepreneurial in
nature and, as such, paeans to "free enterprise" appear increasingly romantic and utopian. This attachment to "free enterprise" (Senator Schmitt has described today's big businessmen
as "supporters of incumbents who are tearing down our free
enterprise system," and fundraiser Richard A. Viguerie has
said that his economic views "are that of a traditional, economic conservative, laissez-faire, minimum government interference in our lives"), according to conservative writer Richard
Whalen, "spares them the difficulty of serious thought." But
"serious thought" assumes that their attitudes toward business
are primarily economic; the attitudes of the New Right toward
big business are rather primarily political, manifestations of
deep-seated hostility to large institutions that threaten their
romantic individualism.

UPHEAVAL VERSUS ORDER

In the unexamined ideology of the New Right there are many
apparent inconsistencies. While the New Rightists attack big
business and the corporate state, they are nevertheless intolerant of the trade union movement, which has evolved to redress
the imbalance between the individual worker who, like the
New Rightist, feels threatened by large institutions, and the
business community. Organizations like the Americans
Against Union Control of Government and the National Right
to Work Committee fight the organized labor movement, de-
picting it as "Big Labor" run by "Labor Bosses" and "Union-
goonism." They continue to resist institutions like the trade

union movement, despite their function of restoring to the individual worker some control over his own life, at a time (ironically) when the Republican party and groups like the American Enterprise Institute are coming to a more enlightened view of unions. The New Rightists invariably point to Great Britain as a society ruined by the growing power of labor, forgetting the conservative defense of organized labor in Frank Tannenbaum's *A New Philosophy of Labor.* In an age in which the extended family has disintegrated under the pressure of industrialism,

> the union returns to the worker his "society. . . ." Institutionally, the trade union movement is an unconscious effort to harness the drift of our time and reorganize it around the cohesive identity that men working together always achieve. Trade unionism is the conservative movement of our time. It is the counter-revolution. Unwittingly, it has turned its back on most of the political and economic ideas that have nourished Western Europe and the United States during the last two centuries. In practice, though not in words, it denies the heritage that stems from the French Revolution and from English liberalism. It is also a complete repudiation of Marxism. . . .

Organized labor, in that view, is one of the institutions in society that create order within chaos, and give meaning to the lives of those who are part of it. The New Right's anticonservative ideology rebels against it; though sympathetic to the individual worker and the individual businessman (the kind "who has met a payroll"), the New Right rebels against the institutions—the organized labor movement and the large corporation—in which the businessman and laborer function.

The New Right's radical individualism and its anti-institutional impulse militate against order and stability, and encourage rootlessness and upheaval—the inevitable consequence of the "free enterprise" the New Right champions. The New Rightists have thus become the celebrants of change, of rootlessness, of progress—all that classical conservatives deplore. It is a reversal of roles. Progress, as Garry Wills has noted, has generally been a "liberal preserve" and only recently has been seized upon by right-wingers who now accuse their liberal opponents of a "failure of nerve" and of a lack of will and a lack of confidence in their ability to face the challenges of the future. Many contemporary liberals have come to embrace "no-growth" economics, austerity, "limits," while right-wingers assert that whatever is technologically possible ought to be done. In the case of nuclear power, for example, liberals are urging caution and prudence, right-wingers urging enterprise.*

Along similar lines, right-wingers have mercilessly ridiculed "eco-freaks" (their term for environmentalists)—those, in their view, who are dedicated to keeping things as they are.

It is in his ability to uphold the non-"Manchester liberal" conservatism of Burke, Disraeli, Irving Babbitt, and others that George F. Will—the New Right's *least* favorite conservative pundit—has made such a significant contribution. Will, in what is considered an unfathomable heresy, takes issue with the New Right's individualist, democratic ideology and, in particular, its notion of the government as Leviathan. At once avoiding the romanticism of some of the dreamier postwar conservative traditionalists, Will has upheld within a distinctly American context the strain of conservatism that is, in its economics, neither plutocratic nor populist. Criticized by many right-wing activists, he has unapologetically conceded that his conservatism is not theirs. Theirs, he has written, is not conservatism at all, but "a radically antipolitical ideology, decayed Jeffersonianism characterized by a frivolous hostility toward the state, and lacking the traditional conservative appreciation of the dignity of the political vocation and the grandeur of its responsibilities." These self-styled conservatives assume that "a large government is an *inherently* liberal device, *inherently* hostile to conservative values."

---

*Involved in the New Right's determination to go forward with nuclear power and other technological advances, it seems, is a concern that America remain a world leader and a fear that, without nuclear power, the United States will be continually dependent upon other (often hostile) countries for its energy sources. America, they believe, must remain "Number One."

But this is only true if freedom is the only conservative value, and if freedom means only the absence of restraints applied by government. And if that is what conservatism asserts, it is a stone-cold anachronism, as dead as the nineteenth century liberalism it resembles. It is an apolitical philosophy irrelevant to the government that has evolved in response to Americans' desires.

True conservatives

distrust and try to modulate social forces that work against the conservation of traditional values. But for a century the dominant conservatism has uncritically worshiped the most transforming force, the dynamism of the American economy.

This uncritical worship of "free enterprise"—"institutionalized restlessness, an engine of perpetual change"—has led to "an anarchy of self-interestedness" that may have reached its low in the much-publicized tax revolt. Even before Proposition 13 swept to victory in California, Will wrote:

What is called "conservatism" might better be called infantilism. Those of us blessed with small children recognize childishness when we see it. Increasingly the nation, like a child, wills the end without willing the means to the end. The end is a full platter of government services. The means to that end is the energetic government that does the inevitable regulating and taxing. Today's "conservatism"? The average voter has looked into his heart of hearts, prayed long and hard, and come to the conclusion that it is high time the government cut his *neighbor's* benefits.

Support of this individualistic, "free enterprise" politics, writes British Tory Henry Fairlie, is "untenable" for true conservatives. American "free enterprisers" have become champions of the "unrestrained individualism that has always been opposed by traditional conservatism."

To almost all that the English conservatism has always loathed in Adam Smith—especially his view of man as individualistic and hedonistic, competitive and acquisitive—the American conservative gives his support.

The American New Rightist, therefore, has placed himself in the unfortunate position, one wholly at odds with traditional conservatism,"of defending a society of isolated atoms," with "too little sense of himself as a social being in a public." This kind of conservative "is reduced to defending the private at the cost of the public, the individual at the cost of the social, self-interest at the cost of communal interest: in short, his concerns are the very opposite of what they should be."

The New Rightist's view of his own government as Leviathan, and his rage against it, are natural outgrowths of his radical individualism—and, being antipolitical, render him impotent before it.

9

Republican Fratricide

announcer: *do you think the time is ripe for a new*
political party?
archy: *it is more than ripe*
it is rotten
—Don Marquis, *The Lives and*
Times of Archy & Mehitabel

Resentments against the East, simmering within the Republican party since the 1940s, boiled over in the late 1970s in a revolt by Midwestern conservatives and impatient New Rightists of the West and Southwest against the party's leadership, perceived by them as too closely affiliated with the East, New York City, the banks, big business, and, of course, the Rockefellers. The result has further weakened a party already weak and at a time when, many serious political scientists believe, the party system in America, so crucial to national political stability, is itself in frightening disrepair.

225

A sympathetic observer of the American Right, Richard J. Whalen, observes in *Taking Sides* (1974) that conservatives outside the East "had long shown a deep-seated inferiority complex growing out of a generation of frustration within the Republican party."

> Money was the taproot of hostility toward New York. Well-to-do conservatives in the Midwest and Southwest had nothing in common with the Populists of yesteryear, except a feeling akin to the old agrarian dread of the money power of the metropolis. Mention of the 'Chase Bank' in conservative circles brought instant recognition; it was the command post of the liberal plutocracy. Goldwater's remark that the country would suffer little loss if the Eastern seaboard were sawed off and set adrift belonged in this context. He first made the quip as a Phoenix department store executive who could not get Eastern banks to accept his commercial paper.

Suggesting the animosity of this struggle was a memo drafted in 1979 by Conservative Victory Fund director Gregg Hilton and circulated among select New Right leaders listing "Grievances against Republican National Committee and other affiliated groups," noting especially the way money was distributed between liberal (Eastern) Republicans and right-wing (Midwestern) Republicans by the National Republican Congressional Committee (NRCC) and the National Republican Senatorial Committee (NRSC):

> 1) The RNC, NRCC, NRSC all raised substantial amounts of money to fight the Panama Canal Treaties. Instead of using one penny to fight the treaties by supporting the [conservative-sponsored] Truth Squad, most of the profits went to feed the bureaucracies of the various organizations, and some even went to people like Howard Baker, Ed Brooke, and Clifford Case and Mark Hatfield, all of whom supported the treaties.
> 2) In 1977 the NRSC raised money by polling contributors on national defense issues. The letter was signed by Howard Baker,

who supported the Panama Canal treaties and is undecided on SALT. A number of contributors were upset to learn that their checks were deposited, but their surveys were thrown out without ever being tabulated. When asked to explain, the NRSC said it was a clerical error, but the individual who threw out the polls said he was told to by his superiors. Clearly, it was nothing more than a gimmick (sic) to get money from conservative contributors and give it to liberal senators. . . .

4) The RNC also attempted to raise money by using labor law reform in one of its direct mail pieces. The RNC didn't explain why NRSC Chairman Bob Packwood and Minority Leader Ted Stevens voted for cloture.

5) So far in 1978, the NRSC and the NRCC has raised more money than it can give to candidates by law. What are they doing with it?

6) One thing the NRCC is doing with their money is hiring political aides for Gerald Ford to help in his 1980 presidential bid.

7) During 1977 and early 1978 attacks on New Right organizations were traced directly back to the RNC. While Bill Brock said he was going to put a stop to the attacks, at a staff meeting, he in fact also joined the attack by saying the New Right was wasting money and that the RNC was more "efficient," a laughable proposition to anyone who has visited the RNC. . . .

10) Press reports reveal that Wilma Goldstein (an RNC aide) told candidates not to use tax limitation and other conservative issues in (sic) their campaigns, and that NRCC field director, March Miller, urged candidates to avoid "traditional outmoded GOP issues such as free enterprise and national defense." . . .

12) The RNC has also initiated a program under the leadership of Pete DuPont to recruit "non-ideological" candidates for state and local offices. Assuming they are successful, (sic) it is only a matter of time before these non-ideological candidates rise through the system and become non-ideological congressmen and senators.

13) Wyatt Stewart, an employee of the NRC, has made a regular habit of attacking New Right organizations by accusing them of being administratively inefficient and eating up most money raised through direct mail costs. In fact the opposite is

true. For example, for the two year period (1976–77) the NRCC gave out approximately 17% of the funds it raised to candidates, while CVF (Conservative Victory Fund) gave 26% and NCPAC (National Conservative Political Action Committee) gave 25%. . . .

16) RNC Co-Chairman, Mary Crisp, is well known for her attacks on New Right groups, CFTR (Citizens for the Republic) and conservatives in general. She also supports extension of the ERA and was instrumental in using RNC facilities to assist the recent march on Washington supporting the ERA.

18) How much money have Charles Percy, Mark Hatfield, Clifford Case, Ed Brooke and other liberals received from the RNC and NRSC? Wasn't it (at least in part) money that was supposed to go to stop the Panama Canal treaties? . . .

24) Any objective source will confirm that the Republican groups sat on their hands and raised money during fights over Paul Warnke, the congressional pay raise, the Carter Electoral Reforms, the Panama Canal treaties, and Labor Law Reform; and that the New Right groups organized and executed most of the activity that was brought to bear.

The message is clear: The Republican leadership, the New Right says, is well aware of the appeal of the right-wing pitch and quite willing to raise money for its campaign coffers on the basis of that pitch. Nevertheless, when the money comes in, the Republican leadership, still under the control of the party's liberal wing and tied to its Eastern, Rockefeller elements, uses the money to advance the careers of the liberal and moderate Republicans.

In July 1979 the New Rightists, at the prompting of Conservative Victory Fund director Gregg Hilton, author of the memo, plotted legal action against the Republican party and the "turkey triumvirate of Brock, Rhodes, and Baker," as Hilton called the GOP leadership, for what the New Rightists believed to be "fraudulent" fund-raising. Hilton and others discussed the plans at New Right "Kingston" meetings, and met with lawyers of the Washington Legal Foundation, the right-wing public interest law firm, to pursue the tantalizing idea. They discarded the plan after the memo was leaked to the Republican National Committee.

THE WAR AGAINST THE ROCKEFELLERS

For almost half a century, the Midwestern and Eastern wings of the Republican party have been engaged in an intense struggle for control of the party, accounts of which by New Rightists have given rise to an entire mythology of recent Republican history. In recent years the hate object of the New Right in this struggle has been Nelson Rockefeller, but he is only a symbol of what Phyllis Schlafly in her 1964 book *A Choice Not an Echo*—a version of that mythology—referred to as "secret kingmakers" of the Eastern business community who have "manipulated and controlled Republican National Conventions" since 1936. That year the "eastern elite," knowing they could not defeat the Midwestern Republicans, then "clamoring for recognition," threw their support to Governor Alfred E. Landon of Kansas. When Landon was defeated, Schlafly wrote, "the New York kingmakers breathed a collective sigh of relief that the Republican Party had escaped passing into control of the midwest." Indeed, the only function of these Eastern Republicans, right-wing theorists believe, has been to deny election and control of the party to its more conservative Midwesterners. As William Rusher wrote in *The Making of the New Majority Party,* the liberal minority within the Republican party "has always been large enough to compel a certain amount of compromise or adjustment *in its direction,*" making it impossible for the party right-wingers to "mount a convincing attack on the nonproducing liberal verbalists and their welfare constituency." The history of Republican failure has been "little more than a record of the compromises made by conservative majorities . . . to appease a liberal minority whose sole effective function has been to insure the defeat of conservatism."

The leader of the Midwestern wing of the party throughout

these years was Senator Robert A. Taft, son of President William Howard Taft, whose presidential ambitions were thwarted five times by the party's liberals. In 1940, to defeat Taft, a conservative isolationist, the Easterners settled on Wendell Willkie, a New York City attorney born in Iowa who became a Republican only months before the GOP convention, and after a spectacular build-up by Henry Luce and Time, Inc., who exemplified the Eastern internationalists. As Schlafly has written:

> The kingmakers did not care whether Willkie won or lost. All they cared was to make sure that they had on both tickets an eastern internationalist candidate who would continue Roosevelt's foreign policy so that the voters would not have a choice on the great issue of entering the European War. Their objective was to make sure that, if by chance a Republican should win, he would be a man the secret kingmakers could control.

The Easterners foiled the Midwestern conservatives in 1944 as well, throwing their support to New York Governor Thomas E. Dewey, who had embraced the internationalism of the big businessmen. That year, Taft had stepped aside to allow Ohio's junior senator, John W. Bricker, also a conservative, to become the candidate. But just before the balloting, Bricker agreed to drop out of the race and accept Dewey's vice-presidential nomination, to Taft's considerable consternation.

In the 1946 off-year elections, the Republicans asked if the voters had "Had Enough?" of postwar shortages. The voters *had,* and the GOP took control of both houses of Congress for the first time since the administration of Herbert Hoover. Yet with the presidency within their grasp, the New York–controlled GOP ignored the advice of Teddy Roosevelt's daughter, Alice Roosevelt Longworth ("You can't make a soufflé rise twice") and nominated Dewey again in 1948, shutting out Taft and the Midwesterners. Once again Dewey failed to capture the White House. In 1952, the party selected popular war hero Dwight D. Eisenhower, born in Abilene, Kansas, but controlled by the New Yorkers. Eisenhower, Schlafly wrote, had not "the slightest idea of the tactics used by the little clique determined to steal the nomination [from Taft] and push him into the presidency." "Fantastic propaganda" was used against the Ohio conservative by the "vicious and dishonest 'hidden persuaders' " of the East.

In 1956, the Eastern elitists, fearing for Ike's health, wanted Richard Nixon, then vice-president and a gut-fighter from the West, off the ticket; they distrusted him, Schlafly tells us, because "he was not a creature of their making, therefore he was not beholden to them." But Nixon, the prosecutor of Alger Hiss, an Eastern elitist (spy or not), proved too popular with GOP regulars, and the Easterners had to wait for 1960. That year, however, Nixon outmaneuvered Nelson Rockefeller, that symbol of the GOP establishment. To conservatives, Rockefeller had come to represent everything liberal in the GOP. He was a scion of great wealth, an internationalist in foreign policy, a "big spender" in policy, a "progressive" sympathetic to the civil rights movement, and devoted to blocking the conservatives. Nixon took pains to make himself acceptable to the Easterners, who clearly preferred him to explicit right-wingers like Goldwater. On the eve of the 1960 convention, after the platform committee had drawn up a document acceptable to moderates and conservatives, Nixon traveled to New York for a secret meeting at Nelson Rockefeller's Fifth Avenue apartment. There the two hammered out a compromise platform of their own, which they proceeded to foist onto the convention. It tilted so far in the direction of the Rockefeller liberals that Arizona Senator Goldwater called it "a surrender to Rockefeller" and the "Munich of the Republican party." Worse yet, he named as his 1960 running mate Henry Cabot Lodge, Jr., "a Boston Brahmin," as William Rusher described him, more liberal "if possible" than Rockefeller. "Once again," wrote Richard Whalen, "someone in New York City had the last word."

The "Rockefeller–Nixon alliance," Schlafly said, "meant that Nixon had paid the price that Taft had been unwilling to pay. He had purged himself of his independence and made himself acceptable to the New York kingmakers." From that moment on, Nixon was never wholly accepted by either wing of the party.

Nixon himself was ambivalent in his allegiances. A small-town boy from Orange County, California, Nixon had begun his political life in the slashing, Old West sheriff style of right-wing politics, carving out a reputation as a "dirty trickster" in congressional campaigns against Helen Gahagan Douglas and Jerry Voorhis. His role in the Hiss case strengthened this aggressive image, and as Eisenhower's vice-president, he won plaudits from the Midwestern conservatives when he staged his "kitchen debate" with Nikita Khrushchev. But on the other "Eastern" side was his "Compact of Fifth Avenue."

The high mark of the postwar period for right-wingers was 1964—a year of disaster for the party itself. The victory of rightist ideologue Barry Goldwater over Nelson Rockefeller at an ill-tempered and stormy convention in San Francisco marked "an historic turning point" in American politics, William Rusher wrote. It demonstrated

> with mathematical finality, that a Republican candidate did not need the support of New York, Massachusetts, or Pennsylvania to win the party's nomination. He didn't even need the backing of that mysterious entity called "Wall Street": There were new concentrations of financial power—in Houston, Los Angeles, and elsewhere—that had money, too, and were prepared to put it where their mouths were. Above all, he didn't need to be a relative liberal, or curry favor with the liberals, to carry a Republican convention. On the contrary, it was conservative slogans and issues and principles that appealed to the coalition newly dominant in the GOP.

That the GOP could not win a national election without a broader constituency seemed not to bother the Right; they seemed to prefer losing, and so embraced a view that was, at heart, antipolitical.

In 1968, the Right was once again out in the cold. Nixon, defeated for the governorship of California six years before, had migrated to New York City and joined a Wall Street law firm, further distancing himself from his right-wing roots. He successfully sought the Republican nomination as the "New Nixon" from his Eastern base, but was briefly challenged by Ronald Reagan, only two years into his first term as California governor and promoted, in vain, by GOP right-wingers like Rusher. The new Eastern Nixon recognized Red China and imposed wage and price controls, but the old Western Nixon surfaced again when he ran for his second term in 1972, setting up his own Committee to Re-Elect the President to circumvent the official Republican National Committee. Those Eastern intellectuals who never bought the "New Nixon" image got a revenge many of them had sought since Nixon was revealed as a "dirty trickster" in his congressional races against Douglas and Voorhis and put the finger on Hiss. Only when the Old Nixon faced impeachment or resignation did the right-wingers reclaim him. Traditional conservatives like George Will and New York Senator James Buckley, however, quickly withdrew their support when the president's flouting of the law became apparent, Buckley angering the New Right when he called for Nixon to resign from the presidency. It responded to the mood of paranoia, blaming the Eastern media and elitists and Republican moderates for the persecution and downfall of a president who had proved himself a vigilante, after all. Once again, the Right proved apolitical, cherishing disgrace and defeat as though it were victory.

It was precisely because Nixon *had* separated his re-election effort (CREEP) from the Republican National Committee that the party itself was able to salvage something of the wreckage he left when he resigned. The conflict between the Midwestern and Eastern wings of the party intensified, however, as both factions scrambled to reclaim the rubble. Gerald Ford, a moderately conservative congressman from Grand Rapids, Michigan, immediately named Rockefeller as his vice-president. In the White House, Ford came under scathing rightist attack despite his moderately conservative record in the House where, many forget, he led the drive to impeach Supreme Court Justice William O. Douglas. Despite a vaguely conservative administration, the Right perceived his presidential and personal style as indecisive and incompetent. His tendency to appoint to government positions politicians and bureaucrats with ties to the GOP establishment prompted the American Conservative Union in 1975 to produce a disapproving study, "My Guys," documenting the "liberal" appointments. Worse still, a revisionist *Conservative Digest* article, under Governor Meldrim Thomson's by-line, said it was a "myth" that Ford had been a "conservative congressman" and has "carefully steered a middle-of-the-road course as president." The truth, he revealed, was that Ford "consistently favored a policy of compromise with the premises of the liberal establishment" and "the troika" that ruled America—"big government, big business and big labor"—and "its faithful servant, the news media." He had maintained "a left-of-center tilt" in his politics and in Congress usually opposed the GOP majority, siding with "the liberal opposition," repeatedly failing to "stand with the people *against* the giant concentrations of power—in government, the media, business, labor, education, foundations and elsewhere."

New Right resentments of the national leadership of the Republican party exploded in 1976 after two deeply disappointing developments. First, Gerald Ford—backed by the Rockefeller forces and the party leadership—edged out Ronald Reagan for the presidential nomination, despite the fact that Reagan had waged a hard-hitting and valiant challenge that actually won a majority of votes cast in GOP primaries. But, more important, in his effort to snatch the nomination from Ford, Reagan, whom most New Rightists favored, selected as his running mate Pennsylvania Senator Richard Schweiker— a politician clearly identified with the moderate wing of the party and, in fact, one of the most liberal members.

In his 1975 book, *The Making of the New Majority Party,* William Rusher excoriated Schweiker, along with Senators

Jacob Javits of New York, Charles Mathias of Maryland, Clifford Case of New Jersey, and Edward Brooke of Massachusetts, for their "purely nominal Republicanism." He linked these politicians either to "the Democratic Party, or the New York State Liberal Party, or Naderist consumerism, or John W. Gardner's 'nonpartisan' agency of liberal good works, Common Cause. They are culturally a world away from the ethos and concerns of social conservatives, and indeed represent much that the latter instinctively oppose." Ford, taking the offensive, called Reagan's selection "extreme," and managed, despite his own conservative reputation, to unite party liberals, moderates, and regulars (many of them conservatives who declined to bolt for Reagan) to win the nomination. Reagan's "sellout"—indeed, his need to balance his ticket with a liberal running mate —convinced right-wingers again of the liberal hammerlock on the Republican party. This was the last straw.

A PARTY OF THEIR OWN

Acting on the age-old dream of right-wingers to have a political party purged of liberals and under their own control, a number of New Right leaders decided to form such a party or, failing that, to take over an already existing splinter party. Sentiment for this kind of move had been brewing for some time; as early as 1975, the subject of abandoning the GOP had been seriously discussed by disaffected conservative Republicans who, at that year's Conservative Political Action Conference in Washington, appointed a Committee on Conservative Alternatives to investigate the possibility. They found much support for the idea, and Republican Congressman Robert E. Bauman of Maryland, founder and former national chairman of YAF and later to become the chairman of the American Conservative Union, summed up the anger of many of the participants when he declared that both major parties are vitually indistinguishable and, in their lack of coherent principled philosophies, corrupt and meaningless. Bauman announced:

It is the present party structure which has failed us all. Its operatives have demeaned a noble electoral system. Its functionaries have debased the currency of political debate through the glib gimmickry of expensive advertising campaigns. Its masters have made the Congress a state for preening demagogues and the presidency an imperial prize. It no longer deserves the allegiance of a free people.

There were tactical considerations as well for a new party, Richard Viguerie wrote in *Conservative Digest* in August 1975: "I understand marketing, and I don't believe that in my lifetime you will ever be able successfully to market the word 'Republican.' You could as easily sell Edsel or Typhoid Mary."

The Committee on Conservative Alternatives, dominated by traditionalist conservatives, failed to reject the new party outright, concluding that the idea should be "studied" further. A working paper distributed at a gathering of the American Conservative Union state chairmen in Chicago, however, called the new party concept "too high a price for conservatives to pay." Despite these poor omens, Viguerie was determined to make the move, and, on the last day of the Republican convention of 1976, he called a press conference in Kansas City to announce his intention to seek a spot on the presidential ticket of the American Independent party, formed in 1968 to aid the presidential ambitions of George Wallace.

Though he had never sought elective office before, Viguerie said he would accept the presidential or vice-presidential nomination of the AIP, apparently because no other prominent right-winger could be convinced to run. Two weeks later in Chicago, Viguerie and a handful of lieutenants launched an eleventh-hour bid to seize control of the American Independent party.

Accompanying Viguerie to the American Independent party convention in Chicago in September 1976 were New Right spokesmen William Rusher, Howard Phillips, Paul Weyrich, and Lee Edwards. As the convention's keynote speaker held forth, to thunderous applause, on the dangers of "atheistical political Zionism" ("the most insidious, far-reaching murderous force the world has ever known"), Viguerie's operatives moved briskly among the far-right delegates in their polyester leisure suits, passing out expensively printed campaign literature. In exchange for nominating Dallas newspaper columnist Robert Morris, a former attorney for the Senate Internal Security Subcommittee and described by Viguerie as "a real responsible intellectual person," as president and Viguerie as vice-president, the New Rightists offered the party use of the lucrative Viguerie mailing lists.

"The idea," reported the weekly *Human Events* a month later, "was to get at least 5 percent of the vote, which would qualify the party for subsidies from the Federal Election Commission both to assist with this year's campaign expenses and to guarantee federal support in 1980 as well. In this way they hoped to utilize the AIP's ballot positions in some 30 to 40 states this year to get a head start for a major new party effort four years down the road."

But the party regulars, a flinty and suspicious lot, resented the newcomers with their three-piece suits and slick campaign literature. They rejected the wooing by Morris and Viguerie to nominate their own favorite, former Georgia Governor Lester Maddox, whose distinction (William F. Buckley, Jr. has written) "lies in his expressed preference for hitting a Negro over the head with an axe rather than serve him a plate of fried chicken." Denied access to the party's organizational apparatus, the New Rightists decamped, later criticizing the party for, as Rusher wrote, "having lost its mind" in nominating Maddox. (If they had found anything objectionable about the party when its keynote speaker delighted the regulars with his anti-Semitic remarks or when the racist Maddox had the floor, they kept their objections to themselves.)

When Viguerie left with his mailing lists—the party never expected to get them anyway—the AIP regulars expressed relief at their escape. The party's chairman, Wisconsin attorney William K. Shearer, commented that he was reminded of "the girl who was targeted for a rape that didn't come off." As for the New Right money, Shearer stated, Viguerie "never gave us any. So it's just like my eating caviar. I haven't tasted fish eggs so I don't miss it." James J. Kilpatrick (hardly a captive of the "left-wing" press) was appalled at the New Right's eagerness to make common cause with the kooky splinter party and steered clear of the convention with its "gun nuts, food nuts, single-taxers, anti-fluoridationists, and a hundred passionate fellows who write in capital letters with red typewriter ribbons."

Thoroughly repudiated, the New Rightists returned to Washington intent on seizing what would be left of the Republican party after President Ford's defeat, and sat on their hands to ensure it. They determined to work within the Democratic party as well. Believing that inflation would skyrocket under either candidate, they hoped to be able to use the issue against the Democrats in 1978 and 1980, rather than defend "liberal" policies of a Republican administration. Indeed, one explanation for the attempt to co-opt the American Independent party is suggested by Howard Phillips's pledge "to work for the Republican Party's defeat" if it appealed to the liberalism represented by Schweiker—and, presumably, Gerald Ford.

During this period of turmoil and disillusionment, the impatient New Rightists would have done well to have reflected on the more truly conservative advice offered by Ohio Congressman John Ashbrook, who in 1972 challenged Richard Nixon for his party's presidential nomination. Commenting after the 1968 GOP victory on George Wallace's American Independent party candidacy, Ashbrook wrote in *National Review* that Wallace's entry into the presidential race

> amply demonstrates a frivolous attitude toward our two-party system, a system which has been a principal foundation of our national political stability. Conservatives should abandon that system only in the last contingency, when the possibility of achieving the conservative goals no longer exists within it. For we should know how unstable the multi-party European gov-

ernments have always been. We do not lightly toss aside our traditional way, the better way by far. There is room in our parties for disagreement, and a man can make his views count within his party—that is, unless his sole objective is personal notoriety and personal power.

Nevertheless, the idea of a new party has yet to die. In November 1979, former New Hampshire Governor Meldrim Thomson announced that he would seek the presidency in 1980 on a new "Constitution party" ticket.

ANTIPOLITICS

Convinced that the political system is corrupt, the New Rightists distrust and resent those who work within it, since those who do must compromise; and compromise means cooperation with the liberal enemy. Only the loners are pure. Consequently, any right-of-center politician to achieve a truly national stature is automatically suspect. "By the time they get into a position to help us, they are no longer one of us," M. Stanton Evans has explained. Those who work with the liberals are "soft" or "squishy."

The implications of the Right's antitraditional politics for the future of the Republican party are immense, given the GOP's current state of disorder and the opportunities for leadership that this disorder presents. With the old powers gone or debilitated, new leaders are emerging, but many of them have already been discarded by the New Right as compromisers to be avoided at all costs.

They don't want as a future party leader, for example, Senator Howard Baker of Tennessee, a relatively conservative politician who has courted a moderate image. Although the son-in-law of the honored GOP conservative and Senate Minority Leader Everett Dirksen, Baker symbolizes, to many right-wingers, compromise itself. He participated in the Senate Watergate Committee's lynching of Richard Nixon, and mention of his name at the 1979 Conservative Political Action Conference in Washington elicited hisses from the delegates. An ambitious politician who cultivates the status of statesman, Baker likes to hold his vote until the optimum moment. He has used this technique, knowing the life-or-death power his position could hold over the Carter Administration's initiatives in, for example, the Panama Canal controversies, but at the last moment he rescued the White House from a humiliating foreign policy defeat. He sought to use his considerable leverage to add amendments to the SALT II package. Such fine-tuning exasperates the New Right; it is a form of political strategy they do not understand. It can and does appear confusing and lily-livered to critics intent on a bold confrontation on principle. The right-wing *Chattanooga News-Free Press,* one of Baker's earliest and strongest supporters, did not endorse his successful bid for re-election in 1978. An editorial said that Baker "has too often misused his position to the detriment of the country," supporting among other mistakes the Panama Canal "surrender," American aid to Communist North Vietnam, "federal invasion of private property rights," a guaranteed annual income plan, and an "unconscionable congressional pay raise." *Human Events* has conceded that Baker has fought "a few good fights" for the GOP, as in the successful skirmish to stop Theodore Sorensen from heading the Central Intelligence Agency. Still, Baker's voting record was graded by the Americans for Constitutional Action as more liberal than 60 percent or more of the other Republican senators. As the *New Guard* noted in 1979:

> While Baker's campaign staff likes to emphasize his "leadership in the Senate," it will have trouble dispelling his negative image as a compromiser. His major problem in seeking the GOP nomination in 1980 will be with the dominant right wing of the party, to whom this image is especially repugnant. Of all the Republican candidates, only John Anderson is to Baker's left.

William Brock, once senator from Texas and later chairman of the Republican National Committee, provokes similar rightist anger for similar political maneuvering. The mention of his name during his tenure at the Republican National Committee also brought hisses and boos at the 1978 Conservative Political Action Conference in Washington. His inexplicable (to the New Right) determination to work with all elements of the Republican party infuriates them; his attempts to "broaden the base" of the GOP suggests a willingness to tolerate liberals.

John Anderson, Republican congressman from Illinois, having taken it upon himself to attack the New Right in public utterances is a special hate object, the object of right-wing purge efforts in 1978 and 1980. He is distrusted also, however, by conservative Republicans for the not-so-subtle ideological changes he has undergone since coming to Washington in 1960. Republicans who challenged Anderson's claim to leadership pointed to the fact that in 1978 he voted more frequently with the Democrats than with his own party colleagues.

Senator Robert Dole of Kansas, who endeared himself to the GOP Right with his slashing campaign as President Ford's running mate in 1975, tried to moderate his tough image in his bid for the nomination in 1980. Although he is anti-SALT and antiabortion, Dole tried, his second time around, to stress the socially beneficial aspects of his free-market economics. The Right viewed him with suspicion for such "pandering."

The New Right appears also to distrust rising Republican Jack Kemp despite Kemp's solidly conservative record in Congress. Kemp has made a mistake, in the view of the rightists, in surrounding himself with neoconservative intellectuals like Irving Kristol, and, rather than railing against the welfare state, preaching a conciliatory economics that holds that, with sufficiently large tax cuts, the level of government services can be maintained at current levels or even expanded. (See Chapter 8.) Still, few political analysts questioned Kemp's own political shrewdness and his aptitude for national party leadership, mentioning him frequently as a natural candidate for vice-president. But that tactical shrewdness has not endeared Kemp to the New Right. He has refused, for example, to exploit highly charged emotional issues such as gay rights and abortion, which makes New Rightists suspect that he is no "conservative" in the Wallaceite sense. Kemp has provided this one area of policy on which Republicans of all persuasions have been able to work together, which reflects his desire to cooperate with the "liberals," rather than drive them from the Republican temple. (In 1978, for example, he infuriated New Rightists by campaigning for the re-election of Illinois Congressman John Anderson, then facing a tough primary challenge orchestrated by the New Right.) The broad policy on which the Republicans united in 1978 was tax reduction, specifically the Kemp–Roth tax cut bill, which promised, with a 33 percent across-the-board tax cut, to create a surge in productivity, raising tax revenues and individual income simultaneously.

Mainstream Republicans saw great potential in such an optimistic view of things, whether or not key economists thought well of it. After Proposition 13's stunning victory in California, the GOP, counting on a national outpouring of angry taxpayers, kicked off a three-day, seven-city, 5,000-mile tour to publicize the Kemp–Roth formula. The Republican pitchmen, including Reagan, Ford, Kemp, Senator William Roth of Delaware, and Baker, hopped from coast to coast in a jetliner called the Republican Tax Clipper. (Conspicuous by his absence was John Connally, who boasted that he had not endorsed the tax cut plan.) The blitz, as it was called by party publicists, met with only limited success, however; in Minneapolis, for example, only about 250 people showed up for a rally that had been publicized on radio and in the newspapers for two days—and that was the largest crowd of the day. "Working people need a break," read banners put up by the Republicans, yet the GOP leaders clumsily showed up in Minneapolis in a chauffeur-driven limousine. The extravaganza ended appropriately enough at Knotts' Berry Farm in Orange County, California.

The New Right has viewed George Bush, the former director of the Central Intelligence Agency, with suspicion, despite the law-and-order image of the CIA. His earlier career in public service—he was ambassador to the United Nations and chief of the United States liaison office in Communist China—suggests an ability to "go along and get along." His failure to move up the electoral ladder—he was defeated twice for the Senate from Texas, in 1964 and 1970, after serving as a congressman from Houston—generated doubts about his presidential prospects. Two of Bush's top aides in his campaign for the GOP nomination in 1980 were two anti-New Rightists—ex-Reagan aide David Keene and Pete Teeley, once an aide to Senator Jacob Javits. But his most severe problem with the Right has been his elitist image. "He was born and raised in patrician Connecticut, the son of a U.S. Senator," the *New Guard* reported disdainfully. "He graduated from Yale University and still maintains a slight New England accent." Worse yet, he served as president of the Council on Foreign Relations, an organization of scholars, businessmen, and politicians, which the Right sees as an effort to control American foreign policy for the benefit of David Rockefeller and the International Conspiracy.

The New Right's on-again, off-again enthusiasm for John Connally of Texas must, in part, be a consequence of his willingness in 1973 to join the Republican party in the depths of Watergate, at what seemed to many to be its darkest hour. It is also a consequence of his general disregard for rigid party fealty. Whatever the cause, the New Rightists seem, in Connally's case, to have underestimated Republican voters who, in primary after primary in 1980, denied Connally their support, a rejection attributable to the Texan's reputation as a slick operator whom they could not trust. Connally, nevertheless, raised money on an appeal to "social issues" through the direct-mail fundraising services of the Richard A. Viguerie Company, but his campaign for the GOP nomination failed to catch on. Connally's consequent withdrawal from the race opened the possibility that those on the New Right—having earlier abandoned Reagan and, to a lesser extent, Crane, in Connally's behalf—would be shut out of the presidential contest or forced to return to Reagan. Thus, such an occurrence would point, once again, to their difficulty in finding an acceptable and credible presidential candidate within the two-party system.

If so, it would represent one of the New Right's fundamental problems—a deep-seated impatience with all political leaders, and leadership in general, an antipolitical (anticonservative) attitude that explains, to a great extent, its inability to function, with any degree of success, in the American party system.

10

Crashing the Democratic Party

Conservatives must learn to disregard meaningless party labels.
— RICHARD A. VIGUERIE

If you can't lick 'em, join 'em.
— OLD ADAGE

The cherished goal of the New Right, repeated throughout its literature, is to forge a "new majority," a grand coalition which, no longer encumbered by sentimental allegiances to such presumably outmoded institutions as the Republican and Democratic parties, can sweep the New Right to power. There exist, the Right contends, millions of Americans who are New Rightists by instinct, waiting for the opportunity to be liberated from their traditional loyalties and ignorant of the choice for freedom the Right offers. Much of the New Right's activities in the late-1970s were devoted to forging this "new majority."

New Rightists had already made inroads in the traditional conservative domain of the GOP. Key to the new effort is the invasion or infiltration of the Democratic party.

Unhappy Democrats, whose loyalty is only to name, can keep the name—the New Right wants only their votes. Those regarded as most vulnerable include Roman Catholics from the urban Northeast who are concerned about the creeping ghettos and busing to inner-city schools, and opposed to abortion and sexual permissiveness; "born-again" Protestants, especially from the Southern Democratic hinterlands, who are alienated by the increasing "urbanization" of values, big government, and big business; disaffected Wallaceites within the labor movement concerned about taxes and recession; and blacks who have achieved middle-class status and are now as concerned as middle-class whites with inflation and crime.

The New Right observed, for example, that labor union members voted for George Wallace in 1968 and Richard Nixon in 1972, abandoning at least in their voting for presidential candidates their traditional Democratic loyalties. Many workers, revolted by the New Left and the counterculture, refused to vote for the Democrats' 1972 presidential nominee, Senator George McGovern of South Dakota; hardhats clashed with anti-Vietnam War protesters on Wall Street in the late 1960s; working families were appalled by the hippie–police confrontation in the Chicago streets during the 1968 Democratic convention. Great cracks, it appeared, had opened up in the Democratic coalition, cracks the New Right watched with close attention and considerable expectation. They are paying similar attention today to further tensions within the Democratic party, hoping to gain, for instance, from the volatile hostilities that developed between Jewish voters and American blacks, fed by affirmative action, and surfacing dramatically when Andrew Young was forced from his position as U.S. ambassador to the United Nations. They see promise, too, in the conflict between white labor unionists and black workers over hiring and promotion and seniority.

The right-wing constituency is those whom political scientist Donald Warren has called "the Radical Center"—those "alienated," "forgotten," "angry," "troubled" Americans who are ripe to engage in backlash politics, and distinguished from the rest of society by their suspicion and distrust of it, by the belief that others are engaged in a conspiracy against them. These are Americans uniquely unable to make common cause within the established system, ill-equipped to engage in the give-and-take politics of cooperation and compromise that coalition-building requires, more attuned to social protest than to the complex process of governing, deeply distrustful of the very nature of coalitions. They put "principle above party." But if the alienated can *become* the society, the core becomes the majority. So New Right leaders hope.

The "new majority" has been described by William Rusher as a union of economic conservatism, "the dominant secular faith of the American middle class," and of social conservatism, "predominantly a movement of the lower middle class and portions of what would be the American 'proletariat' if its behavior warranted that Marxist term."

> Its appeal, therefore, is powerful among those who work with their hands: "hard-hat" industrial workers, small farmers, and the blue-collar population in general. Because of the ethnic character of the migratory waves that filled these important ranks in the population, social conservatives in the Northern states are drawn particularly heavily from Catholic ranks—not only Irish Catholics, who came first and are now widely absorbed into the middle class (and thus into economic conservatism), but Polish, Czech, and other East European Catholics and (last but far from least) Italian Catholics as well.

Murray Friedman has written in *Overcoming Middle Class Rage* (1971):

> Ironically, while Middle Americans have formed, largely, the natural constituency of liberals and the Democratic party historically, it was conservatives and the GOP who first grasped the meaning of their revolt and took steps to capitalize on it.

> The battle plan for the victory of conservatism in 1968—the
> combined vote for Nixon and Wallace was 57 percent—was
> drawn by [Kevin] Phillips.

Exploiting the anxieties of these Americans, Nixon and Agnew
did much to invade traditional areas of Democratic liberal
strength, and talk of the "breakup of the New Deal coalition"
became common in political circles. New Right theorists are
convinced that the old coalition that united the South, the
Northeast, segments of the northern Middle West, blacks,
lower-middle-class Americans, labor union members, and liberal intellectuals is disintegrating, leaving only the liberal intellectuals and what M. Stanton Evans has called "the welfare
majority." The South, which voted for Nixon and Wallace in
1968 and Nixon in 1972, could be salvaged by the Democrats
in 1976 only by nominating a Georgian.

LABOR AND BLACK SUCCESS
IN OKLAHOMA CITY

When the New Right needs a demonstration of its ability to
gain broad-based support from labor union members and
blacks, they invariably present the case of Mickey Edwards, a
Republican congressman from Oklahoma City.

Edwards likes to boast about his success in garnering votes
of blacks and working-class Democrats. He told the 1979 Conservative Political Action Conference in Washington, with a
touch of sarcasm: "Good conservative Oklahoma, people think
—the home of Fred Harris and Carl Albert. Well, in my
district, the registration is three-to-one Democrat. I was the
first Republican elected from it in 48 years. We have enough
of a labor vote that although we have right-to-work in Arkansas,
in Texas and in Kansas—all around us—in Oklahoma, three
times, organized labor has defeated right-to-work." In addition
to a strong blue-collar constituency, Oklahoma's Fifth District
also has a large black community. Roughly 11 percent of Ed-

wards's constituents are black. There are large numbers of black elected officials and an influential black newspaper.

An amiable right-winger who once edited the American Medical Association's monthly journal *Private Practice,* Edwards ran for Congress in 1974 and, like many Republicans that post-Watergate year, he lost. He ran again in 1976, squeaking into office with a meager 51 percent of the vote. But two years later, he won re-election by a landslide, taking not only every blue-collar precinct but every black precinct as well. He won big, for example, in Del City, a suburb with a high concentration of federal employees.

His pre-election polls (taken by conservative pollster Arthur Finkelstein) showed that his strongest single base of support was in households with at least one labor union member.

> Here I was, sitting on this strong base of support, having gotten just forty-nine point nine percent of the vote. You listen to Bill Brock. You know what I had to do, right? I had to move to the left. I had to broaden my base.

Here is how Edwards "broadened" that base. During his first two years in Congress he became an officer of the American Conservative Union. He received nearly perfect voting ratings from the right-wing Committee for the Survival of a Free Congress. He was one of two floor leaders in the House fight to defeat common situs picketing; his record on labor issues was so poor that it provoked the AFL-CIO into naming him as one of the "shameful seven" in Congress. To gain ground with black voters, he said he opposed the District of Columbia voting rights amendment, tried to cut CETA funds, and fought a minimum-wage increase. "I was against every single thing the Black Caucus wanted," he admitted.

When the votes were counted, Edwards picked up 80 percent of the vote. And this, the Right says, is proof that— without compromising its principles—they can win the votes of blacks and blue-collar workers.

What they do not say about Edwards's victory, however,

suggests that much of their optimism may be wishful thinking. Edwards had astoundingly weak opposition. His opponent had spent only about $500 during his primary campaign and won his party's nomination, according to one of Edwards's campaign aides, simply because large numbers of Democrats turned out to vote against his unpopular—but better known—opponent. Edwards's opponent was not even taken seriously by local Democrats in the election itself. Neither the United Auto Workers nor the AFL-CIO's Committee on Political Education gave money to Edwards's opponent. Edwards's former administrative assistant told me that, "In essence, we were unopposed." Edwards was considered such a shoo-in by Republicans that his re-election campaign did not actively seek financial support from the well-heeled New Right's PACs. It was one of the few contests involving New Right candidates that year, in fact, in which right-wing dollars from outside the state did not play a major role. The Edwards campaign, which used the services of Richard A. Viguerie in 1976, conducted its fund-raising drive without Viguerie in 1978, and even the well-padded National Conservative Political Action Committee—crucial to Edwards's 1976 victory—felt that Edwards was such a shoo-in it did not contribute, giving money to races where they felt the money would do more good.

Nevertheless, Edwards did actively court Oklahoma's strong black vote. He hired black staff members and, breaking GOP tradition in the district, established a campaign office in the heart of the city's black community. Edwards was endorsed by the influential daily *Black Dispatch*. Black voters who supported the Democratic candidate for the Senate crossed over to vote for Edwards for the House.

THE YOUNGSTOWN ROADSHOW

In February 1978, New Right leaders, in an effort to broaden their somewhat narrow constituency, trooped off to Ohio, to express solidarity of sorts with the laid-off steelworkers of the

Youngstown Sheet and Tube plant. Led by Congressmen Edwards and Philip Crane of Illinois, and accompanied by Viguerie, Paul Weyrich of the Committee for the Survival of a Free Congress, Howard Phillips of Conservative Caucus, and William Rusher of *National Review,* the New Right delegation held secret closed-door meetings with local labor leaders —and came back to Washington bursting with good news.

The unionists, they reported, were deeply angered about the shutdown of their factories and the loss of their jobs—and the source of their anger was the federal government. The New Right leaders told members of the press corps that the unionists complained of injury to the investment climate caused by unfavorable tax laws; industry's inability to absorb the mounting costs of production imposed by government regulations; lack of a national energy policy geared to production rather than consumption; and inflation caused by deficit financing. These are the same concerns that New Right leaders express. As Edwards explained:

> They were saying: "In order to compete with foreign steel, we need modern equipment. We need to be able to realign the blast furnaces in our steel mills and to get newer, better equipment, and we can't do it because our companies cannot go into the market and borrow money because the money isn't available." "Now I swear to you," Edwards concluded, "that sounds like you were talking to top management, but these were the labor people. They are extremely conscious of the fact that government is eating up all the money."

At the 1979 Conservative Political Action Conference, Edwards said that the unionists also protested congressional failure "to balance the budget. We were dumbfounded. We had to explain to them that we agreed and were fighting to balance it like they wanted!"

Viguerie announced that, as a result of the meeting, he was planning a massive direct-mail campaign to go directly into the homes of unionists across the country, designed to counteract the effectiveness of the AFL-CIO. Weyrich of the Committee for the Survival of a Free Congress simultaneously announced workshops to train congressional candidates to appeal to blue-collar constituencies by stressing shared concerns: jobs, excessive environmental controls, busing, abortion, gun control, and the like. As Congressman Crane put it: ". . . before this century is out, we will all see the battlelines that are being drawn: those who work for a living and those who don't." If all of this proved true, it would, in an amazing political reversal, put conservatives and blue-collar labor on one side, ranged against liberals, labor "bosses," bureaucrats, and welfare families on the other.

No one, of course, can really know whether the claims of coalition were based on fact. Despite the enthusiasm of conservatives who attended, it has been next to impossible to locate a single union member who will admit he attended. One local labor leader refused to comment to the local press, and others denied being anywhere near the meeting. The labor press was generally hostile to the whole affair, and Staughton Lynd, colonial historian and New Left hero, now a labor lawyer in nearby Niles, Ohio, dismissed the meeting in a letter to me as "definitely not a big breakthrough or opening to anything." If nothing else, the meeting was a media event. Jack Anderson devoted a column to it, and it was mentioned in *U.S. News and World Report.* At the very least, it spread the impression that the New Right is trying to work with like-minded blue-collar Democrats and, in politics, perception of events can often be as important as truth.

The Youngstown outing was only part of what was once intended to be a major effort to court the labor union vote, but it was effectively countered by the leadership of the labor unions. In 1977, the AFL-CIO produced and distributed a film, "The New Right Machine," shown to local union members and alerting them to the activities of the New Right and portraying it in terms as lurid as anything in the New Right's own fund-raising letters. The literature of the labor movement in the late-1970s bristled with articles on the New Right, so that many rank-and-filers now know the name Viguerie and are alarmed by the New Right. In *The Evolving Threat of the New Right*, a pamphlet of the labor-oriented League for Industrial Democracy, Arch Puddington wrote:

> The New Right likes to talk about its concern for the needs of working people, a line that has gone down fairly well in the general media. . . . But the fact is that conservatives have devoted as much sweat and money towards defeating situs-picketing legislation, promoting right-to-work laws, and fighting labor law reform legislation as it has towards somewhat better-publicized issues like the Panama Canal treaties and the Equal Rights Amendment.

Ironically, Republicans are more likely to make inroads among labor union Democrats from the relatively sophisticated approach of conservative New York Congressman Jack Kemp, who stresses issues of deep concern to unionists, but which represent neither Old Guard Republican business interests nor New Right reaction.

> The issue facing this country, and especially its backbone, the working men and women, transcends all these political and ideological labels. The issue is whether we will have economic growth and opportunity, or contraction and unemployment. The issue is whether people will look forward to the future with hope and optimism, or despair at the prediction of Alfred Kahn, that "there is no way we can avoid a decline in our standard of living. All we can do is adapt to it."
>
> The Administration thinks we have inflation, apparently, because too many people are working too much, business is doing entirely too much business, consumers are consuming too much, and producers are producing too much. So the Administration's answer is for everyone to do less of whatever it is they're doing, especially holding jobs.
>
> Telling workers to settle for 7 per cent while the government devalues the currency at 13 per cent is robbery. Republicans are quick to defend the profit incentive, but the wage incentive is

no different. Take away either incentive, and you ruin people's hopes and lives as you ruin the economy.

The answer, for business and labor, is economic growth, which can only be stimulated by lowering the tax rates. We haven't had a President since Jack Kennedy who understood that we either all move together as a country, or we don't move at all. Kennedy said, "A rising tide lifts all boats." Economic growth benefits everyone.

Kemp, the former football star, is gaining greater credibility among working-class Americans than the glib New Rightists—and winning a limited acceptance of his ideas among Americans who would otherwise associate Republicans as business touts, opposed to labor's interests. Whether this approach benefits Republicans, or merely finds certain acceptance among Democrats, remains to be seen.

BYPASSING THE GHETTOS

The New Rightists also believe that their program has great appeal for blacks who have achieved middle-class status, and are presumed to be ready, out of concern for inflation and crime, to vote for right-wing Republicans. And so they make gestures in the direction of blacks, quoting whenever possible black neoconservatives like Thomas Sowell, a professor of economics at the University of California at Los Angeles, and Walter Williams, a professor of economics at Temple University. In articles supporting a subminimum wage for teen-agers, right-wing columnists like John Lofton have deplored the high unemployment rate among young blacks, as if a subminimum wage would ease their plight.

But talk is as far as they have gone. The New Right, with the possible exception of a small number of politicians like Congressman Edwards, has done nothing substantive to attract black support and seems not unhappy with the lack of support it receives. Moreover, the Right has criticized the genuine efforts made by the Republican party to attract blacks, initiatives taken not by conservative Republicans but by party moderates like Republican national chairman Bill Brock.

When Brock asked the Reverend Jesse Jackson of Operation PUSH (People United to Save Humanity) to address a meeting of the Republican National Committee, Lofton attacked Jackson.

> Despite what he says [on black self-improvement] the Reverend has: denounced capitalism as a "bad system"; enthusiastically endorsed reverse discrimination calling for quotas in jobs and college admissions for women and minorities; criticized President Ford's effort to reduce Federal regulation of business; and urged passage of a massive, multi-billion dollar federal public service jobs program.
>
> How in the world could any Republican candidate get the Rev. Jackson's vote by endorsing these things without turning his back on the traditional GOP philosophy as regards those issues? The answer is obvious: there is no way. The circle cannot be squared.

And when Brock announced that the Republican convention of 1979 would be held in Detroit—a Democratic stronghold with a large black population—the right-wingers were outraged.

New Rightists seem content to sit back and wait for great socioeconomic changes to take place, after which—they believe—blacks will vote for the right candidates out of self-interest, and without coaxing. These blacks, the theory holds, will become right-wingers out of a desire to keep what they have earned and will share the political and economic views of the GOP constituency. This theory assumes that the black middle class will be indistinguishable from the white middle class. Evidence suggests the contrary.

Charles V. Hamilton, Wallace Sayre Professor of Government at Columbia University and a black political scientist, believes that middle-class blacks may, in fact, be more liberal in their political and economic attitudes than the poorer black community out of which they have sprung. This emerging social and economic group may well be infertile soil for the New Right.

Hamilton believes it would be a mistake to conclude that black middle-class attitudes on economic issues are similar to those of disaffected middle-class whites. "What is important to examine," Hamilton told me, "is not only that blacks have achieved middle-class status but the nature of their relationship to the economy. And, in this case, they are deeply tied to the public sector economy." He says that 67 percent of all black professionals and managers—compared with only 17 percent in the population as a whole—work for the government, and that of black administrators, 42 percent work for the government. Black businessmen, he has found, very often "started through Office of Minority Business Enterprise grants. Many were frequently involved in Great Society programs. Involved as they are in public sector employment, they tend to vote more liberal." Over a twelve-year period, Hamilton studied forty-one ballot issues in New York State to analyze attitudes on economic questions. Of all the groups examined—which included Roman Catholics, Jews, and other ethnic and religious groups—"blacks voted to the left of all other groups. In fact, on every issue except housing, middle-class blacks voted to the left of lower-class blacks."

Hamilton's conclusion that there is little reason to believe that blacks will vote conservatively on economic questions is supported by the results of referenda in the 1978 elections. Blacks in Michigan rejected by overwhelming margins three economic measures favored by the Right—property tax cuts, property tax limits, and a voucher plan for school funding. In Missouri, they opposed a right-to-work law by 93 to 7 percent.

The New Right, indeed, like conservative and moderate Republicans, believes that the key to winning the votes of blacks of all economic levels is to stress private sector job creation and to portray as demeaning public sector employment. Evidence, however, again suggests that this may not work. "Blacks want jobs—period," Kenneth B. Clark, a black psychologist and author, told me. "They don't care whether they are private or public." And they seriously question the sincerity of Republicans who say they want to ease black unemployment. As Clark put it:

> There has yet to be a Republican or conservative politician that I know of who has said: Here is what we are going to do about black unemployment, and then lay out—one, two, three, four —exactly what he is going to do. And until such time, blacks are not going to believe them.

The Right is correct, Hamilton believes, in noting that blacks tend to be more independent now than they used to be in their voting patterns and party registration: "But this follows a national, not a racial trend. Blacks are less Democratic, but they are not more Republican." In New York City, black voters' registration in Harlem in 1965 was 85 percent Democratic, only 7 percent Republican, and 8 percent independent. The registration of independents increased to 28 percent, from 1965 to 1975, while the registration of Republicans remained roughly the same. "The move is from the Democratic side to the independent, but not to the Republican party." Other observers deny that there is any significant movement of blacks away from the Democratic party at all, noting that even if there were, blacks would still remain more solidly Democratic than any other group in the society.

And in those cases in which blacks have voted for Republicans, the New Right has not gained. They have done so only when the candidate offered by the GOP is more liberal than that of the Democrats. The Joint Center for Political Studies, a black-oriented think tank in Washington, in its recent study *Elections '78: Implications for Black America*, acknowledged a new "voter independence and sophistication" among black Americans, suggesting "significant implications for coalition-building, especially between black voters and white Republicans." But the chief beneficiaries of this new independence, based on the results of the 1978 contests, would appear to be liberal to moderate Republicans. When Illinois

Republican Senator Charles Percy defeated right-wing Democrat Alex Seith, Percy won a healthy 32 percent of the black vote. In Pennsylvania, Republican Richard Thornburgh received 52 percent of the black vote in the gubernatorial election, beating right-wing Democrat Pete Flaherty, once mayor of Pittsburgh. These statistics show issue discrimination, not narrow party loyalty, among blacks.

In Tennessee, GOP Senator Howard Baker won 12 percent of the black vote in his re-election bid; Baker, at the time, was under severe attack from the GOP Right for supporting the Carter Administration's Panama Canal treaties. In Mississippi, GOP right-winger Thad Cochran capitalized on the decision by Fayette Mayor Charles Evers to seek the Senate seat vacated by James Eastland, running as an independent. Evers's 23 percent of the vote, which included 95 percent of the black vote, drew off enough support from the Democrat candidate to give Cochran the victory. Evers's role as spoiler thus allowed Mississippi to elect its first Republican to state office since Reconstruction.

But explicitly rightist candidates did poorly compared to their more liberal and moderate GOP counterparts. John Warner in Virginia won only 9 percent of the black vote; Jeffrey Bell in New Jersey won only 7 percent of that vote; John Tower in Texas, 5 percent; Strom Thurmond of South Carolina, 3 percent; and Jesse Helms of North Carolina, 2 percent.

The dominant attitude of the New Right toward blacks is that expressed by Patrick J. Buchanan, in a column that carried the headline: "GOP Vote Search Should Bypass Ghetto." American blacks, Buchanan argued, have been grossly ungrateful for the efforts already made in their behalf by Republicans who by now have done more than enough to seek their support. Recent Republican administrations, he wrote, "were hardly years of oppression for black America." He noted that between 1969 and 1976, a record number of blacks moved into middle- and upper-level civil service jobs, with the Nixon Administration's Office of Minority Business Enterprise helping scores of blacks to start their own businesses. Like Lofton, Buchanan believes the time has come to stop trying to compete with the Democrats for black votes—the GOP won the White House in 1968 and 1972 without them.

While it would be inaccurate to attribute overt racism to much of the New Right, the appeal to fears about busing and quotas and welfare can play on racial anxieties. The disgruntled Wallaceites, who are an important part of their constituency, express considerable status insecurity that for some Americans has a racial base. The New Right, at the least, seems unquestionably insensitive to the interests of black Americans, quite unlike the traditional conservatives who have taken great pains to dissociate themselves from groups like Wallace's American Independent party. Barry Goldwater, for example, in *The Conscience of a Conservative,* declared integrated schools "wise and just" and helped integrate the Arizona Air National Guard and the Phoenix Sky Harbor Airport, although he and other conservatives opposed quotas in the seventies and desegregation in the sixties, believing both to be unwarranted instances of "social engineering" by the federal government. Such positions, though taken with good conscience, pleased racists, on other grounds. Because racial justice to many others seemed to depend on governmental enforcement, conservatives were often thought callous or worse—and were so accused by liberals.

Never was the insensitivity of the New Right better dramatized to me personally than during my stint as an editor of *Conservative Digest* when we were preparing to publish an article about Clay Smothers, a black Wallaceite. One of the editors, emerging from his office, presented the following headline, of which he was obviously quite proud:

CLAY SMOTHERS: A BLACK OF A DIFFERENT COLOR

I politely suggested that I doubted very seriously if I were Clay Smothers I would be honored by the headline. It was eventually changed to:

A BLACK CONSERVATIVE CHAMPION

Less snappy, perhaps, but probably less offensive.

REBELS IN SOUTHIE

Urban Democrats are, like blue-collar labor-union members, middle-class blacks, born-again fundamentalists, and other groups with grievances, the targets of the New Right in their effort to crash the Democratic party.

In a small, drafty storefront on a gritty street lined with run-down bars in a Boston working-class Irish Catholic neighborhood is the South Boston Information Center, headquarters of Southie's foes of "forced busing." On the front of the building hangs a sign:

A CITY IS OCCUPIED
BOYCOTT EXISTS
A TYRANT REIGNS
LAW IS BY DECREE
PEOPLE ARE OPPRESSED
THE SPIRIT OF FREEDOM STILL LIVES

Beside it, painted on a green shamrock, are the words: "With our last breath, we'll say never." Inside, near the rack of right-wing pamphlets, is another sign. "To conquer South Boston by force is only to make a temporary conquest." The South Bostonians even have a song to express their commitment to the cause, a ballad whose lyrics they distribute with copies of a recorded version (to the tune of Galway Bay):

Oh the planes that fly from Logan over Southie
They just see those crowded houses down below
But the people living down there in those houses
Have a spirit that the strangers do not know.

For the strangers came and tried to teach us their way
They scorned us for the things that we hold true

But they'll never break the backs of our resistance
Or force us to do what they want us to.

Jimmy Kelly, a friendly but hard-nosed neighborhood organizer and former dockworker who is the organization's president, sits behind a cluttered desk toward the back of the chilly
building. He reminisces about his youth in Southie and what
it means to him:

> Look, when I was a kid—and this is the same for kids grow-
> ing up around here through generations—every kid I knew had
> one real dream in life. Every kid wanted to go to South Boston
> High and play football. You have no idea what that meant to
> us. People around here loved South Boston High. Everyone
> went there and it means everything to us. Now, it's not possible
> anymore. Kids from Southie aren't allowed in anymore. Every-
> time there is an opening at South Boston High, it is reserved
> for a black kid. Kids from Southie have to be bused out of the
> neighborhood and go somewhere else. That's heartbreaking.
> Something very special has been taken out of their lives.
>   And look at the job situation. Kids growing up around here
> like this neighborhood and they like to stay here. Get married
> and someday buy a house in South Boston, or move into their
> grandparents' house or something, when they die. For years the
> jobs that they all wanted were to be police or firemen. They
> could work here in the neighborhood and the pay was pretty
> good. Good job security. They could save their money and buy
> that house in Southie and then raise *their* kids here. That's all
> they wanted, really.
>   But now the black kids get those jobs because of affirmative
> action. They get first pick. Our kids are shut out of the jobs.
> And you better believe it causes tensions. If there is more
> racism, well, what can you expect? Our kids see the black kids
> getting the jobs they feel entitled to and they can't help but
> associate the problems with blacks. But did the kids from Sou-
> thie cause these problems? No! Judge Garritty did. The govern-
> ment did. They created the problems and they've torn up a
> neighborhood that means more to the people around here than
> they can imagine.

The right-wingers in Massachusetts even have their own monthly newspaper, *The Citizens' Forum,* dedicated "to individual freedom under God, limited government and free enterprise," which alerts readers to the activities of New Right politicians ("Rep. Hansen Seeks Help To End Union Gangsterism" and "Worcester Business Leader Sees Conspiracy Behind US Decline") and promotes Massachusetts New Rightists like Avi Nelson and Edward J. King.

As Gordon Nelson, a six-foot six-inch Jewish stockbroker who is Massachusetts Republican state chairman, told me:

> This state went for McGovern in 1972, but a lot of things have changed since then. When Mike Dukakis ran for Governor in 1974 he ran as a conservative, a cross between Reagan and Goldwater even though he had a liberal voting record in the legislature. That's how much things have changed. On all the major social issues he is a liberal and after he was elected he passed the largest tax increase in state history. Yet when he was challenged in his own party it was from the left—from a McGovernite and she won only seven percent of the vote in the Democratic primary. But challenged from the right within his own party by Edward J. King, he was beaten. Man, liberal's a dirty word in this state now.

Other tensions have contributed to the growing conservatism of Bay State voters—among them, rapidly increasing property taxes, second only to those of California prior to the victory of Proposition 13. In Boston, conservative ideas have gained great credibility, in large part because of the popularity of articulate television and radio commentators like Avi Nelson, son of a rabbi, and David Brudnoy, like Nelson a youthful Jewish intellectual, who inherited Nelson's nightly talk show on WGN-Radio. Avi Nelson and Brudnoy enjoyed enormous popularity among the antibusing forces, whose position was argued on an intellectual level by the two opinion makers. "These guys have had a tremendous influence, not only among the people from Southie but among the students, too. Many of them didn't know intelligent conservatives existed—and they are intrigued by the intellectuality, consistency, and wit of people like Brudnoy," Gordon Nelson said.

The language and temper of South Boston's Irish is not unlike that of the 1950s South when white citizens, nostalgic for past times, fearful of pending change, loss of security and status, and the movement of blacks out of submission and passivity and into competition with them in the schools, in jobs, and in the neighborhood, resisted each forward step with "never!" But the flinty Bostonians prefer to think of themselves as the American patriots of the 1770s, leading a ragtag and courageous revolt, a kind of modern Boston Tea Party, against the federal officials who, like King George III's colonial troops, have begun to tell them how they must live.

The final irony, however, is that greater benefits seem to have been reaped by the Democrats than Republicans during this period of upheaval. The Democrats, running right-wingers like King, have picked up GOP votes without losing Democratic votes. In Massachusetts, many Republicans voted for conservative Democrat Edward J. King over moderate Republican Francis Hatch, as in Pennsylvania, Republican Richard Thornburgh defeated Democrat Pete Flaherty; and as in Minnesota where Democrat Bob Short and Republican David Durenberger faced off after Short ran a right-wing campaign in winning a primary victory over liberal Democratic incumbent Donald M. Fraser. Durenberger, who won, had the support of the Americans for Democratic Action, but received little support from conservative Republicans, support normally guaranteed for the GOP candidate in Minnesota. Only in Illinois, where Seith faced Percy, does the pattern appear reversed, where large numbers of Democrats voted for the more liberal Republican.

As *Washington Post* columnist David Broder noted:

> Everyone of these Democrats who had a contested primary chose to run on conservative issues. Except for Seith, who lost the AFL-CIO endorsement to Percy, all these Democrats have

been able to maintain their conservative positions and still gain endorsements from most unions, from the regular Democratic organizations in their states, and most, if not all, other elected Democrats.

These Democrats have sacrificed some black support—Percy, for example, did very well among blacks—but have made deep inroads into the sizable GOP constituencies. One consequence of this trend could well be to encourage the New Right to concentrate their efforts on remaking the Democratic party rather than trying to defeat it from within the GOP. Given the debilitating effects of the New Right's Kamikaze efforts on the GOP, and the success that the Democrats have enjoyed by running right-wing candidates, they may have no alternative.

11

The Politics of Grievance

"Mistrust those in whom the impulse to punish is strong."

—FRIEDRICH NIETZSCHE,
Thus Spake Zarathustra

If the heart of the New Right is in Orange County, California, its brain is in the Washington, D.C., metropolitan area and its northern Virginia suburbs. There the leaders of the New Right live and work, as they direct their attention to the national scene. While theirs is a grass-roots movement, the leaders urge their foot soldiers to focus their fire upon their senators and congressmen and on the White House, where national policy is made. The New Right organizations are scattered throughout the Capitol Hill area, many offices within walking distance of the Capitol, with New Right businesses—probably for tax reasons—situated in such northern Virginia suburbs as Vienna, Fairfax, and Alexandria. The Richard A. Viguerie Company is located in Falls Church, Bruce Eberle & Associates in Vienna. For the New Right leaders, who rise early from their apartments and houses in Virginia, life is a series of committee meetings, luncheons, receptions, dinners, and conference calls. On Monday, they attend the "PAC luncheon," a meeting of the leaders of rightist political action committees held at the Key Bridge Marriott hotel, across the Potomac River from Georgetown. On Wednesday, they attend a breakfast at the Viguerie company headquarters. On Friday, there is the planning session for the week's legislative activity, held at the Kingston Room of the Congressional Hotel in Washington. On Tuesdays and Thursdays, they can often be seen at the Capitol Hill Club, the dining room of the Republican National Committee headquarters, discussing strategy with GOP New Rightists, in the ambiance of white tablecloths and black waiters or downstairs chatting over burgers and beer at the club's grill.

Busy at all times, the New Rightist professionals are an aggressive, competent, and dedicated corps of skilled political organizers, bright though anti-intellectual. They no longer think only in terms of electing or denying election; their strategy is to take control of all branches of government: the courts through constitutional amendment, the Congress by legislation and election, the executive by one day winning the White House. They seek to mobilize on the local, state, and national levels, to pressure their elected officials in Washington, to push for local and state referenda, initiatives, and constitutional amendments to limit taxes, restore the death penalty, and bring prayer back to the public schools. They encourage their supporters to deluge Capitol Hill with postcards and letters expressing approval of or opposition to legislation.

Once sympathetic congressmen are elected, they are encouraged to attend intensive training sessions conducted by the Committee for the Survival of a Free Congress. Their performance in office is closely monitored. The New Right has formed two unofficial Republican groups, the Republican Study Committee of the House and the Republican Steering Committee of the Senate, paid for by participating GOP members (roughly $100 a month), to provide legislative research and direction to cooperating congressmen. Groups like the Heritage Foundation produce studies to support the New Right's positions.

The New Right stays busy on other District of Columbia fronts as well, working through groups like the Reverend Jerry Falwell's Moral Majority to broaden the constituency for "social conservatism," encouraging action in Washington on issues like abortion, school prayer, and gay rights.

Other organizations, like the National Right to Work Committee, build support for their positions by purchasing advertisements in mainstream, and even liberal, publications like *The New Republic* to broaden the constituency of their cause. Still others, like the American Conservative Union, conduct frequent press conferences to get their views into the newspapers and to create the image of a strong dissenting voice to the policies of the current Democratic administration or the opposing Republican party establishment. The result is a surging undercurrent of political activity which touches many fronts, mobilizing many individuals, and affecting, in countless ways, the attitudes and activities of elected officials.

ELECTORAL VICTORIES

Throughout the mid- and late-seventies, the New Right made great gains in both houses of Congress, by 1980 holding about 40 of 435 seats in the House and 10 of 100 seats in the Senate, controlling, therefore, about one-tenth of both houses.

The ten New Right senators are all Republicans. Jesse Helms of North Carolina and James McClure of Idaho were elected in 1972. Two years later, Jake Garn of Utah joined them. In 1976, the New Right elected Orrin Hatch of Utah, Harrison Schmitt of New Mexico, and Malcolm Wallop of

Washington. In 1978, the Right gained Gordon Humphrey of New Hampshire, Roger Jepsen of Iowa, and William Armstrong of Colorado, and re-elected Helms and McClure. The five winning New Right candidates may have benefitted from low voter turnouts customary during off-year elections. As Maurice Rosenblatt of the Committee for the Study of the American Electorate told *The New York Times,* the nation "may be losing the votes of the broadly concerned citizen, leaving the field to those motivated by narrow, parochial and emotional interest." (Richard Strout, writing as TRB in *The New Republic,* concluded that Jepsen's election was a direct result of this trend.)

If those in office continue to win re-election, and if the Right elects new supporters at the current rate, it would control almost a third of the Senate by the mid-1980s.

The New Right made steady gains in the House as well, and by 1980 they could claim to have elected about 40 congressmen. In 1969, Illinois Republican Philip Crane was elected, an orthodox Republican who became a New Right leader when Richard A. Viguerie's power began to increase. Others clearly part of the New Right include Jim Jeffries, a Republican from Kansas, and Marvin Leath, a Democrat from Texas, elected in 1978, as well as L.A. "Skip" Bafalis of Florida, Robert K. Dornan of California, Mickey Edwards of Oklahoma, George Hanson of Idaho, Henry Hyde of Illinois, Bob Livingston of Louisiana, Larry McDonald of Georgia, J. Kenneth Robinson of Virginia, Eldon Rudd of Arizona, and Steve Symms of Idaho.

In Texas in 1978, the Committee for the Survival of a Free Congress and the National Conservative Political Action Committee—true to the New Right's tradition of backing Democrats and opposing "blue-stocking" Republicans—supported Democrat Kent Hance over Republican George Bush, Jr., son of the 1980 presidential hopeful.

The New Right senators and congressmen have come overwhelmingly from the South or West. Nine of the senators hail from the West—only one, Gordon Humphrey of New Hampshire, elected to represent a New England state. In the House, the South and West also dominate, with small delegations from the Northeast.

BEHIND-THE-SCENES LEADERS

A number of self-appointed leaders not ever elected to public office, though some have run and been defeated, are the real heads of the New Right (the elected officials, very often, appear to be not leaders but "followers out front").

Though tied to the direct-mail fund-raising business, they use their positions with PACs and lobbies to politick. Three fairly representative of the New Right leadership are Paul Weyrich of the Committee for the Survival of a Free Congress; Howard Phillips of the Conservative Caucus, and John T. (Terry) Dolan of the National Conservative Political Action Committee. Of divergent backgrounds, one the son of a German immigrant to Wisconsin, one the son of a Boston insurance broker, one a middle-class New Englander, all have come together to advance the politics of grievance, committed to bringing the New Right to power but with little idea of where they want to lead.

The program of the New Right, said Terry Dolan, would entail sweeping changes in the political system. The New Right is "radical," Weyrich said, "in the same way that FDR's young brain trust was radical—committed to sweeping changes and not to preserving the status quo." Phillips holds fairly standard right-wing views on major policy questions, but is even more radical than Weyrich or Dolan, favoring "a return to Biblical law." Beyond broad support for increased defense budgets and slashing welfare expenditures, New Right leaders seem impatient with the intricacies of public policy. Weyrich, for example, is a self-described "political mechanic" with little knowledge of, or interest in, public policy and political thought.

The personal power of these three leaders is, in part, a

function of who they know—and what they are willing to do to advance the New Right. A cherubic man whose choirboy appearance masks a gift for political hardball, Weyrich, described by an associate as "the foremost survival artist in Washington," owes much of his leadership to his association with brewer Joseph Coors. He met Coors when he was press secretary to Senator Gordon Allott of Colorado. As his unofficial agent in the capital, Weyrich convinced Coors to underwrite the Heritage Foundation and the Committee for the Survival of a Free Congress: He installed himself as a paid employee of both organizations. Phillips, for his part, worked closely with Viguerie on Conservative Caucus activities; in 1977 he helped draft a House resolution calling for the impeachment of United Nations Ambassador Andrew Young (the bill was introduced by Larry McDonald of Georgia, the John Birch Society member). McDonald's move was synchronized with the mailing of 400,000 Conservative Caucus fund-raising letters, resulting apparently in a hefty return.

Paul Weyrich's roots are in the German immigrant communities of Wisconsin; he represents a direct link to the isolationist/populist/Germanophile roots of the New Right. His father, he told me, was a "great admirer of Robert Taft"— beloved by Wisconsin immigrants, of course, for his staunch opposition to United States involvement in the Second World War. He was influenced, he said, by Robert Taft: "I read everything he wrote." (Taft wrote a short tract on isolationism, *A Foreign Policy for Americans,* his only book, except for a collection of his speeches.)

Howard Phillips was educated at Harvard and is probably the brightest of the three, but he has changed his opinions so frequently, associates say, that it is difficult to find any philosophical consistency in them. An outspoken right-winger when he served as Harvard's student body president, he earned a reputation as an equally outspoken liberal when he was chairman at twenty-three of the Boston Republican party. In 1968 he managed the successful senatorial campaign of liberal Republican Congressman Richard Schweiker of Pennsylvania, but when Schweiker was selected as Ronald Reagan's running mate, Phillips denounced the choice as "corrupt," and distributed press releases that "pledged" Phillips to "work for the Republican party's defeat if its appeal to the electorate is premised on the embrace of 'Great Society' liberalism reflected in Dick Schweiker's Senate voting record. . . ." Phillips was not even a member of the Republican party at that time, having left the GOP in 1974 to re-register as an Independent. He changed his registration again in 1978, this time to seek unsuccessfully the Democratic senatorial nomination from Massachusetts; as he explained to *Conservative Digest*, "My loyalty is not to a political party or a personage but to a set of political principles."

David Brudnoy, a libertarian writing in *National Review*, observed that Phillips, in order to deride Elaine Noble, another Democratic candidate,

> imported Anita Bryant to sing on his behalf. But the concert tickets wouldn't sell—of five thousand seats, less than three thousand appear to have been sold, despite weeks of heavy advertising; and a small number of militant homosexuals went whooping against Miss Bryant. This allowed Phillips to cancel the concert and to get what he announced he needed: front-page and prime-time TV coverage. But while Massachusetts isn't *really* the most liberal state in the Union, Bay Staters were not buying the cyncial Phillips ploy. Phillips came in way down, just above Elaine Noble. The Democratic senatorial candidate, by a narrow margin (36 to 31 percent) over State Secretary Paul Guzzi, is Congressman Paul Tsongas. Both are rated perfect by ADA. And that November, Tsongas defeated Ed Brooke, the Republican moderate.

It is difficult to determine what Phillips's "political principles" are, given the frequency with which they seem to change. He did tell me that the only answer for America was "to resort to Biblical law," but was unable to tell me how this could be accomplished, or by whom.

In November 1977, Dolan was involved with then Young

which Congress would be prohibited from going to war, except in case of invasion, without support in a national referendum. "There are those of us," he said, "who believe that the best judges of a nation's welfare are the people who live in it; and once that belief has been set aside, the door is thrown wide open to the most violent excesses of minority rule." A rugged individualist from the American West (Kendall called himself an "Appalachians-to-the-Rockies patriot"), he had the familiar resentment of the East and all that is associated with it; he called it the "world of the Buckleys."

Karl Hess, in 1964 a speechwriter for Senator Barry Goldwater's presidential campaign, began to outrage conservatives in the late 1960s by taking seriously the near-anarchism preached by those on the Right who consider government per se diabolical. He began to flirt with the libertarian Left. Widely dismissed as a crank, Hess stopped paying income taxes and moved to the hills of West Virginia where, in the spirit of the true American individualist tradition, he began to earn his living by welding and writing. In a 1979 article celebrating "the New Populism," Hess praised the Abourezk amendment and assailed the elitist assumptions of David Rockefeller, the big business community, and the Trilateral Commission—even taking potshots at George Will.

In Kendall's day, such heresies were regularly and effectively hooted down by the dominant traditionalists of the Russell Kirk school, who retained enough sentimental attachment to a more aristocratic, European conservatism to find such democratic sympathies a bit too folksy for comfort. Even Barry Goldwater, in *The Conscience of a Conservative,* argued that the Constitution was designed not to establish a democracy, but to frustrate a "tyranny of the masses."

"Majoritarians" and "anti-majoritarians" did agree on this: that the United States was never intended to be and should not be allowed to become a plebiscitary system. Kendall's "majoritarianism," after all, derived from John C. Calhoun's notions of "concurrent" or "constitutional majority." Calhoun, a Southern aristocrat, held that consensus took into consideration "interests as well as numbers," recognizing that any community was made up of "different and conflicting interests" that must be weighed if "the sense of the entire community" is to be determined. This determination is reached, moreover, "through compromise."* Neither Kendall nor Calhoun nor, for that matter, Burke believed in what Irving Kristol and Paul Weaver have called "simple-minded arithmetical majoritarianism—government by adding machine." How, Kendall once asked, could the Founding Fathers have erected barriers to a plebiscitary system when no such system had been conceived until after their deaths? No, American democracy takes form, he argued, not by instant majority rule, but after an involved "process of deliberation among virtuous men representing potentially conflicting and in any case different 'values' and 'interests.'" Conservatives, that is, believe in consensus, not arithmetic.

THE ASSAULT ON FORM

The impatient New Rightists, in their enthusiasm for the methods of direct democracy, risk the unleashing of passions in their disdain for what Tocqueville called "necessary form." Writing in *Democracy in America,* Tocqueville observed:

---

*Calhoun wrote of the two modes of taking the sense of a community:

> But one regards numbers only, and considers the whole community as a unit, having but one common interest throughout; and collects the sense of the greater number of the whole as that of the community. The other, on the contrary, regards interests as well as numbers; considering the community as made up of different and conflicting interests, as far as the action of the government is concerned; and takes the sense of each, through its majority or appropriate organ, and the united sense of all, as the sense of the entire community. The former of these I shall call the numerical or absolute majority; and the latter, the concurrent, or constitutional majority. I call it the constitutional majority, because it is an essential element in every constitutional government—be its form what it may.

Men living in democratic ages do not readily comprehend the utility of forms. . . . Forms excite their contempt and often their hatred; as they commonly aspire to none but easy and present gratifications, they rush onwards to the object of their desires, and the slightest delay exasperates them. This same temper, carried with them into political life, renders them hostile to forms, which perpetually retard or arrest them in some of their projects. Yet this objection which the men of democracies make to forms is the very thing which renders forms so useful to freedom. . . .

The New Right's preference for direct voter participation in matters until recently left, by and large, to the legislative branch reflects "a decline in the credibility of legislative bodies as well," according to Louis L. Friedland, professor of political science at Wayne State University in Detroit. Attempting to limit the judicial and the legislative functions, the New Right leaves only the executive branch and "the people," no checks, no balances—the exact contrary of the eighteenth-century conservatives who worked out the Constitution.

Believing themselves to be shut out of the role they should play in determining the direction of their government, yet committed to the notion that there exists in the country at large a majority of Americans who share their views, these right-wing populists have become fascinated by public opinion polls, which, they believe, should play an ever-growing role in determining positions taken by elected officials. They hail Proposition 13 and similar efforts and denounce the deliberative elites that have traditionally acted as buffers against untrammeled public will.

The growing support among New Rightists for abolishing the Electoral College is part of this trend. Utah Senator E. J. "Jake" Garn, a darling of the New Right, has supported Senator Birch Bayh's bill to abolish the Electoral College, which was defeated in the Senate in 1979. Kevin Phillips has been the most vocal proponent of the direct popular election, which traditional conservatives and some Democrats have warned

against. Phillips believes that the Electoral College discriminates against third-party efforts—which it surely does—by in-
stitutionalizing the two major parties, between which Phillips
sees (in George Wallace's quaint phrase) "not a dime's worth
of difference." Getting rid of the Electoral College, Phillips has
written, "would open up U.S. presidential politics to a broad
majoritarianism appeal that would not have to worry about
possibly losing California or New York by a few thousand
pivotal votes. That support could be made up in Kansas or
North Carolina." A preferable system, he argues, would be to
allow the one-man, one-vote arrangement endorsed by American liberals—a reductionism traditional conservatives have argued could, if applied nationally, wreak radical changes in the
American political system. Bickel wrote:

> The monopoly of power enjoyed by the two major parties would
> not likely survive the demise of the electoral college. Now, the
> dominance of two major parties enables us to achieve a politics
> of coalition and accommodation rather than of ideological and
> charismatic fragmentation, governments that are moderate,
> and a regime that is stable . . . discouraging individual forays
> and hence the sharply defined ideological or emotional stance;
> . . . it makes indeed for a climate inhospitable to demagogues;
> and . . . provides by its very continuous existence a measure of
> guidance to the marginally interested voter who is eminently
> capable of casting his ballot by more irrelevant criteria.

What is the danger of allowing California, for example, to
carry the electoral clout it now enjoys? The state is the home
of an increasing number of minority group members, Phillips
writes, and is therefore, like New York, becoming "a Third
World state." Conservatives working to keep the Electoral
College

> are maximizing the future presidential selection influence of
> potential "Third World" states like California (and New York
> is not far behind). Retention of the Electoral College would
> probably guarantee a minority-oriented presidential selection
> process for the 1980s.

Martin Diamond of Georgetown University wrote that the real issue at stake in the debate over direct popular election of the president is nothing short of the very nature of American democracy. A conservative of the traditional school, Diamond argued that the debate "is not democratic reform versus the retention of an undemocratic system but rather a matter of which kind of democratic reasoning is to prevail in presidential elections—the traditional American idea that channels and constrains democracy or a rival idea that wishes democracy to be its entirely untrammeled and undifferentiated national self." It was precisely the impatient attitude toward such intermediary institutions as the courts or the bureaucracy, Bickel has noted, that gave rise to the abuses of power under the Nixon Administration, a trend he detected, interestingly enough, in the Warren Court. That liberal, more activist Court cut through legal technicalities to get at the substance of things, and it was "utterly inevitable that such a populist fixation should tend toward the concentration of power in the single institution which has the most immediate link to the largest constituency"—the presidency. Expanding the powers of the president has long been an objective of those, from Andrew Jackson to Franklin Roosevelt, who presume to speak for the masses. At the very time when, in the wake of Vietnam and Watergate, liberals have come to be apprehensive about the dangers of "the imperial presidency," the New Right has begun to espouse it, after years of rejection of the Hamiltonian tradition by the conservatives. Conservative intellectuals have shuddered at the prospect of an energetic president using the powers at his command to advance even conservative principles; rejecting Nelson Rockefeller, in part, as potentially aggressive, they eventually turned on the relatively conservative Richard Nixon for many of the same reasons. Yet New Right publicists now stress the importance of capturing the White House, the only institution left that seems to them capable of doing ideological battle with the courts, the Congress, the federal bureaucracy, organized labor, and the news media. Patrick Buchanan, for example, even rejects the notion of an "imperial presidency." Watergate, he told me, was "not at all a product of the 'imperial presidency,' " and the "liberals who are talking that up are doing so for purely political reasons."

> They realize that they have an entrenched liberal Congress and will have it for a long time. They realize too that the mood of the nation is such to elect a conservative president. For those reasons, they want to strip the presidency of its powers.
> . . . I'm not a traditional conservative in this regard. I think that a strong presidency is the only podium from which to put a conservative agenda before the nation.

Illinois Republican Congressman Philip Crane agrees. He has been candid in his approval of the White House as a "bully pulpit" (in the words of Teddy Roosevelt). Another major political candidate, Ronald Reagan, notorious in conservative circles for his lack of interest in the day-to-day details of administration, also favors the "bully pulpit" approach: He is above all an orator and a right-wing evangelist. Like Reagan, John Connally is an accomplished public speaker who owes his popularity more to his ability to arouse his audiences than to administrative competence. William Rusher's approval of John Connally, no "doctrinaire conservative," is rooted in his conviction that Connally would be an energetic, expansive president. "He would be an activist president, which I don't like as a general principle," Rusher told me, "but it might be good now, just what we need to restore our worldly prestige."

A powerful presidency is an inevitable consequence of the populist impulse, as James Burnham warned American conservatives. "Caesarism" is not the contradiction of democracy but its fulfillment, he wrote, "if democracy is understood in terms of a monolithic doctrine of the general will." Once the passion to eliminate the intermediary institutions—or merely to "bypass" them—is unleashed, elections are transformed into "plebiscites the function of which is to acclaim Caesar." (As Disraeli said in his acceptance speech after re-election to Parliament in 1848: "I hope ever to be found on the side of the people and of the Institutions of England. It is our Institutions that have made us free, and can alone keep us so; by the bulwark which they offer to the insidious encroachments of a convenient, yet enervating system of centralization which if left unchecked will prove fatal to the national character.")

The implications of this transition on the Right from Republicans to Democrats (or democratists) are immense. What is at stake is nothing short of what kind of democracy is to prevail in America. The constitutional democracy as envisioned by the Founding Fathers—and here there was little disagreement between Hamilton and Jefferson, Adams and Madison—is at issue. As conceived by the Founders, democracy was limited, restrained by a complex system of safeguards and restrictions. The work of government would be carried forth regularly, routinely, and calmly by constitutionally designated agencies, each as important as the next, each restrained yet accountable to the citizens. The Congress would be a deliberative body, a representative assembly, and on few occasions, indeed, were the people—in the sense of a mass—to become directly involved in the governing process. These included regular election of representatives and constitutional conventions. But even in the latter, the people would work their will through designated representatives.

That said, the New Right would do well to heed the counsel of Will Herberg, who more than twenty years ago in a superb commentary on the career of Senator Joseph McCarthy addressed precisely this question. The American concept of democracy, he wrote in *The New Leader*, has come under increasing assault from "the burgeoning forces of mass-democracy." We have always endured demagogues impatient with constitutional processes and hot for direct action, but today—because of "the phenomenal development of the media in mass communication"—these demagogues represent a real danger to the American political process. This, Herberg wrote, is the real threat of McCarthyism, "government by rabble-rousing" which Herberg thought had been modernized by FDR and Senator McCarthy:

When Roosevelt wanted to get some legislation put through, he virtually bypassed Congress and appealed directly to the people; the people, roused, responded immediately and deluged Congress with hundreds of thousands of letters and telegrams demanding action; and Congress proceeded to pass FDR's "must" legislation literally almost as fast as the bills could be read. What did that mean if not that Congress had ceased to be a *deliberative* assembly and that the legislative process had virtually been taken over by "direct democracy"?

The New Right has unhesitatingly adopted these tactics, through the use of direct-mail solicitation as well as television. Its greatest victories, its apologists say, are the mobilization of millions of Americans in opposition to the Panama Canal treaties, during which controversy they sent millions of angry letters, postcards, and telegrams to Capitol Hill, vowing revenge on senators who dared to oppose them. (Senator James McClure, an Idaho Republican, called for a national referendum on the future of the Panama Canal, Phillips noted in his column.)

If the president wants a given action from the Congress, he need only put his vast propaganda machine into action to deluge congressional offices with telegrams, telephone calls, letters, and (increasingly) personal visits from boisterous constituents. As political technology advances, the possibilities of such action become wider, especially given the effectiveness with which FDR used radio more than forty years ago and more recent presidents have used television. The presidency is viewed by the New Rightists as a position from which opinions are broadcast, deriving its force less from party or executive responsibility than from the broad, moral authority the office commands as the only truly national and plebiscitary spokesman. This, combined with the New Right's impatience with deliberative institutions, sets up a potentially frightening model in which can be discerned roots of Burnham's expansive chief executive whose power is limited only by the general will, which he can manipulate and exploit through the increasingly powerful means at his disposal.

Congressman Paul Simon, the highly respected Illinois Democrat, believes that the New Right represents a small percentage of the electorate but already exercises a disproportionately high degree of political power, as a result of skillful manipulation of popular resentments. When a candidate is on the campaign trail, Simon told me, he is forced to appeal to a broad mass of the voters, to the mainstream of the American electorate, but in Washington, to a great extent, he becomes "responsive to mail, which becomes his barometer of public sentiment in his district or state. The high-powered direct mail campaigns of the New Right can distort his perception of public sentiment by inundating his office with postcards and the like, which suggest stronger feeling on an issue than really exists among the broad spectrum of his constituents."

Simon believes that this is only part of a much larger, and equally distressing, trend. He observes that an increasing number of congressmen, state legislators, governors, and White House aides are taking polls to determine their positions on important questions instead of "asking what is the national need." The New Right may be only part of this development, but its uniquely forceful efforts in this direction can have an undue influence on people who only respond to the public opinion polls; they may follow the New Right's lead because, "having put their finger to the wind, they believe it to be blowing in that direction." The New Right is powerful "out of all proportion to the size of their constituency," he concludes, "because it successfully manipulates public opinion, making it appear that the public opinion is more reactionary than indeed it is."

Yet public opinion, as traditionally understood by conservatives, is not to be measured by opinion surveys or push-button responses. The people (as Bickel once put it) "are something else than a majority registered on election day." Henry Fairlie has written that polls are not an index of public opinion, properly speaking, at all. Public opinion, as understood since the days of the Greek city-states, is not the uninhibited voice of the public, if by that one means a mass of undifferentiated individuals. The public, instead, "is created, and is given voice when it has been filtered through a political process," which resolves contradictions that appear when individuals offer, as in public opinion polls, instant opinions.

> Someone may believe or want A, but also believe or want B; if he finds that A or B are in conflict, he will have to abandon or at least modify one of them. This adjustment of interests and opinions in the individual voter is what takes place when he or she goes to the ballot box [to choose between candidates], just as the adjustment of more general interests and opinions takes place in the traffic and wheeling and dealing of Congress.

The checks and balances of the American system are intended to preserve the process of translating the popular will into public opinion and public policy; representative bodies, dealing with issues by protracted negotiation, filter the popular voice,

> which ensures that moral issues are not frivolously decided, especially by the whim of some majority of the moment.
> If one tried to govern a country by the decisions in referenda, that country would be in a ceaseless state of moral strife and indignation.

A country in which highly sensitive questions are settled by continual referenda would be one of constant moral contention. The New Rightists seem to prefer the fanatics and demagogues—the Anita Bryants, Howard Jarvises, and John Briggses—to the reasoned, responsible leadership associated with classic conservatism. Already such sensitive personal questions as abortion and homosexual rights are put to the public for its approval. We are entering a period when biological discoveries will force many difficult and vital decisions of public policy to be made by the society and the state. When the kind of fury that is aroused by busing or by homosexuality, or—sixty years ago—by Prohibition,

> is let loose on issues of life and death, we will have reason to quail. The thought of unfiltered popular voice playing around

with genetics is terrifying. Then indeed we will be able to say that *vox populi* has become *vox dei,* the voice of the people has become the voice of God.

Nothing less is at stake, as the American Right moves from a traditional conservative defense of representative government against the onslaughts of direct democracy into a celebration of government by rabble-rousing, by adding machine, by majorities of the moment.

"This perfectly timed book alerts Americans to a dangerous distortion sneaking up on us almost unnoticed. The traditional conservative heritage of Edmund Burke, John Adams, and *The Federalist* papers, which conserves law, institutions, and evolutionary due process, is being distorted into a lawless, rabble-rousing populism of the revolutionary Right. Don't vote till you've read Crawford."

Professor Peter Viereck,
Pulitzer Prize-winning author
of *Conservatism Revisited*
(Greenwood Press)

"*Thunder on the Right* is a very solid work. A thorough but very readable account of an important part of the American political drama."

Nicholas Von Hoffman

Notes

EPIGRAPH:

Niebuhr, "Beria and McCarthy," *The New Leader,* 4 January 1954, p. 4.

Chapter 1

THE NEW RIGHT NETWORK

EPIGRAPH: Paul Weyrich, quoted by Alan Ehrenhalt, *Congressional Quarterly,* " 'New Right' Plans Move to Change Congress," 23 October 1976, p. 3027.

REPUBLICAN PROFESSIONAL QUOTED: Eddie Mahe, quoted in Alan Ehrenhalt, "GOP Strategists View 1978 with Lower Expectations, Push Grassroots

Organizing," *Congressional Quarterly,* 11 June 1977, p. 1143.

AMERICANS FOR CONSTITUTIONAL ACTION "AGAINST COLLECTIVE MORALITY . . .": ACA literature quoted by Richard Dudman, *Men of the Far Right* (New York: Pyramid Books, 1962), p. 60.

"MENACE" FROM THE RIGHT: John P. Roche, " 'Menace' from the Right," *Shadow and Substance: Essays on the Theory and Structure of Politics* (New York: Macmillan, 1964), pp. 416–17.

WHALEN QUOTED: Richard J. Whalen, *Taking Sides: A Personal View of America From Kennedy to Nixon to Kennedy* (Boston: Houghton Mifflin, 1974), p. 100.

Information from Annual Report of the American Conservative Union, 1977 and 1978. Numerous interviews, both formal and informal, dating back to 1975.

NATIONAL JOURNALISM CENTER: Author's interview with M. Stanton Evans, 10 May 1979, Washington, D.C. "ACU Education and Research Institute Reports Investigative Journalism Alive and Well," *Battleline,* May 1979, p. 18. Since 1977, the author has been a member of the advisory board of this organization.

CRANE'S CHAIRMANSHIP OF AMERICAN CONSERVATIVE UNION ASSESSED: Author's telephone interview with ACU board member, not for attribution, 12 April 1978, Washington, D.C.

COORS'S POLITICAL ACTIVITIES: Author's interview with Paul Weyrich, 17 May 1979, Washington, D.C. For general background, see three-part series by Stephen Isaacs: *Washington Post,* 4, 6, 7 May 1975; I interviewed a number of persons who said they had been sources for Isaacs's series. On the lobbying of tax-exempt organization: The quotation "of course, was illegal," comes from an interview of January 1979 with the former attorney of the Robert M. Schuchman Foundation, corroborated by a second attorney and former board member of the Schuchman board. Exchange between Coors and board members at Schuchman Foundation took place at board meeting, 24 January 1974, Washington, D.C., described to me in independent interview with several witnesses.

WEYRICH AS "POLITICAL MECHANIC": Author's interview with Paul Weyrich, 17 May 1979, Washington, D.C.

Information on Heritage Foundation taken from its Annual Report, 1977.

MOYNIHAN ON *POLICY REVIEW*: Quoted in "The Heritage Foundation Ready and Able to Meet the Research Needs of America's Key Decision Makers," 1977, p. 1.

HERITAGE FOUNDATION'S "STAFF IDEOLOGY": Quoted in National Information Bureau Inc., report on The Heritage Foundation, #256, New York, 15 February 1979, p. 2.

WEYRICH AND THE AMERICAN LEGISLATIVE EXCHANGE COUNCIL: This discussion is based on documents prepared for Bartnett's attorney given to me by Bartnett; Bartnett's correspondence, files, vouchers for payment to Bartnett, and ALEC telephone bills; author's interviews with Bartnett and with a member of the board.

The quotation from Richard Larry, "Gold rules," for example, was told to me by Bartnett and, later, volunteered me by the board member in spring, 1979.

INFORMATION ON FUNCTIONS OF ALEC: *Strengthening Grass-Roots Government,* a brochure of the American Legislative Exchange Council, Washington, D.C., n.d.

Document given to me by Bartnett with the consent of her counsel, prepared for her counsel in connection with a lawsuit for damages settled out of court.

LETTER FROM USHIJIMA TO IRS: Supplied to the author by Bartnett. Michael M. Ushijima, attorney hired for ALEC tax exemption application, to H. H. Goldberg, IRS Chicago, provided to the author by Juanita Bartnett. Used with the permission of Ushijima.

FORMATION OF COMMITTEE FOR THE SURVIVAL OF A FREE CONGRESS: See *Washington Post* series by Stephen Isaacs, 4, 6, 7 May 1975.

The account of the Committee's origin was corroborated in an interview not-for-attribution with a staff director of a right-wing fundraising group, November 1979.

"RADICALS" IN SENATE: "C.S.F.C. Conservative Register, First Session, 95th Congress, 1977," p. 10.

FUNDRAISING OF NATIONAL CONSERVATIVE POLITICAL ACTION COMMITTEE: "Federal Election Commission, Year-end Report" of the National Conservative Political Action Committee, 1977, filed with the Federal Election Commission.

HUMPHREY'S VICTORY ATTRIBUTED TO NATIONAL CONSERVATIVE POLITICAL ACTION COMMITTEE: *Human Events,* 18 November 1978, p. 3.

DOLAN: Author's interview, offices of NCPAC, 10 January 1979, in Rosslyn, Va.

NBC NEWS ON "MOST ADVANCED" CAMPAIGN: Quoted in fundraising letter for Citizens for the Republic, signed by Franklyn Nofziger, 3 October 1978.

CFTR NEWSLETTER "PRINTS NEWS ONE SELDOM FINDS—BUT SHOULD IN THE MASS MEDIA": Quoted in fundraising package for Citizens for the Republic, 3 October 1978, Los Angeles.

HISTORY OF YAF: Marvin Leibman, 13 January 1979, New York City.

WHALEN ON "CANNIBALISTIC" ATTITUDES: Richard J. Whalen, *Taking Sides: A Personal View of America from Kennedy to Nixon to Kennedy* (Boston: Houghton Mifflin, 1974), p. 119.

BUCKLEY PROGRAM EXCHANGE: Transcript of the television program "Firing Line," No. 77/11, #531. Taped 29 August 1977 and originally released 2 September 1977. Southern Educational Communications Association.

YAF MEMBERSHIP FIGURE: 55,000 is cited in press releases; the number 6582 comes from a YAF memo, "Memo. To: National Board. From: Bob Heckman. Re: State and Chapter Services Report, February 7, 1979." Heckman was director of state and chapter services.

LEIBMAN ON "BORING AND BUREAUCRATIZED": Author's interview with Marvin Leibman, 13 January 1979, New York City.

HUSTON AND PLAN FOR SECRET POLICE: Plan is discussed in *The Final Report of the Select Committee on Presidential Campaign Activities, United States Senate, Pursuant to S. Res. 60, February 7, 1973* (Senate Watergate

Committee), (Washington, D.C.: U.S. Government Printing Office, June 1974), pp. 3–7.

MCCARTHY RECEIVES VOTES AT YAF CONVENTION: Jules Witcover, "It's a Laugher for Reagan at YAF's Mock Convention," *Washington Star,* 19 August 1979, p. A-1.

FIGHT SONG: From "Glory Be, There Goes Another! Songs of the Militant Extreme," compiled by Vincent Joseph Rigdon and Connaught Coyne, for YAF Convention, Houston, 1971. Mimeographed.

PARMENTEL ON YAF: Noel E. Parmentel, Jr., "The Acne and the Ecstasy," *Esquire,* August 1965, pp. 43–44.

RUSHER ON YOUNG REPUBLICANS AS "ANTI-ROCKEFELLER" ALLIANCE: William A. Rusher, *The Making of the New Majority Party* (Ottawa, Ill.: Green Hill Publications, 1975), pp. 42–43.

EVANS ON YOUNG REPUBLICANS' 1963 CONVENTION: M. Stanton Evans, "Battle in the Junior GOP," for release 3 May 1977, Los Angeles Times Syndicate.

CRONKITE MENTION OF YOUNG REPUBLICAN CONVENTION: Transcript of "CBS Evening News with Walter Cronkite," 10 June 1977, pp. 5–6. Ed Rabel reporting.

STONE AND CREEP: See *The Final Report of the Select Committee* (Senate Watergate Committee), No. 93-981, pp. 192–99. The comment on "dirty tricks" is included in the testimony of Herbert L. Porter, 2 April 1973, p. 190; the reference to "some radical group" is on p. 197.

STONE AS NATIONAL YR CHAIRMAN, LEADER OF DIRECT MAIL FUNDRAISING: *YR Political Action Committee Special Report,* Washington, D.C., Fall 1978, p. 1.

BUCHANAN AND BLACK CANDIDATE: *The Final Report of the Select Committee* (Senate Watergate Committee), p. 203.

TRAINING SEMINARS OF COMMITTEE FOR RESPONSIBLE YOUTH POLITICS: Author's interview with Republican activist, not for attribution, 11 March 1979, Washington, D.C.

BLACKWELL AND NIXON'S "DIRTY TRICKS" CAMPAIGN: *The Final Report of the Select Committee* (Senate Watergate Committee), p. 192.

INFORMATION ON PACIFIC LEGAL FOUNDATION: Pacific Legal Foundation, Fifth Annual Report (1978). Robert Lindner, "Conservative Public Interest Foundations Start Having Impact," *The New York Times,* 12 February 1978, "Voice of the Right," *Newsweek,* 9 October 1978, p. 96. "Winning One for the Average Joe," *San Francisco Business,* September 1978. G. Christian Hill, "Businesses Are Finding Environmental Laws Can Be Useful to Them," *The Wall Street Journal,* 9 June 1978.

COMMENTS OF DIRECTOR, OFFICE, PACIFIC LEGAL FOUNDATION: Julian Weiss, *Conservative Digest,* "Pacific Legal Fund Has Impressive List of Victories," June 1978, pp. 50–51.

FLUOR QUOTED ON PACIFIC LEGAL FOUNDATION: *The New York Times,* 12 February 1978.

BELIEFS OF PACIFIC LEGAL FOUNDATION: Julian Weiss, *Conservative Digest,* "Pacific Legal Fund Has Impressive List of Victories," June 1978, p. 51.

POPEO ON NADER: "The Ralph Nader of the American Right," *Conservative Digest,* August 1978, p. 45.

CONSUMER ALERT COUNCIL: Author's interview with Barbara Keating, May 1979, New York City. Tom Faber, "Consumer Alert Celebrates Second Birthday, Is Answer to Nattering Nabobs of Naderism," *Battleline*, April 1979, p. 29. Several brochures of the council.

KEATING ON REGULATION: Author's interview with Barbara Keating, New York City, 13 January 1979.

NATIONAL RIGHT TO WORK COMMITTEE: Jerry Norton, "A Fighter for Freedom," *Conservative Digest,* November 1975, pp. 30–31. Also: issues of the *Right to Work Newsletter.*

HUMAN EVENTS ON BLOCKING OF LABOR LAW BILL: *Human Events,* 8 July 1978, p. 2.

ANTI-UNION LOBBY CALLED "PRO-BUSINESS LOBBY": Author's interview with conservative activist, not for attribution, 18 September 1978, Alexandria, Va.

RIGHT TO WORK GROUP CALLED PART OF "RIGHT-WING FUNDRAISING MACHINE": Author's interview with lobby employee, 5 September 1978, Arlington, Va.

PUBLIC SERVICE RESEARCH COUNCIL SPOKESMAN EXPLAINS TWO NAME POLICY: David Y. Denholm, PSRC representative, quoted in the *Richmond* (Va.) *Times-Dispatch,* 17 October 1978, p. 1-A.

BOOKS BY PHILLIPS: Kevin P. Phillips, *The Emerging Republican Majority* (New Rochelle, N.Y.: Arlington House, 1969). *Mediacracy: Parties and Politics in the Communications Age* (Garden City, N.Y.: Doubleday, 1975).

TROUBLES IN GUN LOBBY: John Chamberlain, " 'Revolt' Put NRA Back on Track," *The Waterbury* (Conn.) *Republican,* 29 June 1977.

BACKGROUND ON CITIZENS COMMITTEE: See *Point Blank,* newsletter of Citizens Committee. For several months in 1975 the author shared office space in Washington, D.C., with John M. Snyder, the organization's Washington representative.

AMERICANS FOR EFFECTIVE LAW ENFORCEMENT: Author's telephone interview with Frank Carrington, 26 January 1979, Washington, D.C.

Annual Report, Americans for Effective Law Enforcement, 1977.

CARRINGTON'S BOOKS: Frank Carrington, *The Victims* (New Rochelle, N.Y.: Arlington House, 1975) and *The Defenseless Society* (with William Lambie) (Ottawa, Ill.: Green Hill Publications, 1976).

CARRINGTON QUOTED: "Champion of the Crime Victim," *Conservative Digest,* December 1976, p. 29.

HISTORY OF AMERICAN SECURITY COUNCIL: Richard Dudman, *Men of the Far Right* (New York: Pyramid Books, 1962), p. 126.

DATA ON EAGLE FORUM: "The New Activists," *Newsweek,* 7 November 1977, p. 41.

MCCORMACK'S VIEWS: "The Right to Life Candidate," *Newsweek,* 9 February 1976, p. 23. "A Long Island Housewife Campaigns for the Presidency on the Anti-Abortion Issue," *People,* 26 March 1976, pp. 31–32.

BRYANT GROUPS: Author's interview by telephone with Ed Rowe, 26 January 1979, Washington, D.C.

FORMATION OF EDUCATIONAL COUNCIL: Letter to author from Jil Wilson, 26 October 1978.

EVANGELISTS: "Mobilizing the Moral Majority," *Conservative Digest,* August 1979, pp. 14–20.

PHILLIPS ON CONSERVATIVE CAUCUS: "Power *Back* to the People," interview with Howard Phillips, *Conservative Digest,* February 1976, p. 8.

CAUCUS ACTIVITIES: Interview with former Caucus organizer, not for attribution, February 1979, Washington, D.C.

"CONTROL OF THE CULTURE": Author's interview with John T. Dolan, 10 January 1979, Rosslyn, Va.

Chapter 2
PLUNDER ON THE RIGHT

MARK RUSSELL SONG: "Rule Reagannia," lyrics provided to the author by Russell's agent.

PLUNKETT ON CAMPAIGN FINANCE: William Riordan, *Plunkett of Tammany Hall* (New York: E.P. Dutton, 1963), p. 76.

ALEXANDER ON "FAT CATS": Stephen Isaacs, "Fat Cat Out; Fund-Raiser Is '76 Hero," *Washington Post,* 16 April 1976, p. 1-A.

VIGUERIE'S BACKGROUND: Since Viguerie did not agree to be interviewed, information about the background of his beliefs has been gleaned from secondary sources, except that learned by the author while working for his magazine in 1975. Sources include Nick Thimmesch, "The Grass Roots Dollar Chase on the Right," *New York,* 9 June 1975, p. 63; *A Modern Horatio Alger,* a brochure distributed by Viguerie backers at the 1976 convention of the American Independent party; and "two Macs," quoted in Ted Knap, "Tough New Up-and-Comer Bucks the Conservative Ranks," *Evansville Press,* 1 January 1976, p. 20.

EFFECT OF WATERGATE REFORMS: Not-for-attribution telephone interview, 12 September 1977, Washington, D.C.

VIGUERIE AS "GENIUS": Author's interview with right-wing fundraiser, not for attribution, 12 April 1979.

STEVENSON ON PACs: "Bill would ban PAC contributions to candidates." Stevenson office press release, 21 March 1979.

STAGGERS'S PAC SUPPORT: "Running with the PAC in Congress," editorial, *The New York Times,* 27 December 1978.

VIGUERIE SPEECH: Address to 1977 Conservative Political Action Conference by Richard A. Viguerie, Washington, D.C., 7 February 1977.

WALTHER ON DIRECT-MAIL FUNDRAISING: Quoted in "Right-to-Work Group Mobilizes Millions," *Conservative Digest,* March 1978, p. 3.

LEIBMAN ON DIRECT-MAIL FUNDRAISING: Author's interview, Marvin Leibman, 13 January 1979, New York City.

RUSHER ON DIRECT MAIL: William A. Rusher, "The 'New Right.' " For release 5 October 1977, Universal Press Syndicate.

DIRECT MAIL IN THE WALLACE AND MCGOVERN CAMPAIGNS: Brian A. Haggerty, "Direct Mail Political Fund-Raising," *Public Relations Journal,* March 1979, pp. 10–12.

PACs GROWTH, 1968 ON: " 'New Right' Pouring Cash Into Campaigns," *Congressional Quarterly,* 21 October 1976, pp. 1–5.

ORDOVENSKY ON NEW RIGHT GAINS: Pat Ordovensky, "Conservative Groups Got Their Money's Worth in Elections," *Conservative Digest,* 9 February 1979, p. 20.

PHYSICAL PLANT OF RAVCO: Described by Nick Kotz, "King Midas of the New Right," *The Atlantic,* November 1978, p. 53.

VIGUERIE AND YAF'S MAILING LIST: John Fialka, "Viguerie: Into Politics by the Back Door," *Washington Star,* 23 June 1975, p. A-10.

EBERLE COMPANY: "The Bruce W. Eberle Story," *Assemblage,* Spring 1979, p. 5.

QUOTE ON H. L. RICHARDSON OPERATION: Interview with conservative fundraiser, not for attribution, Spring 1978, California.

BRIGGS'S USE OF BRYANT MAILING LIST: Author's interview with John Briggs, 13 April 1978, Fullerton, Calif.

LEIBMAN ON RISE OF DIRECT-MAIL "ARMY": Author's interview with Marvin Leibman, 13 January 1979, New York City.

WILL ON "QUASI-POLITICAL ENTREPRENEURS": George F. Will, "Passionate Politics," *Newsweek,* 1 May 1978, p. 96.

DOLAN ON LETTERS AS STIRRING HOSTILITIES: Author's interview with John T. Dolan, 10 January 1979, Rosslyn, Va.

FUNDRAISING LETTER OF AMERICANS AGAINST UNION CONTROL OF GOVERNMENT, signed by David Denholm, n.d.

FUNDRAISING LETTER OF CITIZENS FOR THE REPUBLIC, signed by Lyn Nofziger, 12 January 1979.

FUNDRAISING LETTER OF AMERICANS FOR LIFE, n.d.

FUNDRAISING LETTER OF CONSERVATIVE CAUCUS, signed by Howard Phillips, n.d.

CUNNINGHAM CAMPAIGN: John Judis, "Rightist Populists, Divided Democrats," *In These Times,* 29 June–5 July 1977, p. 2.

KOTZ ON CUNNINGHAM DIRECT-MAIL EFFORT: Nick Kotz, "King Midas of the New Right," *The Atlantic,* November 1978, p. 53.

CUNNINGHAM SIGNS FUNDRAISING LETTER: *Daily Olympian* (Seattle, Wash.), 13 July 1977, p. A-12.

DOLAN AND WEYRICH ON DEBT TO RAVCO: Author's interviews, Dolan, 10 January 1979, Rosslyn, Va.; Weyrich, 17 May 1979, Washington, D.C.

FUNDRAISER EXPLAINS HOW VIGUERIE KEEPS CLIENTS IN DEBT: Author's interview with conservative fundraiser, not for attribution, 12 April 1979.

"CONSERVATIVE WELFARE CLASS": Interview with conservative fundraiser, not for attribution, February 1979, Washington, D.C.

LIVINGSTON FUNDRAISING ARRANGEMENT: News release from the Federal Election Commission, 23 March 1979, Matter Under Review No. 454(77), includes General Counsel's Report signed 23 February 1977 by William C. Oldaker. Also copy of "Agreement by and between Richard A. Viguerie Company, Inc., and Livingston for Congress Committee."

CRYP FUNDRAISING: Year-end report of the Committee for a Responsible Youth Politics, 1976, 1977, 1978, filed with the Federal Election Commission.

NCEC SUIT AGAINST VIGUERIE GROUPS: Federal Election Commission

Matter Under Review No. 297(76). Also, *Campaign Practices Report,* 23 January 1978, p. 4.

PAC MEETINGS: Author's interview with PAC leader, not for attribution, February 1979, Washington, D.C.

COMMENT ABOUT "M-O-N-E-Y": Incident recalled for the author, independently, by two witnesses at Red Fox meeting in March 1976.

DOLAN ON REASONS FOR SETTING UP NCREF: Author's interview with John T. Dolan, 10 January 1979, Rosslyn, Va.

INDEPENDENT EXPENDITURES: Maxwell Glenn, "How to Get Around Campaign Spending Limits," *National Journal,* 23 June 1979, pp. 1044–46.

REAGAN EFFORT BY AMERICAN CONSERVATIVE UNION: Annual Report, 1977, the American Conservative Union. Author's interview, M. Stanton Evans, 10 May 1979, Washington, D.C.

PAC PLANS TO CONTROL SENATE: Fundraising letter of the National Conservative Political Action Committee, [n.d.]. Also, account of announcement, "Conservative group targets $150,000 to oust Sen. Bayh," *Evansville* (Ind.) *Press,* 22 August 1979, p. 3.

ANTI-JAVITS EFFORT: Fundraising letter of the Committee to Replace Jacob Javits with a Conservative U.S. Senator, signed by Robert Carroll, chairman, n.d.

REAGAN GROUP HAS EXCESS OF $250,000: Author's telephone interview with John Laxalt, October 1978, Washington, D.C.

CFTR AND REAGAN CAMPAIGN: "Political Action Committees Mushroom into a Major Force," *Washington Post,* 3 February 1979.

UNITED POLICE FUND: Devine quoted by Harvey Katz, *Give! Who Gets Your Charity Dollar?* (Garden City, N.Y.: Anchor Press, 1974), p. 28. Van Deerlin, *Hearings before the Subcommittee on Consumer Protection and Finance of the Committee on Interstate and Foreign Commerce,* House of Representatives, 94th Congress, 1st Session, 20–22 May 1975. Serial No. 94-35 (Washington, D.C.: U.S. Government Printing Office, 1975). Also, Jack Anderson, "Police Patsy," *Washington Post,* 4 November 1972, p. D-13. "Unconscionable Contract" referred to in letter 27 March 1979 to author from Seig Smith, a former aide to Congressman Lionel Van Deerlin who investigated this group.

CITIZENS FOR DECENT LITERATURE: Documents provided to the author by Lawrence Pratt, assistant attorney general of the State of Ohio. Founder Keating refused to be interviewed. See also: Jack Anderson, "Viguerie: A Modern Wizard of Oz," *Washington Post,* 3 June 1978, p. D-3, and Nick Kotz, "King Midas of the Right," *The Atlantic,* p. 54.

KOREAN CULTURAL AND FREEDOM FOUNDATION: Fundraising letter quoted, n.d. William Claiborne, "New York Accuses Korean Foundation of Charity Fraud," *Washington Post,* 21 February 1977, p. A-3. Charles R. Babcock, "Korean Foundation under Two Probes," *Washington Post,* 31 October 1976, p. 1-A. "Annual Report—Charitable Organization, Korean Cultural and Freedom Foundation, July 1, 1973–June 30, 1975," from the office of William J. Brown, Attorney General of the State of Ohio. Report of the New York State Board of Social Welfare, "Summary of the Information Obtained as a Result of an Examination of the Books and Records of Korean Cultural and Freedom Foundation." Also, copy of the agreement signed between RAVCO and the Korean fund. All in possession of the author.

BIBLES FOR THE WORLD: Report of the Council of Better Business Bureaus, Inc., Philanthropic Advisory Service, June 1978, on Bibles for the World, documents its fundraising. See also Anderson's "Wizard of Oz" column.

VAN DEERLIN ON UNDERGROUND BIBLE FUND: Van Deerlin quoted on "charlatan-like operation" in *Hearings Before the Subcommittee on Consumer Protection and Finance of the Committee on Interstate and Foreign Commerce,* 94th Congress, 1st Session, 20–22 May 1975, Serial No. 94-35 (Washington, D.C.: U.S. Government Printing Office, 1975), p. 129.

VAN DEERLIN AIDE: Author's interview with Seig Smith, by telephone, New York City, 18 March 1980.

CONLAN ARTICLE: John B. Conlan, "Federal Law Threatens Charities," *Conservative Digest,* August 1977, p. 22.

ISSUES BULLETIN ON CHARITY DISCLOSURE: "Disclosure for Charitable Organizations, H.R. 41," *Heritage Foundation Issue Bulletin* No. 18, 2 August 1977.

FRIENDS OF THE FBI: Nick Kotz, "The Troubled Friends of the FBI," *Washington Post,* 21 May 1972, p. 14. Author's interview by telephone with two involved in the operation, not for attribution, 16 March 1980. Washington, D.C. Operation is also cited in Harvey Katz, *Give!,* and Anderson's "Wizard of Oz" column.

FRIENDS OF THE FBI STUDY AND BOOK: *America's Internal Security: Its Dangerous Decline and What to Do About It* (Washington, D.C.: Friends of the FBI, Inc., 1978) (contributors, Allen Brownfeld, Phillip Abbott Luce, Dr. Robert Morris, Herbert A. Philbrick, Otto Otepka); Richard O. Wright, ed., *Whose FBI?* (LaSalle, Ill.: Open Court, 1974).

AMERICANS FOR EFFECTIVE LAW ENFORCEMENT: Author's telephone interview with Frank Carrington, 26 January 1979, Washington, D.C. Basic information is in Anderson's "Wizard of Oz" column, though Carrington fleshed it out a great deal, confirming basics and adding more.

NATIONAL RIFLE ASSOCIATION: Author's telephone interview with H. K. McGaffin, 27 January 1979, Washington, D.C.

GURNEY INCIDENT: Pete Laine, "Gurney Fund-raising Slip-up May Have Violated the Law," *Washington Star,* 29 July 1970, p. A-12.

GUN LOBBY LETTERS: "Lobby to Return Anti-Gun Control Funds," *Washington Post,* 16 January 1978. Jack Anderson and Les Whitten, " 'False Advertising,' " *Washington Post,* 15 November 1977. On "disgruntled" members of Congress, The Hon. Bud Shuster of Pennsylvania, "Interest Group Misuses Members' Names," *The Congressional Record,* 28 October 1977, p. E6659. M. Robert Carr quoted in the *Washington Post,* 16 January 1978, *ibid.* Also, Hon. Robert S. Walker, "Fundraising of the Citizens Committee for the Right to Keep and Bear Arms," *The Congressional Record,* 27 October 1977, p. E6631.

USE OF CONGRESSIONAL LETTERHEADS: "Congressional Letterhead," editorial, *Washington Star,* 29 November 1977, p. 10.

DORNAN, PRATT, AND USE OF LETTERHEADS: *Ibid.*

FINE ON GUN OWNERS: "Gun Owners of America Fined Record $11,000 by Election," *Campaign Practices Reports,* Vol. 5, No. 11, 29 May 1978, pp. 1–3.

WIN-PAC: *Federal Election Commission Year-end Report,* 1977 and 1978, filed by the Western Inter-Mountain Network Political Action Committee.

COMMITTEE FOR SURVIVAL: FEC Reports, 1976, 1977, 1978.

FOOTNOTE ON BURGER FOR SENATE FUNDRAISING: "Fund-Raiser Is Held in Helms' Hill Office," *Washington Star,* 26 August 1976, p. 6. Confirmed in not-for-attribution interview with conservative activist close to the planning of the event, 1979.

GUN OWNERS: Federal Election Commission reports, 1976 and 1978.

GUN LOBBY FUNDRAISING: Federal Election Commission reports, 1976 and 1978.

FUND FOR A CONSERVATIVE MAJORITY: Federal Election Commission reports, 1976 and 1978.

COMMITTEE FOR YOUTH POLITICS: Federal Election Commission reports, 1976 and 1978.

INGRAM LETTER: Quoted in Alan Crawford, "Richard Viguerie's Bid for Power," *The Nation,* 29 January 1977, p. 106. Enclosed in the Ingram mailing was article by James M. Perry, "The Right Wing Got Plucked," *National Observer,* 4 December 1976, pp. 1, 14.

EVANS ON FUNDRAISING: Author's telephone interview with M. Stanton Evans, 10 October 1976, Morgantown, W. Va. Originally quoted in the author's article, "Richard Viguerie's Bid for Power," *The Nation,* 29 January 1977, p. 107.

WINTER ON VIGUERIE: Quoted in James M. Perry, "The Right Wing Got Plucked," *National Observer,* 4 December 1976, p. 14.

CONSERVATIVE VICTORY FUND: Federal Election Commission reports, 1976 and 1978.

LEIBMAN ON FUNDRAISING: Author's interview with Marvin Leibman, 13 January 1979, New York City.

"CLIMBED ON BOARD": Author's interview, not for attribution, 12 September 1977, Washington, D.C.

QUESTIONS FOR DAN CRANE: Questions regarding candidate Crane's direct-mail fundraising effort were raised at a Political Forum at the Charleston, Ill., Holiday Inn, 30 October 1978.

SUBSCRIBER'S LETTER TO *NEW RIGHT REPORT*: Included with answer of 24 January 1979 from Morton C. Blackwell, editor. Circulated among New Right leaders and provided to the author by a recipient.

READER'S LETTER TO *U.S. NEWS*: *U.S. News and World Report,* 19 March 1979, p. 4.

CONSERVATIVE ON "FEELING BAD" ABOUT FUNDRAISING PRACTICES: Author's interview, not for attribution, 10 October 1976, Washington, D.C.

LEIBMAN QUOTED: Author's interview, 13 January 1979, New York City.

VIGUERIE ON DIRECT FUNDRAISING: "Raising Millions of Dollars for Conservatives, The Way It's Done, Interview with Richard Viguerie, Expert on Fund-raising by Direct Mail," *U.S. News and World Report,* 3 March 1979, p. 53.

"UNSUNG MERITS OF CONSERVATIVE PACs": *The New Right Report,* 4 February 1977, p. 3.

STEWART ON FUNDRAISING: "Doubts on Direct-Mail Wizard," *Washington Star,* 9 May 1978, pp. A-1, D-5.

RUSHER ON GOP: William A. Rusher, "Raising Conservative Bucks," *National Review,* 8 December 1978, pp. 15, 31–32.

WEYRICH ON FUNDRAISING: Quoted by James M. Perry, "The Right Wing Got Plucked," *National Observer,* 4 December 1976, p. 1.

DOLAN ON EXPENDITURES: *Ibid.,* p. 14.

Chapter 3
THE NEW OLD WEST

EPIGRAPH: Vachel Lindsay, "Bryan, Bryan, Bryan, Bryan," *Collected Poems* (New York: Macmillan, 1930), pp. 98–99.

WAYNE BOOK: John Wayne, *America, Why I Love Her* (New York: Ballantine, 1979).

REAGAN ON JOHN WAYNE: Ronald Reagan, "Unforgettable John Wayne," *Reader's Digest,* October 1979, pp. 115–19.

DUNLEAVY ON JOHN WAYNE: Steven Dunleavy, *National Star,* 16 September 1975, reprinted as "Bring Back the Heroes," in *Conservative Digest,* November 1975, p. 53.

EASTWOOD ON HIS FILMS: S. K. Overbeck, "Clint Eastwood *Is* Dirty Harry," *Conservative Digest,* June 1977, pp. 12–13.

VIGUERIE ON CONNALLY: Quoted in "John Connally, Superstar," *New Guard,* April 1976, p. 7.

KEVIN PHILLIPS ON CONNALLY: Kevin Phillips, "Can John Connally Pull It Off in '80?" *Anaheim* (Ca.) *Bulletin,* 31 January 1979, p. C-4.

BUCHANAN ON EUROPE: Patrick J. Buchanan, *Conservative Votes, Liberal Victories* (New York: Quadrangle/New York Times Books, 1975), p. 111.

FAIRLIE ON AMERICANS' FEAR OF THE EAST: Henry Fairlie, *The Parties: Republicans and Democrats in This Century* (New York: St. Martin's Press, 1978), p. 72.

WILL ON WESTERN MYTH: George F. Will, "Wagons in a Circle," *Newsweek,* 17 September 1979, p. 116.

TONSOR ON "FRESH START": Stephen J. Tonsor, "A Fresh Start: American History and Political Order," *Modern Age,* Winter 1972, pp. 2–3.

NOBLE ON AMERICAN HISTORY: Quoted by Tonsor, *idem.,* pp. 3–4.

GOLDWATER AND EASTERN SEABOARD: Fairlie, *The Parties,* pp. 72–73.

TAFT ON EUROPEAN QUARRELS, ISOLATIONISM: From James T. Patterson, *Mr. Republican: A Biography of Robert A. Taft* (Boston: Houghton Mifflin, 1972), p. 247.

TAFT ON WELTER OF RACES: Quoted by Fairlie, *The Parties,* p. 87.

FORTUNE ON TAFT: Quoted by Fairlie, *The Parties,* p. 73.

TAFT ON "NEW YORKERS": Patterson, *Mr. Republican,* p. 247.

RIGHT-WING ISOLATIONISM: Ronald Radosh, *Prophets on the Right: Profiles of Conservative Critics of American Globalism* (New York: Simon and Schuster, 1975), pp. 326–27.

DOLAN ON FOREIGN POLICY: Author's interview, 10 January 1979, Rosslyn, Va.

FAIRLIE ON ISOLATIONISM: *The Parties,* pp. 73–74.

SCHLAFLY APPEARANCE ON "FIRING LINE": "The Panama Canal," 77/17, 26 September 1977 (taped).

ATTACK ON BANKS: Matthew Conroy, "A Banker's Betrayal to Hanoi Butchers," *Human Events,* 7 January 1978, p. 10.

WHALEN ON CRITICISMS OF "EASTERN INTERNATIONALISTS": Richard J. Whalen, *Taking Sides: A Personal View of America from Kennedy to Nixon to Kennedy* (Boston: Houghton Mifflin, 1974), pp. 100–01.

HOOVER QUOTED ON "EASTERN INTELLIGENTSIA": James T. Patterson, *Mr. Republican: A Biography of Robert A. Taft* (Boston: Houghton Mifflin, 1972), p. 141.

BUCHANAN ON NEW YORK: Patrick J. Buchanan, " 'The Big Apple' Heads for the Ledge," *Human Events,* 4 March 1978, pp. 13, 18.

ORANGE COUNTY DESCRIBED: Author's visits, April and September 1979. Also, Michael Barone, Grant Ujifusa, and Douglas Matthews, eds., *The Almanac of American Politics, 1978* (New York: E.P. Dutton/A Sunrise Book, 1978), pp. 118–19.

BIRCH SOCIETY BEST SELLER: Gary Allen, *None Dare Call It Conspiracy* (Rosmoor, Calif.: Concord Press, 1971).

INFORMATION ON *SANTA ANA REGISTER* AND LIBERTARIAN PARTY ACTIVITY: Author's interview with Kenneth Grubbs, 13 April 1979, Santa Ana, Calif.

MEYER ON JOHN BIRCH SOCIETY: Frank S. Meyer, "The Birch Malady," *National Review,* 19 October 1965, p. 920.

LIPSET ON JOHN BIRCH SOCIETY: Seymour Martin Lipset, quoted in Laurel Leff, "Whatever Happened to the John Birch Society?" *The Wall Street Journal,* 29 August 1979, p. 12.

ROBERT WELCH ON SCHLAFLY: Welch's comment that Schlafly was "a very loyal member of the John Birch Society" appeared in the JBS *Bulletin,* March 1960, p. 13. On February 17, 1964, she told Group Research, Inc., that "I am not a member at all."

YOUNG AMERICANS FOR FREEDOM SPLIT WITH LIBERTARIANS: Author's telephone interview with Daniel Joy, 30 November 1979, Washington, D.C.

LIBERTARIAN PARTY INFORMATION: Author's telephone interview with Dyanne Petersen, 11 December 1979, Washington, D.C. Pamphlets and brochures of the Libertarian Party provided by Petersen.

NATIONAL REVIEW ATTACK ON LIBERTARIANS: Ernest van den Haag, "Libertarians and Conservatives," *National Review,* 8 June 1979, pp. 725–27.

LARRY FLYNT ENDORSEMENT OF LIBERTARIAN PARTY: Larry Flynt, "No Choice Again," *Hustler,* November 1979, p. 5.

QUOTES FROM JARVIS: References to "rugged bastard" and "messiah or a maniac" appear in "Meet Howard Jarvis," *Time,* 19 June 1978, p. 21. The reference to a junior-high-school boy appears in "Mr. Proposition 13," *Newsweek,* 19 June 1978, p. 25. Reference to "telling the government screw you!" and to the League of Women Voters, appears in *Time,* 19 June 1978, p. 21; to "crock of manure," in *Newsweek,* 19 June 1978, p. 25.

LARSON ON NATIONAL RIGHT TO WORK COMMITTEE: "Private Memorandum to Members," Subject: Freedom to Work Committee of the National Right to Work Committee, from Reed Larson, 7 May 1965. Larson on Morrison and Nathan, *ibid.* Also, 8 June 1965 report of the Better Business Bureau of Metropolitan Washington, signed by Managing Director Leland S. McCarthy. Philip Meyer, "Freedom-to-Work Group Facing Post Office Probe," *Miami Herald,* 22 September 1965. Thomas W. Ottenad, "Fund-Raising Group Is Under Investigation," *St. Louis Post-Dispatch,* 10 October 1965.

BUSINESSMEN FOR GOLDWATER: The BBB Report, Better Business Bureau of Greater Milwaukee, 30 June 1965; Larson memo, 7 May 1965.

FRIENDS FOR HAYAKAWA: Friends for Hayakawa, *Year-End Report,* 1976; *Paso Robles* (Ca.) *Press,* 6 September 1978; Jack Anderson column, "The Prop. No. 13 Man and Some Scams," *Washington Post,* 25 July 1978.

QUOTES FROM DAVIS: "Chief Shoots from the Lip," *Time,* 8 September 1975, pp. 46–47; "L.A.'s Controversial Cop," *Newsweek,* 29 August 1977, p. 55; "The Meanest Police Chief in America: An Interview with Ed Davis," *Conservative Digest,* October 1975, p. 34. The reference to homosexuals and migrant workers appears in the *Charleston Gazette,* 28 February 1978, p. 7-B; to "transvestite morons," in Rowland Evans and Robert Novak, "Ed Davis, Toned-Down Favorite," *Washington Post,* 3 February 1978, p. A-19.

DAVIS LEAVES DEMOCRATIC PARTY: "Names in the News," *Conservative Digest,* November 1978, p. 18.

NEWS LEADER ON HURWITZ: "Students Back Tough Principal's Stand," *Human Events,* 1 May 1976, p. 352. Hurwitz has written a number of articles for *Human Events,* among them: 4 January 1973 and 23 November 1974.

Also, Ken Auletta, "The Last Angry Principal," *New York,* 3 May 1976, p. 45.

LARSON'S "RESPECTFUL NONCOMPLIANCE": Jerry Norton, "A Fighter for Freedom," *Conservative Digest,* November 1975, p. 32.

RAUH ON LARSON: Quoted in *The New York Times,* 4 December 1977, p. D-1.

HEADLINE QUOTED ON AFL-CIO: *National Right to Work Newsletter,* 25 August 1978, p. 6.

DENHOLM ON WORKING NIGHT AND DAY: Fundraising letter signed by Denholm, n.d.

GUN LOBBY BOYCOTT OF CATHOLIC CHURCHES: *Washington Post,* 1 September 1978, p. C-18.

CARRINGTON ON "RIDICULOUS" PROCEDURES: Quoted in Joan Travis, "Champion of the Crime Victim," *Conservative Digest,* December 1976, p. 29. Reprint of an article that first appeared in the *Chicago Tribune,* 4 September 1976.

GROUP NOT "POLICE—RIGHT OR WRONG ORGANIZATION": "Ten Years of Achievement: AELE 1966–1976," a brochure of Americans for Effective Law Enforcement, Evanston, Ill., p. 8.

CHICAGO ACLU SPOKESMAN QUOTED: Travis, *Conservative Digest,* December 1976, p. 29.

DUDMAN ON AMERICAN SECURITY COUNCIL: Richard Dudman, *Men of the Far Right* (New York: Pyramid Books, 1962), p. 45.

AMERICAN SECURITY COUNCIL AND "MILITARY BRASS": Vincent Wilbur, "The New Right vs. The Old Red Menace," *Seven Days*, July 1978, p. 11.

BACKGROUND OF PHILLIP LUCE: Widely publicized for several years, Luce's Communist and radical affiliations are no secret; indeed, he is a friend of the author's, and makes no attempt to hide his past affiliations with organizations he now considers subversive.

LUCE'S BOOK ON CAMPUS RADICALS: Phillip Abbott Luce, *Road to Revolution: Communist Guerrilla Warfare in the U.S.A.* (San Diego: Viewpoint Books, 1967).

Chapter 4
GOOD GUYS AND BAD GUYS

EPIGRAPH: Howard Phillips, quoted in *Political Action Report*, September 1979, p. 5.

FALWELL ON KENNEDY: Quoted in the *Richmond* (Va.) *Times-Dispatch*, 2 May 1979, p. 1.

EVANS'S LAW OF POLITICS: This adage has been expressed to the author on numerous occasions, mostly social.

EDWARDS'S BOOK ON REAGAN: Lee Edwards, *Reagan: A Political Biography* (San Diego: Viewpoint Books), 1967.

VIGUERIE ON GOLDWATER "FACT FROM FICTION": "From the Publisher," *Conservative Digest*, January 1976, p. 1.

CONSERVATIVE DIGEST ON GOLDWATER: Richard A. Viguerie and Lee Edwards, "Goldwater: Leader or Legend?" *Conservative Digest*, January 1976, pp. 6–8.

RUSHER ON GOLDWATER: William A. Rusher, "What's Happened to Barry?" *Conservative Digest*, April 1976, p. 16.

BRUDNOY ON GOLDWATER: David Brudnoy, "The Trouble with Barry." For release 11–12 May 1976.

YAF ON GOLDWATER: "Barry Unfair to Reagan, Conservatives Charge," news release of Young Americans for Freedom, 7 May 1976.

NEW GUARD ON GOLDWATER: Alan Crawford, "The Sunshine Boys Bow Out: Goldwater and Tower—Stage Left," *New Guard*, June 1976, pp. 7–9.

RUSHER LETTER TO *CONSERVATIVE DIGEST*: "Reaction to 'Goldwater: Leader or Legend?' " *Conservative Digest*, March 1976, pp. 2–3.

LOEB LETTER TO *CONSERVATIVE DIGEST*: *Ibid.*

PHILLIPS ON *CONSERVATIVE DIGEST*'S ATTACK ON GOLDWATER: Excerpts printed in *ibid.*

READERS' RESPONSES TO GOLDWATER STORY: *Ibid.*

GOLDWATER SHOULD BE REMOVED FROM LIST OF "FAVORITE CONSERVATIVES," READER SAYS: *Conservative Digest*, December 1975, p. 2.

LOFTON ON GOLDWATER: John D. Lofton, Jr., "Is Goldwater's Support of Ford Fault of Post-Operative Ether Fog?" Column for release 5 July 1976, United Features Syndicate.

KILPATRICK ON REAGAN: James J. Kilpatrick, "The Goldwater and Ford Campaigns: A Difference?" *National Review*, 19 December 1975, p. 1467.

WEYRICH ON REAGAN CANDIDACY ("KINGSTON" MEETING): Author's interview with John Sullivan, 3 May 1976, Washington, D.C.

HOWARD PHILLIPS ON SCHWEIKER CHOICE: 26 July 1976, "Conservative Organizer Denounces Reagan-Schweiker Pact/Howard Phillips Says Foes of Liberalism Should Reject 'Victory At Any Price.' " Press release, for immediate release,

WILLIAM F. BUCKLEY ON SCHWEIKER NOMINATION: William F. Buckley, Jr., "Reagan, Yes, Schweiker, No?" *National Review,* 3 September 1976, pp. 970–71.

KEENE ON RESPONSE TO SCHWEIKER NOMINATION: Alan Crawford, "Richard Viguerie's Bid for Power," *The Nation,* 29 January 1977, p. 107.

ACU ACTIVIST ON SCHWEIKER CONTROVERSY: *Ibid.*

SEARS ON REAGAN'S IMAGE: "With Eye to 1980 Campaign, Reagan Is Considering a Trip to China," *The New York Times,* 20 July 1978, p. A-13.

NEW YORK TIMES ON REAGAN'S IMAGE: *Ibid.*

REAGAN PLAYS DOWN RIGHT-WING IMAGE: "Can a 69-Year-Old Win the Presidency? Reagan Eyes 1980," *The Wall Street Journal,* 19 July 1978, p. 30.

KEVIN PHILLIPS ON REAGAN COMMITTEE: Quoted in Alan Crawford, "Who's New on the Right?" *Inquiry,* 16 October 1978, p. 9.

REAGAN'S RECORD AS GOVERNOR: Statistics drawn from several sources, among them: Eric Garris, "California's Other Governor," *Reason,* July 1975, p. 17; "Enter Reagan," an editorial in *The New York Times,* 20 November 1975; "Inside Ronald Reagan," an interview with Reagan in *Reason,* 15 July 1975, p. 6; "Ronald Reagan: Hubert Humphrey of the Right," *LP News,* the publication of the Libertarian party, November-December 1975, p. 6.

REAGAN SCORED BY *NEW REPUBLIC*: John Osborne, "Back to Reagan," *The New Republic,* 19 June 1976, p. 9.

REAGAN ON WATERGATE: Allan C. Brownfeld, "Rightists' Inconsistent Attacks on Ford," *Phoenix Gazette,* 26 July 1975. Allan C. Brownfeld, "Voters Deserve to Have Reagan Be More Explicit," *Phoenix Gazette,* 17 February 1976.

REAGAN AS COMPROMISER: Ray Cromley, "Reagan's Record Not in Line with Platform," for release 9 July 1976, Newspaper Enterprise Association.

PICTURE ON NOFZIGER'S OFFICE WALL: Richard Reeves, "Why Reagan Won't Make It," *Esquire,* 8 May 1979, p. 7.

NATIONAL REVIEW ON WALLACE: "George Wallace: Moment of Truth," *National Review,* 7 April 1970, pp. 344–45.

KILPATRICK ON WALLACE: James J. Kilpatrick, "The Time Is Not Right," *Conservative Digest,* October 1975, p. 13.

RUSHER ON WALLACE: William A. Rusher, *The Making of the New Majority Party* (New York: Sheed and Ward, 1975), pp. 170–176.

KEVIN PHILLIPS ON WALLACE: Kevin Phillips, "Shaping the Right Deal for America," *Conservative Digest,* July 1975, p. 30. Originally published in *Newsweek,* 19 May 1975.

WALLACE'S RECORD AS GOVERNOR: Peter N. Ehrmann, "Wallace's Southern Shadow," *New Guard,* May 1976, p. 12. Ehrmann quotes the reference to Wallace as "a dangerous left-winger" and a "radical," from Marshall

Frady, *Wallace* (New York: World, 1968), p. 98. The quote that Wallace's programs surpassed "the fondest dreams" of liberals is from Frady, p. 137.

ASHBROOK ON WALLACE: John Ashbrook, "And Anyway, Is Wallace a Conservative?" *National Review*, 22 November 1968, p. 1048.

"AGIN-ISM": Kirkpatrick Sale, *Power Shift: The Rise of the Southern Rim and Its Challenge to the Eastern Establishment* (New York: Random House, 1975), p. 104.

BUCHANAN ON WALLACE: Patrick J. Buchanan, "Wallace: The Most Influential Outsider," *Conservative Digest*, August 1976, p. 24.

LOFTON ON WALLACE: John D. Lofton, Jr., "Wallace Sells Out to Carter, Putting Party Above Principle." For release 18 June 1976, United Features Syndicate.

THOMSON AS GOVERNOR: The reference to sending an aide to examine tax records and Thomson's views on enforcing the constitution appear in John Kifner, "Atom Controversy One of Many of Governor Thomson," *The New York Times*, 11 May 1977, p. A-1. See also: Morton Mintz, "Court Raises Flag in New Hampshire," *Washington Post*, 25 March 1978; Michael Knight, "New Hampshire Governor Strikes a Responsive Chord," *The New York Times*, 30 March 1978, p. 1. "The Gutsiest Governor in America: An Interview with Meldrim Thomson," *Conservative Digest*, August 1975, p. 6.

THOMSON COMPARED TO HUEY LONG: Patrick J. Buchanan, "New Hampshire's Thomson: A Huey Long of the American Right," *Richmond* (Va.) *Times-Dispatch*, 9 September 1978, p. 8.

"MUZZLE" STORY: The "Muzzle" was Daniel Joy, legislative aide to Senator James Buckley, when the author was a speechwriter there. The story was related to the author by Joy.

GALLO EPISODE: Buchanan, *Richmond* (Va.) *Times-Dispatch*, 9 September 1978, p. 8.

THOMSON AND SEABROOK PROTEST: "Thomson Hangs Tough on Seabrook Demonstrators," *Human Events*, 21 March 1977, p. 5.

THOMSON'S ACHIEVEMENTS: David Brudnoy, "How Does Meldrim Do It?" For release 3–4 November 1977.

THOMSON DEFEATED: "The Big Losers," *Newsweek*, 20 November 1978, p. 48. "Conventional Wisdom Shattered in N.H. Race," *Washington Post*, 9 November 1978, p. A-2.

THOMSON WEIGHS PRESIDENTIAL RACE: *Human Events*, 2 September 1978, p. 2.

THOMSON SEEKS PRESIDENCY: "Thomson Joins Presidential Race," *The New York Times*, 1 November 1979, p. A-16.

THE NATION ON HELMS: "The Money Tree," *The Nation*, 30 September 1978, p. 292.

HELMS A "TOTALLY PRINCIPLED POLITICIAN": Flyer distributed by Helms for Senate Campaign, reprint of *Conservative Digest* article, "A Totally Principled Politician," October 1976, p. 8.

HELMS AS "SENATOR NO": *Washington Post*, 6 November 1978, p. 22.

HELMS'S "SPIRITED DEFENSE" ON TOBACCO SUBSIDIES: *The Wall Street Journal*, 25 September 1978, p. 40.

$6.7 MILLION RAISED FOR HELMS'S CAMPAIGN: References to $6 million, *Congressional Quarterly*, 28 October 1978, p. 3113; to $6.7 million, *Washington Post*, 31 October 1978, p. A-12.

ATTACKS ON LABOR: Undated "Senate-Gram" from Helms headquarters in Raleigh, N.C., signed by "Jesse."

HELMS'S CAMPAIGN DEBT: "Helms in the Hole," *Newsweek*, 4 December 1978, p. 37.

HELMS PRAISED BY JOHN BIRCH SOCIETY PUBLICATION: Medford Evans, "The New Conservative in the Senate," *American Opinion*, April 1973, p. 16.

THE "JESSECRATS": M. Stanton Evans, "Senator Jesse Helms: A New Kind of Politician," *Human Events*, 5 August 1978, p. 15.

HELMS CALLS GOP "PARTY OF DISCOUNT DEMOCRATS": Quoted in Free Campus News Service, Sterling, Va., 23 May 1975, Vol. 5, No. 5. Publication of Young Americans for Freedom is now defunct.

BIOGRAPHICAL INFORMATION ON MCDONALD: "Larry P. McDonald, Member of Congress, 7th District of Georgia," mimeographed biography provided by McDonald's office.

MCDONALD'S POLITICAL VIEWS: Author's interview, 6 February 1979, Washington, D.C.

MCDONALD RESOLUTION: "Christian Lobby/Rep. McDonald Introduce Anti-Homosexual Resolution."Press release of *Christian Voice*, for release 24 July 1979, Washington, D.C.

CRANE ON "PHYSICAL STRENGTH": Quoted in *Human Events*, 5 August 1978, p. 637.

LOEB ON CRANE'S "VANITY": "A Stab in the Back," an editorial in *The Manchester Union Leader*, 1 August 1979, pp. 1, 4. See also "Put on the Brakes, Phil," *The Manchester Union Leader*, 26 July 1978, pp. 1, 12.

CRANE–REAGAN DISPUTE: Andrew Mollison, "Panel Created for Centrist Reagan Race," *The Atlanta Constitution*, 8 March 1979, p. A-9.

WILLIAMSON ON REASON FOR CRANE'S CANDIDACY: Author's telephone interview, September 1978, Washington, D.C.

UNION LEADER SERIES ON CRANE: "The Two Faces of Congressman Crane," editorial, *The Manchester Union Leader*, 8 March 1979, pp. 1, 20; and "The Two Faces of Phil Crane: Cleancut Conservative? or Party Playboy?" 8 March 1979, pp. 1, 20. On Crane's administrative problems, see e.g., *Human Events*: George Fowler, "Will a Conservative Capture the 1980 GOP Nomination?" 17 February 1979, p. 1; "Reagan the Man to Beat in New Hampshire," 24 February 1979, p. 3; "Is End Near for Crane's Campaign?" 12 May 1979, p. 5; "Phil Crane Splits with the New Right," 5 May 1979, p. 3; "Is Crane Now Thinking of '84?" 19 May 1979, p. 5; "Chaos in the Crane Campaign," 26 May 1979, pp. 10, 11, 13, 14. See also: "Bickering Racks Crane's Presidential Campaign," *Washington Post*, 5 May 1979, p. 2.

FINANCES OF CRANE CAMPAIGN: The references to $1.7 million, $2 million, and to the size of the debt appear in *Human Events*, 5 May 1979, p. 368.

CONSERVATIVE FUNDRAISING SPECIALIST: Interview with conservative fundraiser, not for attribution, April 1979.

$1 MILLION IN FEDERAL MATCHING FUNDS: "FEC Approves Matching Funds for 1980 Presidential Candidates." FEC press release, 27 February 1980. See also: "Crane Campaign Qualifies for Matching Funds." News from Crane-President-1980, for release 5 February 1980,

KEVIN PHILLIPS AND RICHARD A. VIGUERIE ON CONNALLY: Quoted in "John Connally, Superstar," *New Guard,* April 1976, p. 7.

RUSHER ON "STRONG, ENERGETIC" PRESIDENTS: Author's interview with William A. Rusher, 11 March 1979, New York City.

VIGUERIE SPENDS BETWEEN $35,000 AND $50,000 ON CONNALLY WRITE-IN CAMPAIGN: FEC press report, Summary of 1976 Democratic Primary Write-In Effort for John Connally, 1977.

VIGUERIE AND CONNALLY: "Viguerie Joining Connally Campaign as 'Volunteer,' " *Human Events,* 18 August 1979, p. 3. Also, *Washington Post,* 8 August 1979.

CONNALLY ON ABORTION: "I Might Well Consider Running: An Interview with John B. Connally," *Conservative Digest,* December 1975, p. 12.

SNYDER ON CONNALLY AND GUN CONTROL: Author's interview with John Snyder, Washington, D.C., for *New Guard* article "John Connally, Superstar," *New Guard,* April 1976, p. 8.

CONNALLY'S POSITIONS: On not being a conservative, quoted in *Human Events,* 13 March 1976, p. 5. On détente and longshoremen, *ibid.* " 'I Might Well Consider Running,' An Interview with John Connally," *Conservative Digest,* December 1975, p. 11.

CONNALLY POSITIONS ARE "ANATHEMA" TO CONSERVATIVES: *Human Events,* 13 March 1976, p. 5.

TOPPING ON CONNALLY: Author's interview with John C. Topping, 8 September 1979, Washington, D.C.

CONNALLY'S YOUTH SERVICE PLAN: John D. Lofton, Jr., "Is Connally a Conservative?" *Human Events,* 5 July 1975, p. 11.

FRIEDMAN ON CONNALLY PLAN: Quoted by Lofton, *ibid.*

VON HOFFMAN ON CONNALLY PLAN: Quoted by Lofton, *ibid.*

CONNALLY'S NATIONAL DIVIDEND PROGRAM: Alan Crawford, "The Money's on Connally," *Inquiry,* 8 and 22 January 1979, p. 11.

CONNALLY MEETS WITH NEW RIGHT LEADERS: Rowland Evans and Robert Novak, "Connally's Populist Push," *Washington Post,* 8 August 1979, p. A-21.

HOFSTADTER ON LEADERSHIP: Richard Hofstadter, "Pseudo-Conservatism Revisited—A Postscript (1962)," in Daniel Bell, ed., *The Radical Right: The New American Right Updated and Expanded* (Garden City, N.Y.: Anchor Books/Doubleday, 1962), p. 102.

STUDY OF GOVERNORS: Quoted by M. Stanton Evans, *The Future of Conservatism from Taft to Reagan and Beyond* (New York: Holt, Rinehart & Winston, 1968), p. 80.

SUPPORT FOR AGNEW: Two articles showing early conservative support for Agnew, both stemming from his speech to black leaders, are "Agnew Proves a Big Plus Factor," *Human Events,* 16 October 1968, p. 723; and "Agnew's Successful Debut," *Human Events,* 24 August 1968, p. 532. His remarks to the black leaders were reprinted in *Human Events* as "Gov. Agnew's Controversial Address," 4 May 1968, p. 12. See also: "Agnew: How Conservative?" *Human Events,* 17 August 1968, p. 3.

Chapter 5
PROTECTING HEARTH AND HOME: THE WOMAN'S PLACE

EPIGRAPH: Quoted in James T. McKenna, "The Textbook Revolt in West Virginia," *Conservative Digest,* June 1975, p. 7.

LETTER: Fundraising letter of Christian Voice, signed by Robert Grant, n.d.

EDUCATION AS STATE RESPONSIBILITY: Jo Anne Gasper, *The Right Woman,* 4 April 1979.

EVANS ON BUSING: M. Stanton Evans, *Clear and Present Dangers: A Conservative View of America's Government* (New York: Harcourt Brace Jovanovich, 1975), p. 184.

THE "MIDDLE-AGED" VOTER: Richard M. Scammon and Ben J. Wattenberg, *The Real Majority* (New York: Coward-McCann, Inc., 1970), p. 21.

STATUS FRUSTRATION: David R. Schweitzer, *Status Frustration and Conservatism in Comparative Perspective: The Swiss Case* (Beverly Hills & London: Sage Publications, 1974), p. 5.

MCEVOY ON STATUS ANXIETIES: James P. McEvoy, *Radicals or Conservatives? The Contemporary American Right* (Chicago: Rand-McNally, 1971), p. 151.

SCHLAFLY ON "RIGHTS": Phyllis Schlafly, *The Phyllis Schlafly Report,* Vol. 13, No. 1, Sec. 2, 1979.

EAGLE FORUM: "New Activists: The Single Issue Lobbies," *Newsweek,* 7 November 1977, p. 41.

"I PICK THEM!": Author's interview with Phyllis Schlafly, 10 February 1979, Washington, D.C.

WOMEN ACTIVISTS IN CRANE CAMPAIGN: Author's telephone interview with Judy Mack and Jeannette Boone, 1 November 1978, Danville, Ill.

MAUREEN REAGAN ON ERA: Author's interview, published in *New Guard* as "Maureen Reagan Talks Back: I'm Still a Conservative!" April 1976, pp. 13–14.

JUANITA BARTNETT ON ERA: Author's interview, 10–11 May 1979, Schaumberg, Ill.

SCHLAFLY ON WOMEN AND CAREERS: Author's interview, 10 February 1979, Washington, D.C.

ROWE QUOTED: Author's telephone interview with Ed Rowe, 26 January 1979, Washington, D.C.

THOMPSON ON "COOPERATION" BETWEEN BRYANT AND SCHLAFLY GROUPS: "How to Fight the Homosexuals," *Conservative Digest,* August 1977, p. 3.

RIGHT TO LIFE PARTY: Frank Lynn, "Right to Life Party's Gain," *The New York Times,* 5 April 1979.

DISAFFECTION WITH RIGHT TO LIFE MOVEMENT: "Should it be 'Life for the Right'?" *Chicago Tribune,* 6 May 1979, p. 21.

FIRST-HAND ACCOUNT OF BRYANT'S COUNSELING PROGRAM: Joe Baker, "Inside Anita's Ministries," *The Advocate,* 19 April 1979, pp. 18, 23.

OBJECTIONS TO SCHOOL BOOKS: "NCTE Survey Shows Censorship Increasing in Schools," press release from Public Information Office of the National Council of Teachers of English, n.d.

ALICE MOORE QUOTED: Author's interview with Alice Moore, originally published as "Victory for 'Back to Basics' in West Virginia," *Human Events,* 29 July 1978, p. 15.

SELZER ON WORKING-CLASS OBJECTIONS TO TEXTS: Curtis Selzer, "A Confusion of Goals," *The Nation,* 2 November 1974, p. 430.

FORMATION OF NATIONAL COUNCIL FOR EDUCATIONAL EXCELLENCE: Letter to author from Jil Wilson, 26 October 1978.

ISLAND TREES CONTROVERSY: Quoted in *The Nation,* 27 October 1979, p. 391.

JESUS "NOT A SISSY": Quoted in *Time,* 1 October 1978, p. 68.

FALWELL AT CAPITOL HILL RALLY: Quoted in *Washington Post,* 28 April 1979, p. B-2.

QUOTES FROM THE REV. FALWELL: "The Evangelist and His Empire: Cleaning up America with Jerry Falwell," *Washington Post,* 28 April 1979, p. B-2.

FALWELL ON JEWS: "Va. Preacher's Jewish 'Jest' Stirs Fuss," *Washington Post,* 21 September 1979, p. B-4. "Falwell Apologizes for Remark," the *Richmond* (Va.) *Times-Dispatch,* 21 September 1979, p. B-9.

INFORMATION ON RELIGIOUS LEADERS AND GROUPS: "Building the Moral Majority," *Conservative Digest,* August 1979, pp. 14–19. Also, author's interview with Gary Jarmin at Christian Voice headquarters in August 1979, Washington, D.C.

ROBERTSON ON "HUMANISTIC" INFLUENCE ON AMERICAN GOVERNMENT AND CONTROL BY TRILATERAL COMMISSION: Quoted in *U.S. News and World Report,* 24 September 1979, p. 37.

ROBERTSON ON ABILITY TO "TAKE OVER": *Ibid.*

MORAL MAJORITY'S PLANS FOR FUTURE RALLIES: Quoted in *Conservative Digest,* September 1979, pp. 14–19.

FALWELL TO "TURN THIS INTO A CHRISTIAN NATION": *Washington Post,* 28 April 1978, p. B-2.

WALL STREET JOURNAL ON CHRISTIAN SCHOOLS: *Ibid.*

CONNALLY MEETING WITH EVANGELISTS: "Preachers into Politics," *U.S. News and World Report,* 4 September 1979, p. 40.

CRANE "BORN AGAIN": "Politics: Avocation for Every Believer," *Christian Life,* August 1978, p. 17.

VIGUERIE CALLS FOR NATIONAL DAY OF PRAYER: Richard A. Viguerie, "From the Publisher," *Conservative Digest,* October 1979, p. 48.

REAL ON IMPACT OF FUNDAMENTALIST MINISTERS IN POLITICS: Letter to the author, October 9, 1979.

ACTIVISM OF RIGHT TO LIFERS: "Study shows why single issue supporters have impact far beyond their numbers," *Campaigning Reports,* 20 September 1979, p. 4.

ROSENBLATT IN *NEW YORK TIMES*: Quoted in "Nov. 7 Turnout Was 37.9%, Lowest Since '42," *The New York Times,* 19 December 1978, p. A-13.

HOLT ON WOMEN IN POLITICS: "An Interview with Marjorie Holt," *New Guard*, September 1974, p. 17.

GASPER ON WOMEN IN POLITICS: Quoted in the *Chicago Tribune*, 23 October 1979, p. 4.

Chapter 6
ANTI-ELITISM AND THE NEW CLASS WARFARE

EPIGRAPH: Author's telephone interview with Howard Phillips, Washington, D.C., 23 February 1979.

ROSSITER ON SUPPORT FOR RIGHT AND LEFT: Clinton Rossiter, *Conservatism in America: The Thankless Persuasion* (New York: Alfred A. Knopf, 1962), p. 14.

HOWARD PHILLIPS: Author's telephone interview with Howard Phillips, 23 February 1979, Washington, D.C.

WEYRICH ON "MIDDLE CLASS REVOLT": Author's interview with Paul Weyrich, 17 May 1979.

NASH ON CHANGING CONSTITUENCY OF THE RIGHT: George H. Nash, *The Conservative Intellectual Movement in America Since 1945* (New York: Basic Books, 1976), pp. 250–51.

RUSHER ON PRODUCERS AND NONPRODUCERS: William A. Rusher, "Producers Versus Nonproducers," for release, 26 February 1975, Universal Press Syndicate.

SCHLAFLY AND "THE POWER ELITE": *Conservative Digest* poll of "Favorite Conservatives," March 1978, p. 13.

"ANTI-INTELLECTUALISM" OF THE NEW RIGHT: Hamilton Rogers, "Turning Inside Out," a review of Kevin Phillips's *Mediacracy* in *New Guard*, December 1975, p. 15.

VIERECK ON ANTI-ELITISM: Peter Viereck, "The Revolt Against the Elite," in *The Radical Right: The New American Right Updated and Expanded*, Daniel Bell, ed. (Garden City, N.Y.: Anchor Books/Doubleday, 1962), pp. 91–116.

"NEW CLASS" CONCEPT: Milovan Djilas, *The New Class: An Analysis of the Communist System* (New York: Praeger, 1957).

CHAMBERS ON "PLAIN MEN AND WOMEN": Whittaker Chambers, *Witness* (New York: Random House, 1954), pp. 793–94.

BURNHAM ON "INGROWN EAST": James Burnham, *The Coming Defeat of Communism* (New York: John Day, 1950), p. 277.

KENDALL ON "GOOD SENSE" OF AMERICAN PEOPLE: Willmoore Kendall, "Bipartisanship and Majority-Rule Democracy," *American Perspective*, Spring 1950, pp. 146–56.

SCHLAMM ON MCCARTHY'S SUPPORT: William S. Schlamm, introduction to William F. Buckley, Jr. and L. Brent Bozell, *McCarthy and His Enemies: The Record and Its Meaning* (Chicago: The Henry Regnery Co., 1954), p. xv.

KENDALL ON "*TRAHISON DES CLERCS*": Quoted by Nash, *Conservative Intellectual Movement in America*, p. 232.

HERBERG ON "DEFECTION OF INTELLIGENTSIA": Will Herberg, "Alienation,

'Dissent,' and the Intellectual," *National Review,* 30 July 1968, pp. 738–39.

TONSOR ON LIBERAL "ASCENDANCY": Stephen J. Tonsor, "On Living at the End of an Era," *National Review,* 30 July 1968, pp. 756–58.

HART ON "TREASONOUS" INTELLECTUALS: Jeffrey Hart, "Secession of the Intellectuals," *National Review,* 1 December 1970, pp. 1278–82.

EISENHOWER ON "SENSATION SEEKING COLUMNISTS": Quoted by George Nash, *The Conservative Intellectual Movement in America,* p. 305.

EVANS ON MEDIA BIAS: M. Stanton Evans, *The Future of Conservatism from Taft to Reagan and Beyond* (New York: Holt, Rinehart & Winston, 1968), pp. 103–16.

EFRON BOOK: Edith Efron, *The News Twisters* (Los Angeles: Nash Publishing Co., 1971).

LEFEVER: Ernest Lefever, *TV and National Defense: An Analysis of CBS News, 1972–1973* (Washington, D.C.: Institute for American Strategy, 1974).

KRISTOL AND MEDIA BIAS: Irving Kristol, "Does TV News Tell It Like It Is?" *Fortune,* November 1971, pp. 183, 186.

BUCHANAN ON NEOCONSERVATIVES: Author's interview with Patrick J. Buchanan, May 1976, originally published as " 'The Final Days' and Beyond: An Exclusive Interview with Patrick J. Buchanan," *New Guard,* June 1976, p. 14.

PODHORETZ ON THE RIGHT AND THE NEW DEAL: Author's interview for *New Guard* with Norman Podhoretz, 13 August 1976, New York City. Interview never published.

KRISTOL ON NEOCONSERVATIVES AND JACK KEMP: Author's interview with Irving Kristol, 14 May 1979, New York City.

KRISTOL ON DIRECT DEMOCRACY: *Ibid.*

PHILLIPS ON NEOCONSERVATIVES: Kevin Phillips, "The Neoconservatives: Chiefs without Indians," *Washington Post,* 26 August 1979, pp. D-1, D-4.

BUCKLEY ON "TRANSIDEOLOGICAL FRIENDSHIPS": Author's interview with William F. Buckley, Jr., 11 May 1979, New York City.

PUBLISHER CHIDES BUCKLEY FOR LIBERAL FRIENDSHIPS: The author had numerous conversations of this nature with a newspaper publisher during 1978.

PHILLIPS ON "NOMINAL RIGHTIST" PUBLICATION: Kevin Phillips, "Liberal Hustlers," *Morgantown* (W. Va.) *Dominion-Post,* 19 October 1977, p. 10.

BUCKLEY ON REACTION OF RIGHT TO HIS CAREER: *Ibid.*

HOWARD PHILLIPS ON BUCKLEY: Author's telephone interview with Howard Phillips, 23 February 1979, Washington, D.C.

CONSERVATIVE ACTIVIST ON WILL: Author's interview, not for attribution, 12 January 1979, Washington, D.C.

HUMAN EVENTS ON WILL: "When George Will Writes, Should Conservatives Heed?" *Human Events,* 24 January 1976, p. 5.

BATTLELINE ON WILL: "Will's Will," *Battleline,* April 1977, p. 24.

HUMAN EVENTS ON SAFIRE: "Safire Boasts How He Pushed Nixon Leftward," *Human Events,* 15 March 1975, p. 4.

PHILLIPS ON SAFIRE: Kevin Phillips, "An End to White House Flackery?" *Human Events,* 12 May 1973, p. 6.

Chapter 7
THE JOURNALIST AS MACHIAVELLI

EPIGRAPH: Albert Jay Nock, *Cogitations from Albert Jay Nock,* Robert M. Thornton, ed. (Irvington-on-Hudson, N.Y.: The Nockian Society, 1970), p. 77.

Kevin Phillips, *The Emerging Republican Majority* (New Rochelle, N.Y.: Arlington House, 1969).

BOOK NOT "A STRATEGY": Phillips, Introduction, *Mediacracy: American Parties and Politics in the Communications Age* (Garden City, N.Y.: Doubleday, 1975), p. vii.

PHILLIPS ON SHIFTING BASE OF GOP: *Ibid.,* p. vi.

PHILLIPS ON "UPHEAVAL" OF 1960s: *Emerging Republican Majority, op. cit.,* p. 470.

BOOK DEDICATED TO NIXON AND MITCHELL: *Ibid,* p. 6; proofs "made available" to RNC, *ibid.,* p. 23; prohibitions under which Phillips wrote the book, *ibid.,* p. 23; book distilled into strategy memos, *Mediacracy, op. cit.,* p. vi.

PHILLIPS ON GROWTH OF "KNOWLEDGE" INDUSTRY AND THE "NEW ELITE": *Mediacracy, op. cit.,* pp. 31–38.

PHILLIPS ON REAGAN-WALLACE TICKET: Kevin Phillips, "A Reagan-Wallace Ticket," *Newsweek,* 19 May 1975, p. 13.

CRITICISM OF PHILLIPS'S THESIS: Hamilton Rogers, "Turning Inside Out," *New Guard,* December 1975, p. 15.

RUSHER AS "ACTIVIST": D. Keith Mano, "The Poor Man's Bill Buckley," *Conservative Digest,* December 1975, p. 25.

RUSHER'S MIDWESTERN ROOTS: Author's interview with William Rusher, 11 March 1979, New York City.

RUSHER AS "SENATE RED-HUNTER" AND "BACKROOM POLITICAL OPERATOR": Description taken from mimeographed biography of Rusher, dated September 1978, provided to the author in 1979.

RUSHER'S POLITICAL MANIFESTO: William A. Rusher, *The Making of the New Majority Party* (Ottawa, Ill.: Green Hill Publications, 1975); on GOP "unfittest," p. 14; on Goldwater, pp. 47–48; on "social conservatism," p. 86; on "economic conservatives," p. 87; on "upper-class wasps," p. 84; on Lodge, p. 44; on Kennedy, p. 46; on new party platform, p. 92.

REPUBLICAN CITES "TRADE-OFFS": Author's interview with John C. Topping, Ripon Society president, 10 September 1979, Washington, D.C.

RUSHER ON MIDEAST INVASION: Rusher, *Making of the New Majority Party,* p. 111.

NOVAK ON RUSHER'S BOOK: Robert Novak, "Producers' Party," *National Review,* 6 June 1975, p. 622.

EXCHANGE OVER "MOONIES": The editorial provoking the controversy, "Guyana Holocaust," appeared in *National Review* on 8 December 1972, p. 1524. Rusher's response, a Letter to the Editor, ran under the headline, "Defending Rev. Moon," in the next issue, 22 December 1978, pp. 1571–72. The editors' response to the letter appeared in the same issue, on page 1578, with the headline, "Cult Taxonomy."

RUSHER ON SUPPORT OF "CONSERVATIVE PARTY": Rusher, *Making of the New Majority Party,* p. 9.

GALLUP POLL ON "CENTER PARTY": *Washington Post,* 13 November 1978, p. A-18.

BUCHANAN ON ACTION FUNDS AND "UPPER-MIDDLE-CLASS BIMBOS": Patrick J. Buchanan, "Carter Aides Should Be Axed," *Human Events,* 22 July 1978, p. 15.

SAFIRE ON BUCHANAN: Quoted in "Safire Boasts How He Pushed Nixon Leftward," *Human Events,* 15 March 1975, p. 4.

BUCHANAN'S VIEWS: Patrick J. Buchanan, *Conservative Votes, Liberal Victories: Why the Right Has Failed* (New York: Quadrangle/New York Times Book Company, 1975); on federal bureaucracy, pp. 21, 24; on electoral process, p. 25; on capturing White House, pp. 164–65; on politics of compromise, p. 168; on right to "declare war," p. 8; on unelected oligarchy, pp. 21, 24; on election, p. 25; on confrontation politics, pp. 8, 164, 165, 168.

SHANNON ON BUCHANAN'S BOOK: William A. Shannon, "Conservative Votes, Liberal Victories," *The New York Times Book Review,* 23 November 1975, p. 4.

EVANS'S FIRST BOOK: M. Stanton Evans, *Revolt on the Campus* (Chicago: The Henry Regnery Company, 1961).

EVANS ON "NEGATIVE THINKING": M. Stanton Evans, *The Future of Conservatism from Taft to Reagan and Beyond* (New York: Holt, Rinehart & Winston, 1968), pp. 231, 239, 240, 242.

EVANS ON YOUNG REPUBLICANS: M. Stanton Evans, "Battle in the Junior GOP," for release 3 May 1977, Los Angeles Times Syndicate.

STONE'S OPPONENT AS "ROCKEFELLER FRONT-MAN": Author's interview with M. Stanton Evans, 1 May 1979, Washington, D.C.

EVANS ON HIS OWN CAREER: *Ibid.*

EVANS ENDORSES SEITH IN COLUMN: M. Stanton Evans, "On Supporting Democrats," for release, 26 April 1978, Los Angeles Times Syndicate.

EVANS AND FUNDRAISING LETTER FOR SEITH: "Seith for Senate Committee," signed by M. Stanton Evans, 1978.

EVANS AS ADVOCATE: Author's interview with M. Stanton Evans, 1 May 1979, Washington, D.C.

EVANS DEFENDED: Author's interview with Republican activist, not for attribution, 5 May 1979, Washington, D.C.

EVANS ON SUBJECTS HE DOES NOT WRITE ABOUT: Author's interview with M. Stanton Evans, 1 May 1979, Washington, D.C.

LOFTON ON JERRY RUBIN: *First Monday,* 7 August 1972, p. 15.

LOFTON COLUMN PRAISES CRANE: John D. Lofton, Jr., "Phil Crane Conservatives' Best Bet to Someday Be President," for release 11 February 1977, United Features Syndicate.

CRANE BOOK: Philip M. Crane, *The Sum of Good Government* (Ottawa, Ill.: Green Hill Publishers, 1977).

BROWNFELD HIRED BY NICARAGUAN AGENT: "Supplemental Statement Pursuant to Section 2 of the Foreign Agents Registration Act of 1938, as Amended For Six Month Period Ending April 6–October 5, 1978." Name of Registrant MacKenzie McCheyne Inc., Registration No. 20045, d/b/a Nicaragua Govt. Information Service. Business Address of Registrant 1266

National Press Bldg., Washington, D.C. 20045. Document shows Brownfeld was hired on April 2 and terminated on April 8, having performed "Research."

EDWARDS AND THE AMERICAN-CHILEAN COUNCIL: *Washington Post,* 19 December 1978, p. 18.

LETTER TO *CONSERVATIVE DIGEST* ON "ELITIST CONSERVATIVES": *Conservative Digest,* May 1976, p. 2.

MAGAZINE PRAISED AS "EASY TO READ": *Conservative Digest,* December 1975, pp. 2–3.

REVIEW OF NASH BOOK: Joan P. Lawton, "How Conservatism Grew," *Conservative Digest,* October 1976, p. 54.

MEANY ARTICLE: George Meany, "Détente Has Been a Flop," *Conservative Digest,* May 1975, p. 21. Meany's letter in response was never published.

BLACKWELL ARTICLE SIGNED BY CRAWFORD: Alan Crawford, "A New Option for Conservatives in 1976," *Conservative Digest,* October 1975, p. 45.

ST. JOHN ON THIRD-PARTY CONCEPT: *Ibid.*

CONSERVATIVE DIGEST AS "FRESH BREATH OF AIR": "A *Conservative Digest* Gift Subscription Costs As Little As $7.50," advertisement, *Conservative Digest,* October 1976, p. 42.

NEWSWEEK ON *HUMAN EVENTS: Newsweek,* 6 September 1971, p. 75.

BUCHANAN ON *HUMAN EVENTS:* Quoted in *ibid.*

FUNCTION OF THOMAS WINTER: Author's interview with friend of Winter, not for attribution, 5 May 1978, Washington, D.C.

RYSKIND ON "FAIR CRITICISM": Author's interview, Allan Ryskind, 3 April 1979, Washington, D.C.

MCDONALD CRITICIZES *HUMAN EVENTS:* Author's interview, Larry P. McDonald, 6 February 1979, Washington, D.C.

VIGUERIE ON *HUMAN EVENTS:* Sarah Ban Breathnach, "Keeping Right," Washington *Post/Potomac,* 26 November 1978, pp. 38–39.

AD FOR KLAN MEMBERSHIP: "Confederate–KKK Paraphernalia," *Human Events,* 1 April 1978, p. 16.

NEW RIGHT REPORT PREDICTS WAGE AND PRICE CONTROLS: *The New Right Report,* 22 September 1978, p. 1.

KILPATRICK LETTER TO *NEW RIGHT REPORT: The New Right Report,* 18 March 1977, p. 6.

SULLIVAN ON *THE NEW RIGHT REPORT:* "It's not journalism at all . . ." from author's interview with John Sullivan, 10 May 1979, Washington, D.C.

MCGOFF AND THE SOUTH AFRICAN GOVERNMENT: "McGoff tied to S. African scandal," *Editor and Publisher,* 9 June 1979, p. 4. John Consoli, "U.S. Publisher Implicated in S. African PR Scandal," *Editor and Publisher,* 7 July 1979, pp. 34–35. John Consoli, "McGoff Denies Any Links to South African Gov't.," *Editor and Publisher,* 21 July 1979, p. 7. "McGoff Makes Reply," *Fairfax* (Va.) *Globe,* 19 July 1979, p. 1. For S. African government transfer of $11.5 million, see *Washington Post,* 3 April 1974, p. 1. The comment from McGoff on "utter nonsense" appears in *Editor and Publisher,* 9 June 1979, p. 14.

Author's interview. See reference to investor group, in Karen Rothmyer, "The McGoff Grab," *Columbia Journalism Review,* November–December 1979, pp. 33–39.

ON MCGOFF'S EFFORT TO BUY *THE TRIB:* Author's interview with Leonard Saffir, by telephone, Washington, D.C., 11 March 1980.

SAFFIR ON SCAIFE AND MCGOFF: *Columbia Journalism Review,* November– December 1979, pp. 37–38.

MCGOFF FIRES MICHIGAN EDITORS: "2 Editors Dismissed in Articles Dispute," *The New York Times,* 26 June 1977, p. 15.

MCGOFF GUILTY PLEA: "McGoff Faces Disorderly Conduct Charge in Aspen," *Editor and Publisher,* 20 January 1979, p. 3, and "McGoff Pleads Guilty in Colorado Case," 24 March 1979, p. 22.

"POLITICS AND RELIGIOUS NEWS" AND *FAIRFAX* (VA.) *GLOBE:* Author's telephone interview with Mary Jean Maroney, 3 March 1979, Washington, D.C.

KINSOLVING AND STATE DEPARTMENT FLAP: "Press Group Expels Rev. Kinsolving for S. African Payments," *Washington Post,* 10 February 1977, p. A-24. "Kinsolving Defends S. African Payment," *Washington Post,* 10 March 1977, p. C-9. Kinsolving told his own side of the story—there was no dispute over the facts—in the *Fairfax* (Va.) *Globe* under his own by-line on 3 February 1977.

LEGISLATIVE AIDE ON *WASHINGTON WEEKLY:* Author's interview, not for attribution, 15 February 1979, Washington, D.C.

AIM'S FUNCTION: This is described in an undated brochure published by *AIM* for Fairness, Balance and Accuracy in News Reporting," *AIM* pamphlet, Washington, D.C. (n.d.)

IRVINE BIOGRAPHY: John Rees, "An Exclusive Interview with Reed Irvine," *The Review of the News,* 24 January 1979, p. 3.

EVANS ON *AIM:* M. Stanton Evans, "Accuracy In Media," for release 16 June 1977, Los Angeles Times Syndicate.

BRADLEE LETTER TO IRVINE: Hangs on wall of *AIM* office, Washington, D.C.

QUOTES FROM LOEB: Quoted in Kevin Cash, *Who the Hell Is William Loeb?* (Manchester, N.H.: Amoskeag Press, Inc., 1975). Also in "Presidential Hopeful Phil Crane Is the Latest Victim of a New Hampshire Loebotomy," *People,* 26 March 1979, pp. 45–46. Also, *Newsweek,* 28 February 1972, p. 51.

LOEB'S PROLABOR VIEWS: Author's interview, 3 April 1979, Pride's Crossing, Mass.

LOEB ON NEW RIGHT: *Idem.*

NEW GUARD ON LOEB: Jerry Norton, "Who the Hell Cares Who the Hell Is William Loeb?" *New Guard,* May 1976, p. 30.

LOEB ON ROCKEFELLER: *People,* 26 March 1979, p. 46.

PHILLIPS ON THE FIRST AMENDMENT: Kevin Phillips, "Is the First Amendment Obsolete?" *Human Events,* 13 January 1973, p. 37.

Chapter 8
THE RAGE AGAINST LEVIATHAN
EPIGRAPH: Former Police Chief Ed Davis, *Washington Star,* 26 May 1978, p. A-7.

NOCK: Albert Jay Nock, *Our Enemy, The State* (New York: W. Morrow and Co., 1935).

WEYRICH ON FREE ENTERPRISE: Author's interview, 17 May 1979, Washington, D.C.

ACCOUNT OF MRS. TED STEVENS'S DEATH: *The New Right Report,* Vol. 7, No. 3, 14 December 1978, p. 1.

SONG OF YOUNG AMERICANS FOR FREEDOM: "God Bless Free Enterprise," lyrics printed on mimeographed song booklet, "Glory Be, There Goes Another," distributed at 1971 convention in Houston.

ORIGINS OF "FREE ENTERPRISE": Peter Viereck, *Shame and Glory of the Intellectuals: Babbitt Jr. and the Revolt Against Revolt* (New York: Capricorn Books, 1965), p. 259.

FRIEDMAN ON "LIBERAL VALUES": Milton Friedman, *Capitalism and Freedom* (Chicago: University of Chicago Press, 1962), p. 5.

KIRK ON "CORROSIVE" CAPITALISM: Quoted in George H. Nash, *The Conservative Intellectual Movement in America Since 1945* (New York: Basic Books, 1976), p. 81.

NISBET ON LAISSEZ-FAIRE: *Ibid.*

CHAMBERS ON "ANTICONSERVATIVE" NATURE OF AMERICAN ECONOMY: Quoted in Nash, p. 255. Letter from Whittaker Chambers to William F. Buckley, Jr., quoted in *Odyssey of a Friend: Whittaker Chambers's Letters to William F. Buckley, Jr., 1954–1961* (New York: Putnam, 1970), p. 216.

BUCKLEY ON "THEOLOGY" OF FRIEDMAN: William F. Buckley, *The Governor Listeth: A Book of Inspired Political Revelations* (New York: Putnam, 1970), pp. 129–134.

NEW "LIBERAL" ESTABLISHMENT: Author's telephone interview with Gregg Hilton, 4 October 1979, New York City.

NEW RIGHT AND BIG BUSINESS: Author's interview with Julian Gammon, 10 February 1979, Washington, D.C.

BUCHANAN ON BIG BUSINESS: Patrick J. Buchanan, "Does Big Business Deserve Our Support?" *Conservative Digest,* April 1977, p. 6.

SOLZHENITSYN CRITICIZES AMERICAN CAPITALISTS: Quoted in Buchanan, *Conservative Digest,* April 1977, p. 7.

RYSKIND ON CUBAN TRADE: Allan Ryskind, "The Iron Grip of Communism on Cuba," *Human Events,* 24 June 1978, p. 12.

BUCHANAN ON BIG BUSINESS: Buchanan, *Conservative Digest,* April 1977, pp. 8, 11.

COORS BEER ADVERTISEMENT IN HOMOSEXUAL PUBLICATION: The ad appeared in *The Advocate,* 5 April 1979, p. 14.

FALWELL AND BRIGGS RESPOND TO COORS AD: Quoted in *The Spotlight,* 21 May 1979, p. 13.

BIG BUSINESS AND "BIG MEDIA": Buchanan, *Conservative Digest,* April 1977, pp. 7–8.

RUSHER ON THE NETWORKS: William A. Rusher, *The Making of the New Majority Party* (Ottawa, Ill.: Green Hill Books, 1975), pp. 102–03.

CRITICISM OF BUSINESS PACs: Morton C. Blackwell, "The Sorry Record on PACs," *Conservative Digest,* April 1977, p. 9. Originally published in *The New Right Report.*

BUCHANAN CALLS FOR "NEW TREATY": Buchanan, *Conservative Digest,* April 1977, p. 11.

LAXALT ON FORTUNE 500: Quoted by Kevin Phillips, "The Fortune 500 Fights Back," *Morgantown* (W.Va.) *Dominion-Post,* 25 November 1977, p. A-10.

WEYRICH ON "MOBIL OIL BILLBOARDS": Quoted in "Right On for the New Right," *Time,* 3 October 1977, p. 26.

BUCHANAN ON GOP AS "VOLUNTEERS": Patrick J. Buchanan, "Does Big Business Deserve GOP Support?" *Human Events,* 25 December 1976, p. 1.

LAXALT ON BIG OIL: "Laxalt Asks Oil Company Audit," press release, Sen. Paul Laxalt, 23 May 1979.

PHILLIPS ON ATTACKS ON MULTINATIONALS: Kevin Phillips, "The Fortune 500 Fights Back," *Morgantown* (W.Va.) *Dominion-Post,* 25 November 1977, p. A-10.

HATCH ON "GUTLESS WONDERS": Quoted in the *Washington Star,* 3 July 1978, p. D-12.

CHAMBERLAIN ON "RIGHT WING POPULISM": John Chamberlain, "Big Business Losing Friends," *Human Events,* 3 April 1977, p. 7.

SCHMITT ON BUSINESS LEADERS: Quoted in the *Washington Star,* 3 July 1978, p. D-12.

VIGUERIE'S ECONOMIC VIEWS: Quoted in "The 'New Right' Plans Move to Change Congress," *Congressional Quarterly,* 23 October 1976, p. 3029.

WHALEN ON "FREE ENTERPRISE": Richard J. Whalen, *Taking Sides: A Personal View of America from Kennedy to Nixon to Kennedy* (Boston: Houghton Mifflin, 1974), p. 123.

TANNENBAUM ON LABOR UNIONS: Frank Tannenbaum, *A New Philosophy of Labor* (New York: Alfred A. Knopf, 1952), pp. 3–5 and 198–99.

WILLS ON "PROGRESS": Garry Wills, "The Conservatives Discover Progress," *Chicago Sun-Times,* 29 May 1978, p. 22.

WILL ON "DECAYED JEFFERSONIANISM": George Will, *The Pursuit of Happiness and Other Sobering Thoughts* (New York: Harper & Row, 1978), pp. xvi, 176–77, 186, 191–92.

FAIRLIE ON "LAISSEZ FAIRE": Henry Fairlie, *The Spoiled Child of the Western World: The Miscarriage of the American Idea in Our Time* (Garden City, N.Y.: Doubleday, 1976), pp. 276–79.

Chapter 9
REPUBLICAN FRATRICIDE

EPIGRAPH: Don Marquis, *The Lives and Times of Archy and Mehitabel* (Garden City, N.Y.: Doubleday, 1950), p. 301.

WHALEN ON "DEEP-SEATED HOSTILITIES": Richard J. Whalen, *Taking Sides: A Personal View of America from Kennedy to Nixon to Kennedy* (Boston: Houghton Mifflin, 1974) pp. 100–01.

MEMO: "Grievances against Republican National Committee and other affiliated groups," n.d. Copy in author's possession provided by a recipient.

HILTON ON GOP LEADERSHIP: Author's telephone interview with Gregg Hilton, 4 October 1979, New York City.

GOP HISTORY: Phyllis Schlafly, *A Choice Not an Echo* (Alton, Ill.: Pere Marquette Press, 1964), pp. 30–34, 43–44, 47, 53, 55, 75.

RUSHER ON FUNCTION OF LIBERAL REPUBLICANS: William A. Rusher, *The Making of the New Majority Party* (Ottawa, Ill.: Green Hill Publications, 1975), pp. 13, 77, 15.

NIXON AND ROCKEFELLER MEETING: William Safire, "Compact of Fifth Avenue," *The New Language of American Politics: An Anecdotal Dictionary of Catchwords, Slogans and Political Usage* (New York: Random House, 1968), pp. 87–88. Goldwater's reaction quoted by Schlafly, p. 75.

RUSHER ON GOLDWATER'S NOMINATION: Rusher, *The Making of the New Majority Party*, p. 44.

WHALEN ON SELECTION OF LODGE: Whalen, *Taking Sides*, p. 101.

SCHLAFLY FINDS "MEANING" OF ROCKEFELLER-NIXON AGREEMENT: Schlafly, *A Choice Not an Echo*, p. 75.

RUSHER ON GOLDWATER NOMINATION: Rusher, *The Making of the New Majority Party*, pp. 47–48.

JAMES BUCKLEY CALLS FOR NIXON TO RESIGN: Quoted in *Watergate: Chronology of a Crisis* (Washington D.C.: Congressional Quarterly, 1975), p. 103.

STUDY OF FORD APPOINTMENTS: Compiled by Peter K. Monk, John S. Buckley, and James E. Cavanaugh, "My Guys: A Look at President Ford's Appointments," The American Conservative Union, 2 February 1976.

FORD ATTACKED BY *CONSERVATIVE DIGEST*: Meldrim Thomson, "Ford: The Myth and the Reality," *Conservative Digest*, September 1975, pp. 8, 14.

RUSHER ON "NOMINAL" REPUBLICANISM: Rusher, *op cit.*, p. 88.

BAUMAN ON PARTY SYSTEM: Robert E. Bauman, "The Present Party System Has Failed. . . . ," *New Guard*, April 1975, p. 11.

VIGUERIE ON MARKETING THE GOP: Richard A. Viguerie, "From the Publisher," *Conservative Digest*, August 1975, p. 1.

COMMITTEE TO "STUDY" THIRD PARTY OPTION: *Washington Post*, 17 February 1975, p. 1.

ACU WORKING PAPER: "Should Conservatives Form a Third Party?" *Human Events*, 20 November 1976, pp. 1, 6, 17.

VIGUERIE ANNOUNCES CANDIDACY: "Richard Viguerie Seeks Vice Presidential Nomination," *The American Independent.* August 1976, p. 2.

KEYNOTE ADDRESS ON "ZIONISM": Quoted in " 'New Majority' Attempt Fizzles in Chicago," *Human Events*, 11 September 1976, p. 3. Also, Stephen Isaacs, "Newcomers' Hopes Are Scuttled at 3d-Party Convention," *Washington Post*, 29 August 1976.

VIGUERIE ON MORRIS: Quoted in Stephen Isaacs, "Maddox a Favorite as Third Party Meets in Chicago," *Washington Post*, 27 August 1976, p. 3.

PLAN OF VIGUERIE BACKERS: " 'New Majority' Attempt Fizzles in Chicago," *Human Events*, 11 September 1976, pp. 3–4.

BUCKLEY ON MADDOX: William F. Buckley, Jr., "The Chicago Convention," *National Review*, 1 October 1976, p. 1083.

AIP "LOST ITS MIND": William A. Rusher, "Footnotes to History," column, for release 10 September 1976, Universal Press Syndicate.

SHEARER ON NEW RIGHT INVASION OF PARTY: *Human Events,* 11 September 1976, p. 4.

KILPATRICK ON AIP: James J. Kilpatrick, "Gauzy Aggregation on the Far Right," *Washington Star,* 26 August 1976.

PHILLIPS ON AIP VENTURE: Quoted in "Howard Phillips Denounces Reagan-Schweiker Pact," *The American Independent,* August 1976, p. 3.

ASHBROOK ON WALLACE CANDIDACY: John Ashbrook, "And Anyway Is Wallace a Conservative?" *National Review,* 22 November 1968, p. 1048.

THOMSON AND CONSTITUTION PARTY: "Thomson Joins Presidential Race," *The New York Times,* 1 November 1979, p. A-16.

EVANS ON LEADERS ON THE RIGHT: The author has heard this stated in varying forms on numerous occasions.

TENNESSEE PAPER ATTACKS BAKER: Quoted in *Human Events,* "Conservative Paper Won't Back Baker," 5 August 1978, p. 7.

HUMAN EVENTS ON BAKER'S RECORD: "Should Baker Be Re-Elected Senate Majority Leader?" *Human Events,* 25 November 1978, p. 4.

NEW GUARD ON BAKER: "Campaign 1980: GOP Marathon," *New Guard,* Summer 1979, p. 24.

REPUBLICAN BANNERS SAY "WORKING PEOPLE NEED A BREAK": Quoted in "GOP Grabs Tax Cut and Runs with It to Seven States," *Washington Post,* 23 September 1978, p. A-2.

BUSH AS ELITIST: "Campaign 1980: GOP Marathon," *New Guard,* Summer 1979, p. 25.

Chapter 10
CRASHING THE DEMOCRATIC PARTY

EPIGRAPH: Quoted in "From the Publisher," *Conservative Digest,* February 1976, p. 1.

MIDDLE AMERICANS: Donald I. Warren, *The Radical Center: Middle Americans and the Politics of Alienation* (Notre Dame and London: University of Notre Dame Press, 1976).

RUSHER ON TWO KINDS OF CONSERVATIVES: William A. Rusher, *The Making of the New Majority Party* (Ottawa, Ill.: Green Hill Publications, 1976), pp. 86–87.

FORGOTTEN AMERICANS: Murray Friedman, *Overcoming Middle Class Rage* (Philadelphia: Westminster Press, 1971), p. 36.

"WELFARIST" CONSTITUENCY: M. Stanton Evans, *The Future of Conservatism: From Taft to Reagan and Beyond* (New York: Holt, Rinehart & Winston, 1968), p. 67.

EDWARDS ON WINNING: Speech by Mickey Edwards, 1979 Conservative Political Action Conference, 9 February 1979, Washington, D.C.

"WE WERE UNOPPOSED": Author's interview with former Edwards aide, not for attribution, February 1979, Washington, D.C.

YOUNGSTOWN ROADSHOW: "Can Conservatives Successfully Woo Labor?" *Human Events,* 11 March 1978, pp. 184–85.

EDWARDS ON STEELWORKERS: Quoted in *Human Events, ibid.*

CRANE ON DIVISION IN AMERICAN POLITICS: Philip M. Crane, "Blue Collar

Constituency Is Really Conservative," *Conservative Digest,* April 1978, p. 6.

"NO BIG BREAKTHROUGH": Letter to author from Staughton Lynd, 14 October 1978.

ANDERSON ON YOUNGSTOWN: Jack Anderson, "The Republican Right Courts the Labor Vote," *Washington Post,* 26 February 1978.

LABOR FILM: According to a press release issued by the AFL-CIO's Committee on Political Education, producer of the film *The Right-Wing Machine,* the New Right is trying to "create and manipulate fear, confusion, distrust and hate." The film says: "This is a horror film; not the usual kind featuring haunted houses, creepy creatures, ghosts or ghouls. The stars are people who could be your neighbors . . ." The organizations of the New Right, it alleges, "overlap, interlock, coordinate and multiply like rattlesnakes!" It concludes: "We are the principal target of the right-wing machine. But we can beat it."

REACTIONS OF LABOR UNIONS AND LIBERAL GROUPS: The National Committee for an Effective Congress has issued a pamphlet dedicated to the *Right Wing Political Machine,* which is "Aiming for the Most Conservative Congress Money Can Buy." On 29–30 August 1978, the Industrial Union Department of the AFL-CIO held a conference in Washington on "The Radical Right Wing in America." At it, Senator Howard Metzenbaum said on 29 August that "the people behind Joe McCarthy were out to eliminate organized labor as an influence in America," forgetting that McCarthy enjoyed the strong support of organized labor in Wisconsin. William P. Winpisinger of the Machinists' union referred to "its spiritual predecessors in Hitler's Germany, Mussolini's Italy and Franco's Spain," calling anti-ERA activist Phyllis Schlafly "a rich bitch" bankrolled by "corporate fat cats." Americans for Democratic Action, in a fundraising package similar to NCEC's, published *A Citizen's Guide to the Right Wing.*

PUDDINGTON ON THE NEW RIGHT: Arch Puddington, "The Evolving Threat of the New Right," *The American Federationist,* August 1978, pp. 1–4.

KEMP ON LABOR UNIONS: "Needed: A Coalition Between Labor and the GOP," a speech to the Forty-fourth Convention of the National Longshoremen's Association of the AFL-CIO at Miami, Fla., 16 July 1979. Reprinted in *Human Events,* 22 September 1979, pp. 10–14.

LOFTON ON JESSE JACKSON: John D. Lofton, Jr., "GOP Shouldn't Try for Black Vote by Outpromising Democrats," for release 27 January 1978, United Features Syndicate.

HAMILTON ON BLACK MIDDLE CLASS: Author's interview, 4 February 1979, New York City.

CLARK ON BLACK VOTER BEHAVIOR: Author's interview, 10 October 1979, New York City.

HAMILTON ON BLACK VOTER BEHAVIOR: Author's interview, 4 February 1979, New York City.

INFORMATION ON BLACK VOTER BEHAVIOR 1978: *Election '78: Implication for Black America* (Washington, D.C.: Joint Center for Political Studies), January 1979, pp. 2–28.

BUCHANAN ON BLACKS AND THE REPUBLICAN PARTY: Patrick J. Buchanan,

"GOP Vote Search Should Bypass Ghettos," *Charleston* (W. Va.) *Daily Mail,* 16 February 1977.

GOLDWATER ON INTEGRATION: Barry M. Goldwater, *The Conscience of a Conservative* (Shepherdsville, Ky.: Victor Press, 1963), p. 37.

HEADLINE ON SMOTHERS'S ARTICLE: Published as David Brudnoy, "A Black Conservative Champion," *Conservative Digest,* November 1975, p. 45.

SOUTH BOSTON INFORMATION: Author's visit to South Boston Information Center, March 1979.

SONG LYRICS: Provided to the author by the South Boston Information Center.

KELLY ON BUSING IN SOUTH BOSTON: Author's interview with Jimmy Kelly, 2 April 1979, Boston, Mass.

CONSERVATIVE JOURNALISM: *The Citizens' Forum,* A Monthly Review of the News Dedicated to Individual Freedom Under God, Limited Government and Free Enterprise, March 1979.

NELSON ON GOP IN MASSACHUSETTS: Author's interview with Gordon Nelson, 2 April 1979, Boston, Mass.

BRODER ON PARTIES: David Broder, " 'Victory Formula' for the Democrats," *Washington Post,* 29 October 1978, p. C-7.

Chapter 11
THE POLITICS OF GRIEVANCE

EPIGRAPH: Friedrich Nietzsche, *Thus Spoke Zarathustra* (London: Penguin, 1968), p. 124.

ROSENBLATT QUOTED: "Nov. 7 Vote Turnout Was 37.9%, Lowest Since '42," *The New York Times,* 19 December 1978, p. A-13.

STROUT ON JEPSEN'S ELECTION: TRB, "The Silent Majority," *The New Republic,* 25 November 1978, p. 2.

DOLAN: Author's interview, 10 January 1979, Rosslyn, Va.

HOWARD PHILLIPS: Author's telephone interview, 23 February 1979, Washington, D.C.

WEYRICH INTERVIEW: Author's interview, 17 May 1979, Washington, D.C.

WEYRICH AS "SURVIVAL ARTIST": Author's interview with Louis Ingram, 3 May 1979, Washington, D.C.

TAFT'S BOOK: Robert A. Taft, *A Foreign Policy for Americans* (Garden City, N.Y.: Doubleday, 1951).

PHILLIPS ON SCHWEIKER NOMINATION: Press release for immediate release, 26 July 1976, "Conservative Organizer Denounces Reagan-Schweiker Pact/ Howard Phillips Says Foes of Liberalism Should Reject 'Victory at Any Price.' "

PHILLIPS'S LOYALTY NOT TO POLITICAL PARTIES OR PERSONAGES: Quoted in "Conservative Phillips Goes After Ed Brooke," in *Conservative Digest,* July 1978, p. 18.

PHILLIPS'S CAMPAIGN AGAINST ELAINE NOBLE: Noble is quoted as acknowledging Lesbianism in "A Gay Pol's Run for the Senate," *US,* 11 July 1978, p. 41.

BRUDNOY ON PHILLIPS'S CAMPAIGN: David Brudnoy, "One Hand Clapping," *National Review*, 13 October 1978, p. 1268.

PHILLIPS ON "BIBLICAL LAW": Author's interview, 23 February 1979, Washington, D.C.

DALTON RACE AND ROBINSON LETTER: *Washington Star*, 30 September 1977, p. C-1; 22 October 1977, p. 10; *Washington Post*, 4 October 1977, p. C-1.

DOLAN ON DIRECT-MAIL APPEALS: Author's interview, 10 January 1979, Rosslyn, Va.

"WE'RE GONNA BLOW YOUR HEADS OFF": Quote from National Right to Work Committee fundraising letter, n.d.

"WE'RE GOING TO DEFEAT THE BASTARD": Quoted by Michael Novak, "Abortion Foes Win Big," *Dayton Journal-Herald*, 24 November 1978.

IOWANS FOR LIFE ROLE IN CAMPAIGN: Ward Sinclair, "Anti-Abortion Activists Help Scuttle Clark in Iowa," *Washington Post*, 9 November 1978.

DES MOINES REGISTER SURVEY: Quoted by TRB, "The Silent Majority," *The New Republic*, 25 November 1978, p. 2.

TRB ON JEPSEN VICTORY: *Ibid.*

JEPSEN COMMENTS: "An Interview with Roger Jepsen," *The Review of the News*, 28 March 1979, pp. 31–42.

CONSERVATIVE DIGEST ON HASKELL: "Elections '78: The Senate Races to Watch," *Conservative Digest*, November 1978, p. 9.

HASKELL CALLS ARMSTRONG "ON THE FRINGE": Quoted in *Washington Post*, 18 October 1978, p. A-3.

THE FEAR BROKERS: Thomas McIntyre, *The Fear Brokers* (New York: Pilgrim Press, 1979).

MCINTYRE CAMPAIGN: Marquis Childs, "McIntyre's Stand Against the Radical Right," *Washington Post*, 14 March 1978, p. A-17.

REPUBLICAN BILLBOARDS IN MINNESOTA ELECTIONS: Quoted in *Washington Post*, 9 November 1978, p. A-12.

MITAU ON "ERA HAS ENDED": Quoted in "Humphrey-Mondale Party in Shock," *Washington Post*, 9 November 1978, p. 1.

BOSCHWITZ ON ANDERSON: Madeleine Nash, *Washington Star*, 8 October 1978, p. A-3.

SYMMS'S LETTER ON BROOKE RE-ELECTION BID: *Washington Star*, 28 January 1978, p. 3.

GOP LEADERS "SANDBAGGED" NELSON'S CAMPAIGN: *Human Events*, 30 September 1978, pp. 3–4.

GEORGE WILL ON SEITH-PERCY RACE: George F. Will, "Not Only the Faces Are Changing," *Washington Post*, 12 November 1978, p. B-7.

SCHLAFLY ROLE IN SEITH CAMPAIGN: Basil Talbott, Jr., "Seith-Schlafly Squeeze Play," *Chicago Sun-Times*, 2 November 1978, p. 63.

GOLDWATER DEPICTED AS "NUCLEAR MADMAN": "Capitol Briefs," *Human Events*, 18 November 1978, p. 2.

TEXT OF SEITH ADVERTISEMENT: *Washington Post*, 3 November 1978, p. A-1.

BUCKLEY ON SEITH CAMPAIGN: William F. Buckley, Jr., "Running," for release 21 November 1978, Universal Press Syndicate.

TEXT OF PERCY APOLOGY: *Washington Post,* 3 November 1978, p. A-1.

BUCKLEY ON PERCY'S ELECTION: "Running," *op cit.*

"NEGATIVE ADVERTISING": Rowland Evans and Robert Novak, "Percy: The Lesson of '76," *Washington Post,* 6 November 1978, p. A-23.

SEITH RACE: David Axelrod, "Seith Off and Flying for Senate," *Chicago Tribune,* 28 September 1979, p. 3.

BELL "CRAZY" TO SEEK SEAT: Nofziger quoted in *Philadelphia Inquirer,* 8 June 1978, p. D-1.

BELL CAMPAIGN APPEAL: Fundraising letter for Bell for Senate campaign, n.d.

GOP "INERT": Bell quoted in "Case's Loss Laid to Lax Effort Against Conservatives," *The New York Times,* 8 August 1978, p. 44.

RUSHER COLUMN: William A. Rusher, "Money May Make the Difference in N.J. Race," *Human Events,* 21 October 1978, p. 17.

GAHAGAN CAMPAIGN: "Will Maine Elect an Independent U.S. Senator, Too?" *The New Right Report,* 26 June 1978.

COHEN CHALLENGED BY RIGHT: Rowland Evans and Robert Novak, " 'New Right' Fights Cohen," *Washington Post,* 8 September 1978, p. A-13.

JOLY QUOTED: "Will Maine Elect an Independent U.S. Senator, Too?" *The New Right Report,* 26 June 1978.

GAHAGAN CHARGES SABOTAGE: *Political Action Report,* September 1978, p. 5. "Maine Senate Candidate Claims Sexual Abuse," *New Times,* 16 October 1978, p. 14.

BRODER ON ANDERSON: Quoted in *Human Events,* 4 March 1978, p. 3.

ANDERSON'S APPEALS TO DEMOCRATS: "Anderson Aided by Huge Demo Crossovers," *Human Events,* 1 April 1978, p. 3.

THE NEW YORK TIMES HEADLINE: *The New York Times,* 23 March 1978, p. A-1.

DOLAN ON ANDERSON: *Human Events,* 4 March 1978, p. 3.

PHILLIPS ON GOP LIBERALS: Kevin Phillips, "Cannibals and Elephants," 25 November 1977, King Features Syndicate.

MCGOVERN ON LIBERAL SETBACKS: Quoted in *Human Events,* 30 September 1978, p. 3.

ACU ACTIVIST ON NEW RIGHT CAMPAIGNS: Author's interview with Daniel Joy. Quoted in Alan Crawford, "Richard Viguerie's Bid for Power," *The Nation,* 29 January 1977, p. 106.

KEENE ON BUSING: Author's interview for Crawford, *The Nation, ibid.*

EFFECT OF RIGHT-WING CHALLENGES: J. Brian Smith, "Dinosaurs and Neanderthals," *The Nation,* 9 September 1978, p. 206.

DEMOCRATIC GAINS: "Liberals Upset by Primary Trends," *Human Events,* 30 September 1978. p. 3.

Chapter 12
POPULIST PAST, NEOPOPULIST PRESENT

EPIGRAPH: Kevin Phillips, "Who Is a Liberal, What Is a Conservative? A Symposium," *Commentary,* September 1976, p. 88.

HENRY WALLACE ON TAFT: Quoted in James A. Patterson, *Mr. Republican:*

A Biography of Robert A. Taft (Boston: Houghton Mifflin, 1972), p. 386.

VIERECK ON MCCARTHYISM: Peter Viereck, *The Unadjusted Man: A New Hero for Americans* (Boston: Beacon Press, 1953), p. 180.

FAIRLIE ON AMERICAN POPULISM: Henry Fairlie, *The Parties: Republicans and Democrats in This Century* (New York: St. Martin's Press, 1978), p. 121.

HOFSTADTER ON POPULISM: Richard Hofstadter, "North America," in *Populism: Its Meaning and National Characteristics,* Ghita Ionescu and Ernest Gellner, eds. (New York: Macmillan, 1969), pp. 9–10.

HOWARD PHILLIPS ON JACKSONIAN DEMOCRACY: Howard Phillips, "Jacksonian Democracy Offers Precedent for the 'New Majority,'" *Human Events,* 5 October 1974, pp. 18–19.

WHITAKER'S BOOK: Robert D. Whitaker, *A Plague on Both Your Houses* (Washington, D.C.: Robert B. Luce Co., 1975).

RUSHER ON WHITAKER: Quoted in promotional flyer for *A Plague on Both Your Houses,* n.d.

WHITAKER ON POPULISM: "What Do You Mean . . . Populist?" *Conservative Digest,* July 1975, p. 41.

BILLINGTON ON NATIVISM: Ray Allen Billington, *The Protestant Crusade: A Study of the Origins of American Nativism* (New York: Macmillan, 1938), p. 322.

GREELEY ON KNOW-NOTHINGISM: Quoted by Billington, *The Protestant Crusade, op. cit.,* p. 417.

NATIVIST PLATFORM: Billington, *Protestant Crusade, op. cit.,* p. 210. The quote is from the 1844 platform of the American Republican party.

MCEVOY ON WALLACE AND GOLDWATER: James McEvoy, III, *Conservatives or Radicals? The Contemporary American Right* (Chicago: Rand-McNally, 1971), p. 153.

JERRY SIMPSON QUOTED: Mark N. Summers, *A Student Cartoonist's View of Great Figures in American History* (New York: Washington Square Press, 1972), p. 161.

VIERECK ON BRYAN: Peter Viereck, *Conservatism: From John Adams to Churchill* (Princeton, N.J.: D. Van Nostrand Company, 1956), p. 97.

DIETZE ON DEMOCRACY: Gottfried Dietze, *America's Political Dilemma: From Limited to Unlimited Democracy* (Baltimore: Johns Hopkins Press, 1968), pp. 14–15.

MORLEY ON BRYAN: George H. Nash, *The Conservative Intellectual Movement in America Since 1945* (New York: Basic Books, 1976), p. 212.

BRYAN'S "GOSPEL OF SERVICE": Paul Glad, *The Trumpet Soundeth: William Jennings Bryan and His Democracy, 1896–1912* (Lincoln, Neb.: University of Nebraska Press, 1960).

"POPULISM GONE SOUR": Peter Viereck, "The Revolt Against the Elite," in *The Radical Right: The New American Right,* updated and expanded ed., Daniel Bell, ed. (Garden City, N.Y.: Anchor Books/Doubleday, 1962), p. 94.

MENCKEN ON BRYAN: "W.J.B.," in *A Mencken Chrestomanthy,* H. L. Mencken, ed. (New York: Alfred A. Knopf, 1949), pp. 245–46.

COUGHLIN'S VIEWS: Sheldon Marcus, *Father Coughlin* (South Bend, Ind.: Notre Dame University Press, 1973). Reference to "decentralization of wealth," p. 43; "wealth and intellect," p. 73; "money-hoarding" dynasties, p. 76.

HEARST: Raymond G. Swing, *Forerunners of American Fascism* (New York: Julian Messner, 1935), p. 137.

LONG AND CONSTITUTION: Mark N. Summers, *A Student Cartoonist's View of Great Figures in American History* (New York: Pocket Books, 1972), p. 245.

WILL ON HUEY LONG: George F. Will, *The Pursuit of Happiness and Other Sobering Thoughts* (New York: Harper & Row, 1978), pp. 35–36.

BUCKLEY ON MCCARTHY: William F. Buckley, Jr., *Up From Liberalism* (New York: Bantam Books, 1968), p. 9.

EVANS ON MCCARTHY: "The Buckley Roast," tape recording of remarks before Young Americans for Freedom, 27 August 1977.

HERBERG ON RABBLE-ROUSING: Will Herberg, "Government by Rabble-Rousing," *New Leader,* 18 January 1954, p. 15.

WILHELMSEN ON LIBERALISM: Quoted by Clinton Rossiter in *Conservatism in America: The Thankless Persuasion* (New York: Alfred A. Knopf, 1962), p. 256.

ENGLISH ON FUNCTION OF CONSERVATISM: Rossiter, *ibid.,* p. 256.

ROSSITER ON "DILEMMA" OF CONSERVATISM: Rossiter, *ibid.,* p. 54.

KEVIN PHILLIPS: "Who Is a Liberal, What Is a Conservative? A Symposium," *Commentary,* September 1976, p. 88.

WEYRICH: Author's interview, 17 May 1979, Washington, D.C.

KIRKPATRICK: Jeane Kirkpatrick, "Why the New Right Lost," *Commentary,* February 1977, p. 39.

WALLACE ON BOOK: Quoted in publicity flyer for *A Plague on Both Your Houses,* n.d.

WHITAKER ON WALLACE: "What Do You Mean . . . Populist?" *Conservative Digest,* July 1975, p. 41.

HOY ON "NATIONALIST" PARTIES: Letter to author, 27 September 1978.

"THE PARANOID STYLE": Richard Hofstadter, *The Paranoid Style in American Politics, and Other Essays* (New York: Alfred A. Knopf, 1965).

SHILS ON IDEOLOGICAL "EXTREMISTS": Edward Shils, *The Torment of Secrecy: The Background and Consequences of American Security Policies* (New York: Free Press, 1956), p. 234.

VIERECK ON "CONSPIRACY-HUNTING": *The Unadjusted Man,* p. 189.

Chapter 13
RAMPAGEOUS DEMOCRACY

EPIGRAPH: Frank Meyer, "The Mandate of 1968," *National Review,* 19 November 1968, p. 1170.

BUCKLEY ON PLEBISCITARIAN GOVERNMENT: William F. Buckley, Jr., "Running," for release 21 November 1968, Universal Press Syndicate.

BURNHAM ON DEMOCRATISM: James Burnham, *Congress and the American Tradition* (Chicago: The Henry Regnery Co., 1959), p. 41.

"DEMOCRATIC" NATURE OF AMERICAN SYSTEM: Quoted by George H. Nash in *The Conservative Intellectual Movement in America Since 1945* (New York: Basic Books, 1978), p. 241.

KENDALL ON ATTITUDES OF FOUNDERS: Quoted by George H. Nash in *op. cit.*, p. 240.

BRIGGS ON HOMOSEXUALS: Author's interview, 13 April 1979, Fullerton, Calif.

REAGAN ON PROPOSITION 6: "Two Ill-Advised California Trends," *Los Angeles Herald-Examiner,* 1 November 1978, p. A-19. Also, "Reagan Sees It Right," *Los Angeles Times,* Part II, p. 6.

BRIGGS AND MEDI-CAL: *Santa Ana Register,* 15 March 1979, p. 1.

ABOUREZK ON NATIONAL VOTER INITIATIVE: Quoted by Karl Hess, "The New Populism," *Penthouse,* February 1979, p. 60.

ABOUREZK ON LIBERALS: Quoted in *Newsweek,* 22 May 1978, p. 22.

PHILLIPS ON NATIONAL INITIATIVE: Kevin Phillips, "Voters Will Be Heard," *Tallahassee Democrat,* 4 September 1977.

BUCHANAN ON AVOIDING REPRESENTATIVE GOVERNMENT PROCESSES: Patrick J. Buchanan, "Letting the Voters Become Lawgivers," *Chicago Tribune,* 20 December 1977, Section 3, p. 3.

RUSHER ON PLEBISCITES: William A. Rusher, "A National Voter Initiative?" column for release 15 September 1978, Universal Press Syndicate.

BICKEL ON VIRTUES OF CONSERVATIVE ATTITUDES TOWARD GOVERNMENT INSTITUTIONS: Alexander M. Bickel, *The New Age of Political Reform: The Electoral College, the Conventions, and the Party System* (New York: Harper Colophon Books, 1968), p. 3.

HIMMELFARB ON "MASS-MAN": Gertrude Himmelfarb, "The Prophets of the New Conservatism," *Commentary,* January 1950, p. 78.

BOZELL'S BOOK: L. Brent Bozell, *The Warren Revolution: Reflections on the Consensus Society* (New Rochelle, N.Y.: Arlington House, 1966).

BERGER'S BOOK: Raoul Berger, *Government by Judiciary: The Transformation of the 14th Amendment* (Cambridge, Mass.: Harvard University Press, 1977).

CONSERVATIVE DIGEST ON JERRY BROWN: "Would You Believe Carter and Brown?" *Conservative Digest,* June 1976, p. 6.

WILL ON ECONOMIC POLICY: "Constitutionalizing Economics," *Washington Post,* 8 February 1976, p. A-25.

BURKE ON THE ENGLISH PEOPLE: Edmund Burke, *Reflections on the Revolution in France* (London: Penguin, 1969), p. 181.

KENDALL'S VIEWS: Much of the information on Kendall's life and thought is taken from Nash, *op. cit.*, pp. 227–252.

HESS ON ELITISM: "The New Populism," *Penthouse,* February 1979, p. 53.

GOLDWATER ON DEMAGOGUES: Barry Goldwater, *The Conscience of a Conservative* (Shepherdsville, Ky.: Victor Press, 1960), p. 18.

CALHOUN'S "CONCURRENT MAJORITY": Viereck, *Conservatism,* pp. 149–51.

KRISTOL AND WEAVER ON "MAJORITARIANISM": Irving Kristol and Paul Weaver, "A Bad Idea Whose Time Has Come," *The New York Times Magazine,* 23 November 1969, p. 156.

KENDALL ON "PROCESS OF DELIBERATION": Quoted in Nash, *op. cit.*, pp. 227–52.

TOCQUEVILLE ON "FORM": Quoted in Viereck, *Conservatism,* p. 146.

FRIEDLAND ON LEGISLATIVE BODIES: Quoted in *Newsweek,* 22 May 1978, p. 22.

GARN ON ELECTORAL COLLEGE: Statements on Senate floor, Washington, D.C., *The Congressional Record*, 15 March 1978, p. 2842.

KEVIN PHILLIPS ON ABOLISHING ELECTORAL COLLEGE: Kevin Phillips, "Abolish the Electoral College!" *Morgantown* (W.Va.) *Dominion-Post*, 15 July 1977, p. A-18.

BICKEL ON THE ELECTORAL COLLEGE: Alexander Bickel, *The New Age of Political Reform*, pp. 14–15.

PHILLIPS ON "THIRD WORLD" STATES: Kevin Phillips, "Abolish the Electoral College!" *op. cit.*

DIAMOND ON ELECTORAL COLLEGE: Martin Diamond, *The Electoral College and the American Idea of Democracy* (Washington, D.C.: The American Enterprise Institute, 1977), pp. 11–12.

BICKEL ON ABUSES OF NIXON ADMINISTRATION: Quoted by George F. Will in *The Pursuit of Happiness and Other Sobering Thoughts* (New York: Harper & Row, 1978), p. 51.

BUCHANAN ON "IMPERIAL" PRESIDENCY: Author's interview published in *New Guard* as " 'The Final Days' and Beyond, An Exclusive Interview with Patrick J. Buchanan," *New Guard*, June 1976, p. 13.

CRANE ON PRESIDENCY AS "BULLY PULPIT": *The Tomorrow Show*, 7 August 1978, NBC Television. Crane was guest.

RUSHER ON CONNALLY: Author's interview, 11 March 1978, New York City.

BURNHAM ON "CAESARISM": Burnham, *Congress and the American Tradition*, p. 299.

DISRAELI ON "INSTITUTIONS": Quoted in Robert Blake, *Disraeli* (New York: St. Martin's Press, 1967), p. 257.

GOVERNMENT BY RABBLE-ROUSING: Will Herberg, "Government by Rabble-Rousing," *The New Leader*, 18 January 1954, pp. 15–16.

MCCLURE ON PANAMA CANAL: Author's interview with Tod Neuenschwander, press secretary to Senator McClure, Washington, D.C., 14 March 1980.

SIMON ON POPULAR VOICE: Author's interview, 2 February 1979, Washington, D.C.

BICKEL ON MAJORITY: Alexander Bickel, "Edmund Burke," *The New Republic*, 17 March 1973, p. 32.

FAIRLIE ON POLLS: Henry Fairlie, "Galluping Toward Dead Center," *The New Republic*, 8 April 1978, p. 20.

FAIRLIE ON POPULAR VOICE: Henry Fairlie, "The Problem of Putting Propositions to the People," *Washington Post*, 21 November 1978, p. B-8.

Index

churches, fundamentalist, 159; *see also* fundamentalist ministers
churches, gun lobby and, 108, 109
Citizens Committee for the Right to Keep and Bear Arms, 32–3, 68–9, 70, 108–9, 139
Citizens for Decent Literature, 61–2
Citizens for the Republic, 17, 60, 119; fundraising letter from, 53
Clark, Kenneth B., 256–7
Clark, Richard, 162, 273–4
class hostility, 5; *see also* antielitism
Cochran, Thad, 258
Cohen, William, 284–6
Committee for Responsible Youth Politics, 25, 57, 71
Committee for the Survival of a Free Congress, 15–16, 48, 55, 70, 72; Democrat supported by, 268; training sessions by, 266; *see also* Weyrich, Paul
Committee to Re-Elect the President (CREEP), 23–4, 25, 43, 122, 194, 233
communist countries: business interests and, 214; U.S. diplomatic relations with, 119, 139; *see also* Soviet Union
Congress: constitutional provision for, 327; fundraising appeals and, 68–9; New Right strategy for, 266–7; "radicals" in, 16; Westerners in, 83–4, 268–9; *see also* congressional elections
congressional elections: campaign fundraising for, 45, 47–8, 59–60, 70; liberal losses in, 287–8; New Right victories in, 267–9, 272–7
Connally, John B., 111–12, 138–42, 162, 201, 326; political style of, 81, 91, 123; withdraws from 1980 presidential race, 243–4
Conservative Caucus, 38, 39–40, 54, 130; *see also* Phillips, Howard

Conservative Digest, 10, 30, 168, 198–9, 298–9
conservative intellectuals, 166–7, 176–80, 320, 325; neoconservative, 7, 169, 173–5
Conservative Political Action Conferences, 219, 235, 241, 251
Conservative Victory Fund, 15, 58–9, 72; *see also* Hilton, Gregg
conservativism (and conservatives): Burkean tradition of, 166, 169, 222, 303, 317; direct democracy and, 311–12, 331; economic philosophy of, 211–13; liberalism and, 304–6; New Right and, 7, 10; New Right's antielitism and, 165–6, 169, 176, 180, 185–6; New Right's individualist ideology and, 221–4; philosophy of government of, 317; populism and, 165–7, 303–7; racism and, 259; *see also* conservative intellectuals; Midwestern conservatives; "social conservativism"
conspiracy theories, 308–10
Constitution (U.S.), 319, 323
constitutional amendments, proposals for, 319–20; *see also* antiabortion amendment; national initiative amendment
constitutional democracy, 327
Consumer Alert Council, 27
Coors, Joseph, 10–11, 12, 15, 215–16, 270
Coughlin, Charles, 299–302
Council on Foreign Relations, 243, 309
Crane, Daniel B., 73, 150–1, 283
Crane, Philip, 89, 123, 130, 135–9, 268, 326; as ACU chairman, 9–10, 196–7; as "born-again" Christian, 162; Reagan and, 118, 135–6; in Youngstown delegation, 251, 252
Cranston, Alan, 59

Alan Crawford is a former editor of *New Guard,* the journal of Young Americans for Freedom, and has been assistant editor of *Conservative Digest.* He was an aide to Senator James Buckley.